The Birth of the Craft Brew Revolution

Ben Novak

The Birth of the Craft Brew Revolution

Ben Novak

The Nittany Valley Society
State College

Published in the United States of America
by The Nittany Valley Society, Inc.
www.nittanyvalley.org

ISBN 10: 1484076265
ISBN 13: 978-1484076262

Novak, Benjamin
The Birth of the Craft Brew Revolution

Cover Photograph © William Ames
First Edition

Contents

Foreword

Cheers! Prost! Salute! To Your Health! Whatever words you give it, when vessels of hand-crafted quality beer are touched together and the eyes of the men and women who hold them meet, something magical happens — a long and frustrating day brightens, worries soften, stresses chill, and friends (or soon to be friends) connect, and The Life becomes *La Vie*. Yes, they're the same, but doesn't the French spelling just sound more beautiful?

Beautiful isn't used much when it comes to beer or beer drinking. This is almost an absolute truth when referring to big-batch, small-taste beers and the drinking of them. However, as I discovered long ago and continue to discover today, when you drink a quality craft-brewed beer (even alone), *beautiful* can sometimes be heard as an audible response. You might think I'm some sort of a beer guru like Ben. I'm not. But like Ben, and in part because of Ben, I do consider myself a beer *geek* — one who appreciates beer way more than usual. But this wasn't always so.

In the preface of my own book, I tell the story about how, via a personal encounter with a guy who wrote a beer column in our local newspaper, my worldview of beer and, may I dare say, my life in general, changed forever. Ben's articles appeared for a number of years, and many people throughout Central Pennsylvania and beyond became "aware," if you will, that beer can be more than just beer. Fact is, I think Ben was ahead of his time. Back then (and I'm talking the early 1980s) "beer geeks" didn't even exist. Thanks to Ben, and others like him, it's now a common title, and I'm proud to be one. So what was once just a beverage to quench my thirst has become a *beautiful* way to drink in *La Vie*.

The following is an excerpt from my first book "going LOCAL! An Adventurer's Guide to Unique Eats, Cool Pubs & Cozy Cafes of Central Pennsylvania," where I first acknowledge Ben and the impact he had on me.

***

When it comes to good beer, there are no maybes. My discerning taste began with an encounter I'll never forget. The place and situation rest in my mind like the memories you get when you put on your favorite sweater or pair of shoes — you remember exactly where you got them and where they've taken you.

I was just 21 at the time, full of life and eager to let fly my new rights to purchase alcohol. In those days, my beer of choice was Stroh's. I kept a can of it in my truck for years (the same can!) as my "Emergency Beer" in case I was in a situation where I really needed a beer and didn't have one. One day though, I walked into a local historic tavern just down the street from where I now live.

Duffy's Tavern had a six-pack cooler in the back, and there I found my precious brew — Stroh's in cans. I grabbed a six-pack and started toward the bar to pay. As I walked, I heard a voice behind me say, "Excuse me, are you going to buy that beer?" I stopped, ready to flash my ID and prove my manhood (at least my 21-hood), and saw a group of "older people," probably in their thirties, sitting there. The guy said again, "Are you sure you want to buy *that* beer?" A bit confused and put off, I said, "Yeah, why?" He then enlightened me about a new genre of craft-brewed beers, hand-made in small batches by brewers who were passionate about yielding a brew that would make the medieval monks salivate.

He then did something that will go down in the annals of history. He said, "Let me buy you a six-pack of a new and really good beer, brewed in a tradition of purity and excellence." Well, what choice did I have? Here's a random guy, offering to buy me beer, and from his short dissertation, a damn good one too. He walked my Stroh's back to the cooler and returned with something called Samuel Adams, which I had never heard of. But I thanked him, tucked it under my arm, and walked away. When I left I was thinking "What a nut!" and "What a nice guy!" at the same time. I jumped in my truck, grabbed an opener, took a swig and drove away. Kidding! Honestly, I don't remember drinking it at all, but what I do remember is throwing my good ol' "Emergency Beer" away shortly thereafter.

I hope that ending wasn't disappointing, but the gist of it was that it's not the taste I remember, but the act of a stranger who took the time to enlighten a young, naïve buck, and set in motion a love and appreciation for what passionate brewers and winemakers can create. He also helped me think twice and even refuse big-batch, small taste beer companies, wine and food makers, who think more about the bottom line than they do about what's in the bottom of their kettles.

Almost a week or so after that fateful encounter, I picked up our local paper to see the face of the guy who had bought me the beer. Turns out he was a local lawyer named

Ben, who also wrote a beer column for the paper. "That's the guy!" I exclaimed, and realized what a fortuitous encounter that had been.

***

Now 30 years later, that same Ben asked me to write a foreword for him for his own book — a collection of the very same articles that inspired me to appreciate craft beer and craft food, if you will, and to write about both. My books have become something like regional best sellers, and folks from all over the Keystone State have in turn become foodies and beer geeks. Now instead of a meaningless toast where everybody looks at his or her can, bottle, or glass, they're now looking each other in the eye and toasting with passion.

Ben Novak was ahead of his time when he started his beer column in the *Centre Daily Times* years ago, but it was perfect timing for me. This is perfect timing for you. Drink in *La Vie* with Ben and let him inspire you and guide you to a new appreciation of an old and sometimes trivialized drink. Cheers, Prost, Salute, To Your Health, or whatever you say, your appreciation of what's in-hand, who you're with, and how good life can be, will go from big batch, small taste, to intimate and full of flavor.

How beautiful!

Ken Hull
Boalsburg, PA

Author's Preface

The Big Bang in Beer History

The "Big Bang" in beer history, with which this book is concerned, occurred in the early 1980s. Before 1980, the entire universe of beer had contracted to a set of tastes and styles of beer the size of a tennis ball. In 1980, there were less than fifty breweries in the entire United States, and they all produced only one style of beer: the classic American light lager, such as Budweiser, Miller, Schlitz, Stroh's, Pabst, etc.

Europeans who visited America constantly ridiculed the blandness and sameness of our beer choices. Americans who visited Europe always returned with highest praises for the beers they encountered there. The universally stated description of American beers in general was "making love in a canoe," which cannot be explained directly, except to say that it refers to doing something "close to water."

Then suddenly the tennis ball exploded to create — seemingly out of nothing — a vast new universe of thousands of small breweries, known as microbreweries, popping up all across the country, each making beers and ales so new (to Americans) and different in tastes and styles (many original), that it made many a beer drinker believe that there just had to be a God.

Prehistoric Beer History

Of course, unlike the physicists' Big Bang, there is a lot of history prior to beer's Big Bang. In a nutshell, it runs like this. From the time of the first colonists at Plymouth Rock and Jamestown, to about the time of the Spanish-American War (1898), beer was as American as apple pie. Clearing forests, forging steel, mining coal, and building railroads across the continent made men thirsty. From what statistics we have, Americans drank two or three times the amount of beer we drink today. Breweries grew up everywhere to slake their thirst. Every town, it seemed, had its own local brewery; there were at least 3,000 in the US around the turn of the century.

But as with all good things, some people were against it. As the 20th century dawned T-Totalers were gaining strength. (The phrase "T-Totaler" arose from the original Temperance Movement, which sought to get people to sign a pledge to abstain. At its inception, however, the pledge was primarily aimed only at hard liquor. By signing it one was not obligated to abstain from beer and wine. However, one could pledge to abstain from all alcohol by adding a "T" after one's signature, committing one to total abstinence.) In 1920, we got Prohibition. That, of course, went over like a lead balloon. Fourteen years later, a thirsty majority of the American people repealed the 18th Amendment. Beer was back.

But for our purposes, it wasn't quite back the way it was before Prohibition. Of the approximately 3,000 breweries that existed in 1920, barely 750 reopened after Prohibition ended in 1934. But the important thing is that in those fourteen years much of the craft of brewing was lost. When the breweries that survived reopened it was the middle of the Great Depression. People just wanted beer — lots of it and cheap. In fourteen years most of the master brewers found other work or just largely disappeared.

But there were two other factors also working against variety over the next half century from the 1930s to the 1980s: advertising and marketing.

Advertising. Advertising costs hit small breweries hard. By the early 1950s, for example, both Budweiser and Schmidt's of Philadelphia were selling about two million barrels a year, and each had to make a decision about the future. Schmidt's decided the way to compete was to keep the price low. Budweiser decided that people don't drink beer, they drink advertising. By the mid '80s, Schmidt's was filing for bankruptcy, and Budweiser was selling fifty million barrels a year. Few small breweries ever had a choice. Unable to afford expensive advertising campaigns, most could only pray that one of the giants would buy them up.

Marketing. Following World War II, many states liberalized their beer laws to allow supermarket sales. This was one of the worst things that ever happened to small breweries and variety. "Why?" you might ask.

Well, it worked this way. Before supermarket sales, men bought most of the beer, either in their pub or from some distributor whose place of business was usually a dingy drive-thru warehouse where some guy in dirty clothes took a case of beer from a shipping palette and loaded it in your trunk. You wouldn't send your wife there, and women didn't like to go — let alone be seen — there. With the advent of supermarket sales, however, this changed. The little missus could just pick up the beer along with the groceries. Convenient!

But it brought a major change in what beers were bought. A little known marketing fact of the time was that while two-thirds of all beer was *drank* by men, with the advent of shopping centers and supermarkets, two-thirds was now *bought* by women. And what beers did the little missus buy for her hubby? Not the local brand she never heard of, but some name brand she saw advertised on the telly.

So, generally wherever supermarket sales were permitted, local breweries bit the dust. On the other hand, where the men still bought beer at dingy old distributors, they continued to order their local favorites. Thus, for example, of the 50 or so breweries left in the entire United States in 1980, seven were located in just one state, Pennsylvania — which fought off allowing supermarket sales of beer until well into the 21st century.

All this goes to explain to the reader how and why, from a beer lover's point of view, just about "nothing" existed prior to the early 1980s.

Fueling the Explosion

If beer's Big Bang was an explosion, it was fueled by changes in the law — as well as a few loopholes — that proved crucial to creating the vast variety of beer and breweries in the US that we all enjoy today. The first change is easy to understand.

Homebrewing Legalized. Not only was there nothing before the Big Bang (characterized by a mass-produced blandness), but it was also illegal to brew your own personal beer at home.

Homebrewing had been made illegal by the original federal regulations adopted in the 1920s to carry out Prohibition. When the 18th Amendment was repealed, however, a mistake in transcription left the regulation prohibiting brewing beer for private use still in effect. The government got around to repealing the regulation in 1978, unleashing a whole new interest in beer. People could now think of brewing, and when they actually brewed their own beer, the next thought was of selling it.

(An interesting fact of homebrew history is that Steve Jobs and Apple Computer got their start in the 1970s at meetings of the Silicon Valley Homebrew Computer Club. So, Apple lovers can also thank the Big Bang in Beer for their iPads and iPhones.)

Tied Houses. Beer brewing and marketing has centuries of history and has lived through just about every abuse known to marketing in general. One of the worst problems encountered in the 19th century was called "tied houses." This occurred when big breweries tried to buy up pubs so that only their particular brew was sold in them. You can easily imagine how this practice skewed the market by keeping both competition and variety out.

The solution to tied houses was laws that divided beer marketing into three *tiers*: breweries, distributors, and retailers (the latter including pubs, restaurants, package stores, etc.) These laws prohibited any person or entity from having an economic interest in more than one tier, effectively preventing, for example, brewers from owning pubs.

Since many of the first microbreweries were conceived as brewpubs where the beer was both brewed and served, they had to overcome the tied houses laws. They did it in two ways.

Taproom Exception. Breweries had a long tradition of having a taproom at the brewery where both employees and the public could enjoy beer brewed on premises. An exception was therefore written into the tiering laws that permitted each brewery to have a taproom on premises.

Many of the first brewpubs of the microbrewery movement came into existence under this exception; they applied for a brewery license instead of a retail license, enabling them to sell their beer on premises. Of course, this limited them considerably, because they could only sell their own product. But such was the thirst for better beer that many of these early brewpubs thrived, convincing others that the market was thirsty for new tastes and styles of beer.

Microbrewery Legislation. It soon became clear that the taproom exception did not cover everything that was needed. In 1982, California passed a new enabling statute specifically authorizing commercial microbreweries, which were defined as breweries producing fewer than 15,000 bbl per year. Model legislation quickly spread to other states.

With a sound legal foundation, microbreweries suddenly began cropping up all across the country. Evoked by an overwhelming rebellion against blandness and fueled by a favorable legal climate, the Big Bang in beer exploded onto the American scene with the same gusto as the early pioneers spread all across the continent to settle the lower forty-eight and form the nation we are proud of today as the United States of America.

The Big Bang Explodes

The first year that the Big Bang in beer registered on seismographs was 1982. In that year, there were approximately 44 known microbreweries in the entire United States. That was also the first year of the Great American Beer Festival (sponsored by the then-fledgling American Microbrewers and American Homebrewers Associations). It was held in Denver, and its purpose was to showcase the new microbrewers and their new styles of beers and ales coming onto the market.

In that first year, the Great American Beer Festival featured 22 new microbreweries presenting 40 different beers to be judged in competition. Total attendance was 800. This was what could be called the first emanation of particles from the Big Bang in beer that would produce the galaxies of beer tastes and styles that we have today.

By 2011, just 33 years after the first Great American Beer Festival, the total number of known microbreweries in the US had skyrocketed from approximately 44 to 1,973 members of the Association. The number of microbrewers attending this 2011 Great American Beer Festival (held in Seattle), had grown by almost 1,200 per cent — from 40 in 1982, to 496 in 2011, while the number of beer aficionados attending grew from 800 in 1982 to 49,000 in 2011.

Clearly, the universe of beer appreciation in America has expanded exponentially.

Present at the Creation

I wish I could fully convey the excitement that existed when all this was new. I traveled around the country to visit the pioneers who were following their love of the craft to build new microbreweries in the fields of Iowa, across the Rocky Mountains, in upstate New York and Vermont, and in Delaware and Pennsylvania. For each, it was a risky venture; many failed to generate enough sales or financing. But everyone I met had that original pioneering look in his or her eye to become a dedicated and determined craftsman or craftswoman. They were truly great people to know. I wish I could have told you about all of them; I was doing research on several of these when the column ended (for reasons I will describe shortly).

In particular I will never forget Ed and Carol Stoudt of Stoudt's Brewing Company in Adamstown, PA. I met Ed in about 1986 at a conference on brewing in San Francisco — one of several conferences Ed traveled to the West Coast to learn about the feasibility of brewing his own beer. I spent many days with him at the conference and later. Ed wanted to have a brewery to go with the restaurant inherited by his wife and him — Stoudt's Black Angus Steakhouse.

What I did not know till later was that while Ed was the financial and planning brains behind it, but it was really Carol who wanted to do the brewing. On many occasions I visited Adamstown to eat in the restaurant, attend Stoudt's annual summer Gemutlichkeit Festival in their bier garten, and to watch the brewing process. Carol hired a trained master brewer, Scott Stover, to assure expertise, but Carol was eager to learn. In 1987, Ed and Carol opened the first microbrewery in Pennsylvania since Prohibition. They quickly produced beers that not only won awards but also won the acclaim of beer drinkers. Soon after creating a viable bottling process, Stoudt's beers were being distributed all over Pennsylvania.

The example of Ed and Carol's dedication would be duplicated by thousands of new brewers across the country in the explosion of the Big Bang in brewing. I only wish that my column had continued so that I could have published the story of Ed and Carol, as well as scores of other early pioneers.

A Happy Ending

The columns collected in this book are part of that initial explosion of interest in beer. Like Ed and Carol, I was one of the early people who caught the excitement, although I was more of an appreciator of craft brewing than a brewer. I could enjoy the crafted results, and report on both the pioneering efforts of those early dedicated craftsmen, and their results. Today we all know the end of the story — Americans now have thousands of craft breweries offering up all the tastes, styles, and craftsmanship a true beer lover could ever want.

Although the Big Bang that started the universe occurred some 13 or 14 billion years ago, we know it happened because astrophysicists have found traces of the initial explosion still flying through space. In the case of beer's Big Bang, this collection represents traces of what things were like in the beginning.

Ben Novak
Ave Maria, Florida
July 2012

Introduction

The materials you are about to read were, in their time, unprecedented. Assembled and reprinted here is the complete set of the first regular newspaper columns on beer ever published in the United States or, as far as I am aware, anywhere else in the world.

It all began in the summer of 1984 because the local weekly wine columnist, Gene Borza, complained to the editor, Bill Welch, of the local county newspaper, the *Centre Daily Times*, that Gene felt overburdened by producing a new wine column every week and wanted to cut his work in half by going bi-weekly. Unfortunately for Bill, however, this left a big hole in the layout of the Sunday local section.

As luck would have it, Bill was in the habit of eating dinner frequently at Ye Olde College Diner on College Avenue in State College, PA, where two friends and I also ate regularly. Jeff Stover was a new lawyer at my law firm of Ben Novak & Associates, Attorneys-at-Law, and Daniel was a Frenchman trained as a chef at the best culinary schools of France who had just bought the diner at a bankruptcy sale. With Daniel now the owner, obviously the cuisine at the diner was not simply diner fare — which explains why the editor of the newspaper as well as many other local notables began eating there regularly.

In any event, Jeff, Daniel, and I had just returned from attending the Great American Beer Festival together in Denver, Colorado, and were regaling Bill with news of new microbreweries opening across the country, and all the new tastes and styles of beer and ale now flooding from the purple mountain majesties across the fruited plain.

Bill immediately grasped that the solution to his problem lay at hand: he asked whether any of us would write a bi-weekly column on the new beers coming onto the scene. I volunteered. Thus an entirely new and unprecedented type of newspaper column was born: a column devoted solely to the appreciation, art, craft, and enjoyment of beer.

Having agreed to write a column on beer, the first problem was to how to write it. There was no precedent to go by. Though it was to alternate on a biweekly basis with a wine column and was devoted, like a wine column, to the art and enjoyment of an alcoholic beverage, I knew from the start that it could not be written with anything like the same tone and attitude.

The Challenges of Writing the First Beer Column

The Wine Column Challenge

At that time, wine columns had been standard features in many of the big city newspapers for decades. They were written for distinct audiences of elites who generally set the tone and standards of social life. But they were much more widely read by people who wanted to show some class. Simply put, for anyone who entertained regularly for business or social climbing reasons, the wine column was a "must." Of course, wine columns also attracted a good part of their audience from those who just wanted to know how the other half lived. Obviously, a beer column would not appeal to any of these audiences. Beer was about as plebeian as anything could be.

The first challenge, therefore, was the problem of finding, defining — or developing out of thin air — an audience: Why would anyone want to read about beer? At that time there was simply no status to beer, and thus no reason to talk about it. And even if you did, what was there to say once you listed the ingredients and described the technical details of the brewing process? With a wine, it was enough to *ooh* and *ahh* about its floral bouquet, rich body, complexity, or vintage. But to talk about these in relation to beer was to invite ridicule.

The Educational Challenge

It may be difficult to imagine today, but back then all that just about anybody knew about beer was Bud, Miller, and Stroh's (which was our local shorthand for all American beers). When friends heard I was going to write on beer, the most frequent question I got was: "What is there to write about?" Another friend asked, "Isn't that like writing on different flavors of soda pop?"

The second problem therefore was educating a readership that there was more to beer than the almost indistinguishable mono-taste of American beers. Compared to a wine column audience, for example, where one could assume that almost everybody knew the major differences in wine (the reds you serve with red meats, the whites with white meat); you could count on your nose the number of people who knew the difference between a lager and an ale.

One reason for this: With only one style of beer, why should anyone care? I doubt that one person in fifty could name the four basic ingredients in beer, and fewer still knew anything more about the styles of beer than light and dark — where light referred to color and not calories. With homebrewing made illegal since Prohibition began in 1919, almost no one had any reason to know anything much about how beer was made.

What this meant was that there was no vocabulary generally known to talk about the differences in beers and ales. The entire subject had to be built from scratch.

Conceptualizing the First Beer Column

Since this was to be a long-running column produced bi-weekly, I had to develop a strategy to bring my audience up to speed. At first, they would be puzzled by the mere existence of a beer column. I had to convince them that there was something of value about it.

Of course, the main thing I had going was the microbrewery revolution. The big news was that these new breweries came into existence to bring out entirely new beer styles and tastes. Throughout the life of the column (practically three years), the constant theme was the appearance of something new amidst the old and familiar.

Beyond that, however, I developed several principles for how I talked about beer. As you peruse the columns in this book, it will help to see the overall strategy.

The first principle of the column was to *report something new*. The microbrewery revolution offered new types and styles of beers and ales to report on, explain, and describe.

This would give a hook upon which to educate the beer drinking public on the differences in beer and how to appreciate them.

The second principle was: *at all costs, don't ape the competition*. The competition was the wine columns, because whatever I wrote back then would be immediately compared to them. This leads to several corollary principles.

Have a sense of humor. Wine columns are generally very serious and pretentious. A column on beer has to convey a totally different attitude. A beer column, I decided had to be humorous and fun, entirely self-deprecating and non-pretentious.

Don't be judgmental. Wine columns are filled with statements about what the author likes. I resolved never to judge a beer based on my taste, but only to describe it as objectively as possible and quote what other's have said about it. The purpose in either case was not to establish a taste comparison, but to help the reader know what to look for (i.e., taste for) in a new beer — what was distinctive about it.

Tell the brewer's story. There is really not much to tell about a wine but what the sun and the rain did to a grape one year. But beer is different, it entails understanding what the brewer conceived when he brewed the beer. For every beer is different, not so much based on climate or soil, but based on what the brewer wanted it to be. Therefore, to appreciate any beer, one has to know something about the brewer and his or her goals in producing that particular brew. The principle was simple: to appreciate a beer is to taste the story in it. (This later served as the rejoinder to a jab from the wine columnist, a sort of in-joke that is explained below.)

Tell the story of beer and ale in history and society. The final corollary is that just as there is a story to each individual brew, there is also a great story of the role of beer and ale in history. For example, each baseball game is not only the story of the teams and coaches in that particular game, but also the story of baseball itself. When a person enjoys a beer, therefore, he or she is becoming part of a long history of beer and brewing and the role it has played in our culture. I thought it was important to add this dimension.

Highlights

I am particularly proud of the first six columns of the series, because in them I hit almost every one of the themes and principles I just described. (In discussing them, however, the reader should know that I did not write the headlines. Although I provided a title to each column, the headline editor always rewrote them.)

The first column, *Revolution in Brewing Keeps the Customer Satisfied (9/9/1984)*, sets the theme for the rest of the series: there is something new going on in the beer market. Here I list four different factors that are changing everything that one may have thought was unchanging. These include: 1) the microbrew revolution giving birth to new brewers and new styles of beer and ale; 2) the invasion of new imports to the US making available tastes and styles not previously available; 3) the new recognition of regional breweries that kept their old tastes despite the mergers and consolidations that homogenized the market; and 4) the response of the Big Six in brewing that did not ignore the changes, but began to bring out variety in their offerings. In subsequent columns I tried to embellish on each of these developments.

The second column, *For What Ales You: A Guide to Different Beer Types (9/23/1984)*, was my first educational column, in which I give a brief guide to several of the main types or styles of beer and ale.

The first two columns were straightforward and factual, and it was time to introduce the fun. The third article, *Raging Debate over How to Pour Beer Coming to a Head (10/7/1984)*, was written specifically to inject a note of self-deprecating humor into the column, and to assure beer drinkers that this series was not going to be serious and pretentious in tone like a wine column. For, if it sounded at all like a wine column, I was sure I would lose my readers.

Brewery Goes Full Steam Ahead (10/21/1984), the fourth column, introduces the theme of talking about a beer by telling the brewer's story. There were many reasons why I chose to tell the story of Fritz Maytag and the Anchor Steam brewery. First, the Anchor Steam Brewery, after Maytag took over, really became the model for other microbrewers, and became the flagship of the movement (even though another microbrewery predated it). Of all the microbrewers, Maytag was the most dedicated, passionate, and most of all articulate and successful. Another reason is historical, in that Anchor Steam beer is the only recognized original style of beer from America (even though no one today knows how the original was made — go figure). There was also a practical reason; Anchor Steam was one of the few microbrewery beers that was locally available, which meant that my readers could sample what I was writing about.

I particularly enjoyed writing the fifth column, *Flavor of American History: Beer, Ale in the Colonies (11/4/1984)*. This is the first of my articles telling the story of beer in a way to make its history part of an ongoing tradition. Frankly, too, I wanted to have some fun with the local Women's Christian Temperance Union, which was still a force in central Pennsylvania; several townships around State College still banned the sale of alcoholic beverages. The fact that the earliest colonists, including the Pilgrims, considered beer important was a revelation that made a whole lot of beer drinkers in my reading area much more comfortable.

My sixth column, *Stalking Some Great Native Beers in Denver (11/18/1984)*, returns to the microbrewery revolution by reporting on the Great American Beer Festival that my friends and I were telling the local newspaper editor about when he asked one of us to write a column on beer. At that time, there were only about 44 microbrewers in America. That was truly at the beginning of the revolution, for today that number reaches into the thousands. This is the first of many articles surveying the field in order to describe the new styles and identify the new offerings by brewers.

The column *Porter: A Hearty Drink with Strong History and Tradition (12/2/1984)* was one of the most popular I ever wrote. People loved the history and the poetry, the tradition mixed with humor and irony connected with this nectar of the gods. I shall talk about this column again under my most popular columns.

Finally, my first annual Christmas column on beer was the first of three annual Christmas columns while the series ran. It had a special function of adding a note of reverence and awe that was appropriate to the season, but also vital to the concept of the column itself. You see, I wanted to be irreverent about beer; but I learned long ago that in order for irreverence to work, one must first have something to revere; without it, irreverence falls flat. Few things ever pleased me as much as when Luther Harshbarger, the head of Penn State's religious studies department, congratulated me for managing to insert good theology into an article about beer. What I wrote in my Christmas columns seems as wonderful, cozy, and familiar at Christmas today as it did more than a quarter century ago. These columns are *Joy of Christmas Spirits (12/16/1984), Yule Ales Add to Advent Spirit (12/1/1985),* and *This Season Brews Fond Memories (12/17/1986).*

The Initial Reception

For the first month or two after the column began to appear, almost no one mentioned it to me. I thought I was writing into the void. I think they simply did not know how to take it or to respond to anything so new, different, and unexpected as a regular newspaper column on beer.

But by Christmas, these seven articles clearly established the column as humorous, interesting, fun, and knowledgeable. People relaxed and began telling me how much they enjoyed them. Suddenly all kinds of people — perfect strangers — were coming up to me on the street with good words about it. The ice was broken and the barriers came down. It took four months, but from Christmas on I made new friends all over the county.

Fruitful Errors, Inside Jokes, and High Points

How a clerical error led to my columns starring in Journalism class. In a column on Budweiser on Feb. 10, 1985 I wrote that, under the German Purity Law of 1516, "beers can contain only four ingredients: barley malt, hops, yeast, and water." However, either I or my secretary or the newspaper copyist who retyped it for publication (this was before electronic copies could be sent and everything was delivered in hard copy to be retyped into the printing process), added a comma after "barley." Who of these first added the unwanted comma was never discovered, but when the editor read it, she compounded the mistake into downright error. She read the list of five items separated by commas and changed "four" to "five," so that the sentence now read "beers can contain only five ingredients: barley, malt, hops, yeast, and water." I, of course, was mortified. It now looked like I intended to say beer contained five ingredients, something that would make me look quite ignorant to my growingly knowledgeable readers.

So, I planned a whole article for Aug. 1, 1985 to clarify all the typos, clerical errors, and just plain mistakes that had crept into the column, to which my editor gave the title *Summer Dog Days Are for Washing Up the Wart Tun*.

The upshot is that these two columns, the one with the misplaced comma leading to a major error, and the article explaining it, were used by Professor Tom Berner in journalism courses at Penn State University for more than two decades to demonstrate how something as small as a misplaced comma can significantly change the meaning of an article and result in embarrassment.

Inside joke: sparring with the wine columnist. Some time after my beer column appeared, the wine columnist, Gene Borza, who was a good personal friend, took a good-natured jab in his column at the very idea of a column on beer appreciation—which to the cultured palate of the elite was entirely too plebeian. So, in my next column, *Beer Tasting: Learning to Appreciate a Brewer's Taste (9/8/1985)*, I responded. You would not know that the following was a response to a jab from the wine columnist because it is not mentioned in my column, which is why I refer to it as an inside joke. But to those locally who read both columns regularly, it was obvious.

In any event, here is my response. Comparing a wine tasting to a beer tasting, I delivered my own put-down by noting that there is nothing more to appreciating wine than the sensual tasting of "what the sun and the rain did to a grape one year." Then I delivered the coup de grace by distinguished beer appreciation from wine appreciation by explaining that:

> *"...beer is much more of an art. What you taste in a beer is the taste a brewer intended to put there. So the object of a beer tasting is not so much to judge a taste but to learn to appreciate another man's taste, namely the brewer."*

Gene Borza immediately called me when my article, appeared and laughingly said *"Touché."*

High Point: finding my articles laminated in a bar outside San Francisco. In the summer of 1986, I took a motorcycle trip across the US. Traveling 9,000 miles in 37 days I dipped my foot into both oceans, and visited microbreweries from Iowa to Minnesota to Idaho and Washington state, and then south to California. One of the high points, however, came as I began my return trip by cutting through the hills east of San Francisco. There I stopped at a popular country bar and ordered a beer. I noticed the barmaid (who later turned out to be the owner), seeming to stare at me. Soon, she walked over and picked up a laminated stand-up on the bar, looked at it, then carried it over to ask, "Are you the guy in this picture?"

I'll be darned if it wasn't a copy of one of my articles. "Yup, sure is," I replied. That was all it took for her to treat me like royalty. She explained that my articles were being handed out at the annual San Francisco Beer Festival. She then introduced me to everybody in the bar and announced, "All the drinks you want are on me."

The saloon she owned was great, with a large, well-appointed western-style atmosphere, and a long bar with about 12 taps dispensing local microbrewery beers. When I commented on her choice of beers, she explained that the week before the bar had just celebrated "Bud's Gone Day," referring to the day that all the national beers were replaced by local microbrewed beers. On the bar were a set of about twelve cups filled with different kinds of hops, each labeled. You could actually take a hop and chew it, tasting and comparing it with all the others. There was a second row for different barley malted at different temperatures so one could compare all the differences.

She also told me her own story. She had worked as a waitress and barmaid for about 20 years, scrimping and saving every penny to buy that particular bar. She was determined to make it the best bar for good beer in the valley. She was a real aficionado. I have to say that it felt good to be treated as a celebrity by such a wonderful person, and to know that the fame of my column had reached the West Coast. But the real honor was just to meet such a dedicated beer aficionado willing to work herself to the bone to reach her ambition. After all, she was the kind of person I was really writing for.

Most Popular

You may want to know the most popular articles at the time. The articles that received the most response by far were:

Yuengling Beer: The Pearl of Pottsville (2/9/1986). Part of the reason for the popularity of this column is that State College, PA, lies at just about the western edge of the D.C. Yuengling Brewing Company's regional area. But that is not all the story. It is difficult to believe in today's world how much loyalty and affection people can have for a particular local beer. Of all my columns, none received as many thanks and outpourings of feeling as this paean to the pearl of Pottsville.

Next come the three articles on McSorley's Ale House and Saloon. These are entitled *A Legend in a Bottle (9/7/1986)*; *Memories Abound: Many Drawn to Famous N.Y. Saloon (9/21/1986)*; and *McSorley's Character (10/5/1986)*. McSorley's is without a doubt the most sacred institution in America that even today is visited as a pilgrimage. I received dozens of calls and ran into many dozens of people after these appeared who could not wait to tell me they had been there.

As mentioned above, my column on porter, *Porter: A Hearty Drink with Strong History and Tradition (12/2/1984)*, seemed to be the article that broke the ice and brought forth the first fulsome positive responses to the series. People finally grasped the fun and humor of the stories, and seemed for the first time to relax and enjoy them. For some the last little rhyme in the column caught on, and I was to hear many say in reverent tones in my presence — either to me or to their beer — "Oh, my soul, can this be porter?"

Undoubtedly, the most literary of all my columns was the ironic mockery of light beers in my introduction to dark beers entitled *Dark Beers: Courage to Peer into a Glass Darkly (2/24/1985)*. Professors of English, philosophy, and writing courses used it as a model in classes, and critics of popular culture thought it was a classic; see also the follow-up containing Dr. Mourant's enquiry about light dark/beers, in *Light-Dark Beers: The Possibilities Are Endless (5/13/1987)*.

My Favorites

Beyond all these, the articles I wrote on particular new beers were the most gratifying, and evoked the strongest response over time. People seemed to like to read the stories behind how a brewery was founded and how a new beer that was once only a dream in a future brewer's mind came to be reality. These were, above all, the columns that fixed in readers' minds the idea that the true enjoyment of beer lay in tasting the art, craft, and the story of the brewer in one's stein. Among the best of these are:

Giving Up the Rat Race for a Great Glass of Beer (1/13/1985); the story of Matthew Reich and New Amsterdam Beer;

British Ales Invade Manhattan (2/24/1985); the story of two Englishmen founding the Manhattan Brewing Company;

Penn State Alumni Brew Outstanding Beer (8/25/1985); the story of Jim Kollar and Chesbay;

Spirit of Cincinnati Brewing Available in Centre County (9/22/1985); the story of Christian Moerlein and Hudepohl Brewing Company;

Challenge and Tradition at Blitz Weinhard (11/3/1985); the story of how brewing an ancient recipe saved the Blitz Weinhard Brewery;

Saranac: Unveiling a Taste Imported from the Past (12/29/1985); the story of another old recipe brought to life by the F. X. Matt Brewery;

A Revolutionary Beer Lager Result of 6 Generations of Brewing (1/26/1986); the story of Jim Koch's founding of the Boston Brewing Company and the creation of Samuel Adams Boston Lager;

Scientists Become Brewers (2/23/1986); and *Boulder Beers: Product of Quality and Idealism (3/9/1986)*; the story of how two nuclear- and astro-physicists founded the Boulder Brewing Company, helped by an idealistic stock broker;

Sierra Nevada Brewers Get Their Start Scrounging in Junkyards (4/6/1986); and *Sierra Nevada: Ales Brewed in the West (4/20/1986)*; the story of Ken Grossman's dream as a 13-year-old to brew beer and the founding of one of the most successful microbreweries in America;

Brewer Follows in Footsteps of His Famous Ancestor (8/10/1986); and *New Lager with Old-Time European Taste is Brewed in Pennsylvania (8/24/1986)*; the story of Thomas V. Pastorius and the founding of Penn Pilsner;

Thomas Hardy Beer Arrives in America (8/24/1986); the story of how an ancient beer with the most beautiful description in literary history came to be brewed again;

Writer Pleasantly Surprised by New Beer (3/4/1987); and *Catamount Brewery: Young Men's Dream Realized (4/15/1987)*; the story of two academics' dream of fresh beer for New England; and finally, the already-mentioned first article on a brewer's story:

Brewery Goes Full Steam Ahead (10/21/1984); the story of Fritz Maytag and the flagship brewery of the microbrewery revolution, Anchor Steam Brewery.

History of the Beginnings of the Craft Brew Revolution

I assume that for many, indeed for most of the people who choose to buy and read this book, their major interest is historical. They want to know what the revolution in American beer tastes was like at the beginning. For such readers, these articles constitute a sustained view of the development of this revolution when it was new. In 1984, when this revolution had barely taken off, there were fewer than 50 known microbrewery startups. By the time these columns ended in 1987, this had increased to over 100. Today, of course, there are thousands. So, for anybody really interested in what it was like when all this started, this collection presents one of the few attempts at the time to report about this revolution to a general audience of ordinary people, instead of in beer publications or books aimed at people already interested in beer. At that time, I was simply not aware of any other sustained effort like it.

Why These Columns Ended

For anyone who reads these articles to the end, the question will hopefully arise: why did the series end so abruptly? Did the author lose interest? Was there insufficient reader interest? Was there a fight with the editor? The answer is: none of the above. Rather, the reason is simply the march of globalization. The *Centre Daily Times* was founded in 1896 and continued as a family-owned newspaper until 1979, when it was bought up by Knight-Ridder. For the first several years thereafter the local management remained in place. But in late 1986, Knight-Ridder really began to take over. One result was the termination of all the local columns. This included the food writer, the beer and wine columns, and several others. I was quite sad at this turn of events, for I greatly enjoyed writing on beer.

One other question that might cross the mind of the reader is: what was I paid to write these columns? The answer may be embarrassing in today's crass commercial world: the only pay that I or the other local columnists received was a free subscription to the *Centre Daily Times*. However, at that time, it was considered an honor to serve the community by writing for the local newspaper. (Even though it was bought in 1979, it was still considered as a family and community newspaper because the same management stayed in place until about 1987. Soon after 1987, however, not only the local columnists but also the local management was gone.)

As I ended all the articles, I shall end this introduction: Ein Prosit der Gemutlichkeit!

Revolution in Brewing
Leaves the Customer Satisfied

September 9, 1984

Editor's Note: On Tap is a regular feature on beer that will occur every other Sunday. Ben Novak, 41, a State College attorney, has been a brewing aficionado since his college days. He estimates he has sampled more than 200 brands of beer from 15 countries.

Surely if there is one thing that a man ought to be able to take for granted, it is the cold one he reaches for while watching the game.

For well nigh a half century in America a person was able to walk into his favorite tavern and place his order by simply asking for a "beer". He could be pretty confident that whatever brand was served would be a familiar taste. Ninety-five percent of all the beer produced in America was the same lager type and pilsener style, so his taste buds were well protected from surprise.

For half a century the beer industry reflected the market's penchant for a single type of beer. For several decades after Prohibition, which ended in 1933, the existing breweries in America bought one another and consolidated into a few giant companies.

For a while the beer industry was beginning to look like the fast food industry: a small number brands available everywhere, and everywhere the same. But that was just the foam in your stein. Underneath a revolution was brewing. A revolution was demanded by consumers — both women and men — for flavor, variety, and deep rich taste in their beers.

The revolution of American beer has happily erupted on four fronts. The battle for your taste buds is on and good news is found on just about every battlefield.

First, a whole new breed of "microbrewers" has entered the beer industry. These are young men who have started small breweries producing less than 10,000 barrels a year. They produce less than one percent of the beer in America, but they are challenging the giants to meet new standards of quality and real beer flavor.

The microbrewers are leading a return to beers with deep, rich taste. They have captured the attention of the media, which are rushing in to provide information on a new growth industry. And they have captured the attention of beer lovers around the world, anxious to taste the most touted results of new Yankee abilities in an international field where America has not been considered in the running since Prohibition. Already some of the new microbrewery beers have been recognized as "world class".

The second "front" of the beer revolution in America has been the invasion of imports. More than 400 brands are registered for importation and they are rapidly developing a beachhead. In the larger cities such as New York and Los Angeles, up to 20 percent of the beer being consumed is imported.

The imported beers have found a ready market in America for a wide range of tastes. These include not only the Old World Brews of Bohemia, Britain, Bavaria, and the Netherlands but also the fine brews developed in the New World such as Dos Equis from Mexico, and the great brews from Canada, Australia, Japan, and the Philippines.

The third "front" of the American beer revolution is the resurgence of the few small local breweries that have survived both Prohibition and the pressure to merge with the giants. These are the "regionals" who've stuck it out, usually with only a small band of loyal customers to support them.

Ausburger, brewed by the Joseph Huber Brewing Co. of Monroe, Wisc. is one of the most well-known of the regional "world class" beers.

Pennsylvania is fortunate to be the home of one of the largest numbers of the independent regionals in the country. These include D.G. Yuengling of Pottsville whose porter has become almost a cult beer in three states; the Jones Brewing Co. of Smithton, which makes Stoneys, Old Shay, and Esquire (the latter being one of the smoothest beers in the world); Latrobe Brewing Co. famous for Rolling Rock; Straubs of St. Mary's, perhaps the most famous of all; The Lion Inc., of Wilkes-Bare, brewer of Gibbons, Liebotschaper, Stegmaier and Esslinger; Pittsburgh Brewing Co., the pride of western Pennsylvania, maker of Iron City Beer and Christian Schmidt, maker of Schmidt's of Philadelphia, Prior Double Dark and McSorley's Cream Ale.

These independent regional breweries like their counterparts in many other states, are making a comeback, justifying their perseverance in preserving the brewer's art and the tradition of regional tastes.

The fourth "front" in the great American beer revolution has been the response of America's own giant breweries. Unlike the Big Three of the American automobile industry, the Big Six of the American brewing industry — Anheuser Busch, G Heileman, Stroh, Miller, Pabst, and Coors — are moving quickly to meet the challenges of imports and demands of many consumers for more taste in beer.

Ein Prosit der Gemutlichkeit!

For What 'Ales' You:
A Guide to Different Beer Types

September 23, 1984

If you have read any beer labels lately, or have simply noted the beer "types" mentioned in their names, you will have noted a baffling variety of categories. Moosehead calls itself a "lager," while Molson Red Label is an "ale"; Miller Lite styles itself a "Pilsner," and Guinness is, of course, a "stout." Stroh is now marketing a "marzen" beer. The beer judged by some critics as the best America has to offer is Anchor "steam beer."

Ausburger beer comes as both a "Dark" as well as a "Bock." And Colt 45 is "malt liquor."

It sounds almost as confusing as wines. But it is not. There are just two basic types of beer, called lagers and ales. Once you understand the difference between these two the rest comes easily.

Traditionally, all beers — both ales and lagers — are made from only four ingredients: barley, hops, yeast, and water. In Germany, under very strict laws, no other ingredients are permitted to be added.

In the brewing process, barley is converted to malt, which is then dried and cured and heated. The degree to which the malt is roasted when heated determines whether the beer will be light or dark. Hops, which are a climbing, perennial plant, are added to impart the bitter flavor to beer. Finally, yeast is added as the fermenting agent.

The Three Big Factors

In this process, a change in three factors determines whether the beer is an ale or lager: The type of yeast; the temperature at which it is fermented and the length of the aging process.

Ales, which use the oldest type of brewing process, are "top fermented." This means that the type of yeast used to make ale rises to the top and floats during the fermentation stage. The ale type of yeast will ferment at a relatively higher temperature. Because of this higher temperature ales could be brewed year round. Finally, ales need to be aged for a short period of time, when only a few days to at most a few weeks.

Lagers on the other hand use a "bottom fermenting" yeast. The lager type yeast sinks to the bottom of the vat during fermentation. This yeast works at a much lower temperature than ale yeast. Before the days of refrigeration lagers could only be made in the cold months of the year. The word "lager" comes from the German word "to store." Lager beers are normally stored and aged for much longer periods of time than ales. Michelob, for example, is lagered, or aged for 32 days, while Pilsner Urquell, the most famous lager in the world, is lagered for three months.

For most of history, ales were the only type of beer that could be practically produced. It was not until the discoveries of Louis Pasteur that the study of fermentation became possible. His discoveries opened up the possibility of separating the lager-type strains of yeast and of preserving them in refrigerated conditions. These advances were first incorporated into beer production by Gabriel Sedlmayr in Munich in the 1820s. The result made Munich the beer capital of the world, a title it holds to this day.

But the crown of perfection for 19th century beer was won by Czechoslovak breweries in two little towns called Pilsen and Budweis. The beers brewed there beginning in 1842 were the lightest, clearest, most golden, sparkling beers in the world. The style of beer from these two towns became the most popular in the world.

"Pilsner-style" was widely copied and is a name found on many American beer labels even today. It denotes the style of beer drunk by about 95 percent of all American beer drinkers. The name of the original beer from Pilsen is Pilsner Urquell, which simply means, " Pilsner from the Original Source."

"Budweis" was the name of the town and of the beer from which Adolphus Busch took the name "Budweiser" for the beer he introduced to the American public in 1876. Today, Budweiser is the largest selling beer in the world.

Generally lager beers are lighter in color, lighter in taste, and lighter in alcoholic content than ales. However, if the malt is roasted at roasted at higher temperatures the result will not be the light "Pilsner" type but a "dark" beer known as "Munich Dark". When made very strong and very dark it is known as a "Bock" beer, named for the kick of a billy goat.

Ales can be categorized in three types: Pale ale, porter, and stout. Pale ale is the traditional beverage in Britain where, contrary to American custom, ales constitute about 80 percent of the beer consumed. Bass Ale is a good example of a pale ale. Porter is made by the ale process, but with the use of a highly roasted malt. Porter generally has a strong coffee type taste. Stout, which is the Irish contribution, has an even fuller body and a heavy bitter, burnt-chocolate taste.

Because lager beer needed a colder temperature to age, it could not be brewed in the 19th century during the summer months. The last batch of the Spring was brewed in March. It had to be brewed with a higher alcohol content in order to help it last through the summer. Since it was brewed in March the Germans called it "Marzen" beer and it was the beer drank at the following fall harvest and at Oktober-fest.

"Steam beer" is America's contribution to the art of brewing. In turn-of-the-century San Francisco, refrigeration was simply unavailable. Even the winters there were too warm. A way was found to give San Franciscans the fashionable lager beer of the day, but lagered at ale temperatures in special vats. The process produced a lively head, which was dubbed "steam" when the kegs were opened. Today, Anchor Steam Beer from San Francisco is rated by critics as one of the top five beers in the world.

Ein Prosit der Gemutlichkeit!

Raging Debate Over How to Pour Beer Coming to a Head

October 7, 1984

There are always three ways to enjoy beer: Your way, my way and the expert way.

Undoubtedly your way is the best. I like to think that my way is pretty reasonable. But the experts, as always, do not agree on anything, so it's a lot more fun to talk about their ways.

The great controversy among the experts is over the question of how to pour beer in a glass. In Jonathan Swift's famous book, "Gulliver's Travels," the wars between the little people of Lilliput and Blefuscu were fought between the "big-endians" and the "little-endians" over the great issue of which end of an egg one should crack open to eat. In our time this momentous issue has been replaced as the great divider among men and nations by the greater issue concerning the amount of foam on top of one's stein.

Actually, the argument breaks down, or shall we say, rises to the issue of "head." The "big head" experts demand that their beer shall be poured down the middle of the glass, splashing at the bottom, and raising a blooming and beautiful head of foam. The "little head" experts tilt their glasses and let the beer run down the side to minimize the foam.

Big Header's Position

The big headers insist that splashing pour is essential to release the flavor. Ed McMahon says that it's the way to release the "tiny little taste buds" in beer. Howard Hillman, the author of "The Gourmet Guide to Beer" argues that "unless a beer is sufficiently aerated, it will not release enough CO_2 or aeromatics."

Of course, if a beer does not release enough CO_2 before it reaches one's mouth, then all the CO_2 gas will have to be released in one's stomach. Since mass production beers are not naturally carbonated, but rather full of artificial, chemical carbonation, it is argued that the bloated feeling that some people get from drinking beer is the result of the way their beer is poured.

The big headers also put forward two other arguments for pouring their beer happily and splashingly down the center of the glass. First, they argue that the action of releasing the head in the form bubbles, also releases the aroma of the beer to be savored by the true lover of hops and malt.

Second, they argue that a good head is the pride of a brewer's art. The ideal head is composed of extremely small heads (bubbles), and is very thick. I have been told that the perfect head is one on which one can write one's initial and it will still be there when the beer underneath has been quaffed (I have not yet found a head on a beer thick enough to hold an initial through to the bottom, but I keep looking and writing my initials in the foam).

Little Head Arguments

Whether the big headers are right or not, they constitute a small minority in this country. The vast majority of beer drinkers in this country are "little-headers." Most folks tilt the glass and let the beer run down the side, attempting to stir up as little head as possible.

The most respected world expert on beer, Michael Jackson of England (not the Michael Jackson), sides with the Americans. He argues a really good beer will produce a good head without being poured splashingly down the center.

"Served that sort of violence," he writes, "any beer will produce an instant head, but not an honest one."

The biggest reason that most people do not like a big head of foam on their stein is, of course, that they do not like to get foam on their face when they drink. The biggest headers usually foam at the mouth at the mere suggestion of this argument.

With mass produced, artificially carbonated beers, however, there is a more cogent reason for pouring beer slowly down the side of a glass. Artificial carbonation is easily injected into the beer before bottling and is just as easily released when poured. Thus pouring the beer down the side of the glass helps keep the beer from losing its chemical carbonation and keeps it from going flat in your glass.

Beer in cans often has less artificial carbonation injected into it by the manufacturer than the same beer in a bottle. This is because can beer is expected to be drank directly from the can, rather than poured into a glass. Canned beer, therefore, can go flat much more quickly and ought to be poured to minimize the head.

How much head should you want on your beer? Be careful: the answer to that question may have been one of the underlying, very deep, unknown causes of the two world wars. The Germans like lots of head, usually at least 2 inches on a 22 oz. glass. The English on the other hand want their glasses filled to the brim, and then insist that the head form above the level of the rim.

Most Americans have sided with the English on making sure the beer filled their glasses to the brim. But few Americans expect a head to form above the rim anymore. This probably says a lot about artificial carbonation than it does about good head.

In the Netherlands where the brewer's art is highly prized, the Dutch say that a good head on a beer should be "two fat fingers thick."

It is my impression, however, that it is hard to write one's initial in the foam with fat fingers.

Ein Prosit der Gemutlichkeit!

Brewery Goes Full Steam Ahead

October 21, 1984

In 1965, young Fritz Maytag, the heir to the Maytag washing machine fortune, was drifting around San Francisco. He was 28 years old and had a degree from Stanford in Asian studies. But the Vietnam war, which was just heating up, was not where he wanted to use his talents.

One evening he decided to go back to visit one of his old college haunts, the Spaghetti Factory, for old time's sake. As a student he had remembered downing schooners of the local brew there. At dinner, he heard that the Anchor Steam brewery was for sale. The next day he visited it and on an impulse, bought it.

Making beer was not as easy as making washing machines. Maytag had to learn not simply a technique but an art. The company steadily lost money for the next eight years. But, fortunately Maytag was not a quitter. By 1973 he had developed an almost perfect beer and, what was equally good news, a profit for the first time.

The result of Maytag's investment in superb beer is still ongoing. Since he proved that a beer with taste could make it, 15 new microbreweries have opened up across the country. Some of these already closed, usually because of under capitalization, but nine are still operating and eight more are scheduled to fire up their brew kettles in 1984. Maytag, a perfectionist who also owns and runs vineyards and wineries, was challenged by the brewing business. William Mares, in his book "Making Beer" quotes the philosophy that made Maytag take on the challenge.

"Beer is just beer," Maytag once explained. "That's part of the problem and part of the fun of it. Wine making is anything you want to make of it, but beer is beer. That's one reason I like making beer. On the one hand, it's the common man's drink. Nobody will pay a dollar a bottle for any great quantity of it. On the other hand its much harder to make than wine, takes more art and science."

Maytag's Anchor Brewing now makes five highly rated brews. Anchor Steam Beer is, of course, the flagship of his fleet. It is a lager beer, but aged at higher temperature than is traditional. It has a dark copper color and real beer taste. Michael Jackson lists Anchor Steam Beer as one of the top five beers in the world.

Anchor also makes a superb porter. Originally Anchor's porter was a bottom-fermented "porter like" beer. But Anchor has recently installed a new top fermenting ale facility, and Anchor's porter is now a real top-fermented porter.

In 1983, Anchor also started continuous production of its famous bicentennial top-fermented brew, Liberty ale. This ale has a unique flavor and aroma obtained by a process rarely used in America known as "dry hopping." In this process while, fresh hops are specially added to the aging tanks during fermentation.

Anchor has also revived another old brewing tradition — the production of special beers commemorating holidays and important events. Anchor's holiday brew is its Special

Christmas Ale. The 1983 edition of this annual specialty won fourth place at this year's Great American Beer Festival.

Anchor also makes a "barley wine" to commemorate special events. A "barley wine" is so called because it has a high alcoholic content, a fruity aroma, and a rich lingering taste. Anchor's brand is known as Old Foghorn after the British tradition of giving barley wines humorous names. It has an alcoholic content of 10.5 percent.

The 1983 batch was brewed on April 7, 1983, the 50th anniversary of the end of Prohibition. Each bottle from that batch had a small card affixed which read "Jubilee Ale, April 7, 1933-1983." In celebration of the most important date in American brewing industry history.

It may be interesting to know that barley wines are ales sold in small six or seven ounce bottles known as "nips." This is probably the source of Rolling Rock's slogan, "The little nip in the green pony bottle."

Anchor Brewery's beers and ales are now available in 22 states, but not yet in Pennsylvania. Fortunately Fritz Maytag intends to expand sales to every state in the Union.

Ein Prosit der Gemutlichkeit!

Flavor of American History:
Beer, Ale and the Colonists

November 4, 1984

It has been said that, "To speak of the origins of brewing in America is to speak of the origins of the nation itself."

There is more than a little truth in this.

So if you want to share some of the real flavor of American history, sit back, fill up a fine tankard of good English ale and relax. We will talk together of some of the unsung facts about the place that humble beer has occupied in the founding of America.

The Jamestown Beer Shortage

The subject of beer was among the most conscious concerns of America's first colonists. When the ship which had brought the first settlers to Jamestown in 1607 lifted anchor to make the return voyage to England, one of the settlers realized that the colony's planners had forgotten something: "There remained." He sadly wrote, "Neither tavern, beer house, nor place of relief."

It was well known, indeed taken for granted long before the founding of Jamestown, that ale was the "Naturall drinke" for an "Englysshe Man." The experience of the New World was a difficult transition for the new settlers who complained bitterly that "our drinke was water."

Although ale was frequently sent on the supply ships to Jamestown, the Governor and Council of Virginia resolved to find a more permanent solution to the pressing problem of providing "naturalle drinke." In 1609, the Council voted to advertise in England for two brewers to be sent to the colony.

But the situation was not immediately solved, and a Spanish visitor to Jamestown in 1613 wrote the following report to his government:

"There are about 300 men there more or less (who) have nothing but bread or maize, with fish; nor do they drink anything but water — all of which is contrary to the nature of the English."

And Sir Francis Wyatt was still writing at about 1624 that there had been great sickness in the colony for "want of beer."

By 1629 it is recorded that peace had been brought to the hearts and hearths of the Virginia colonists. Captain John Smith writing his general history of Virginia in that year boasted that the colony had built two brewhouses, and he further described the means by which the English colonists achieved naturalness again:

"For drink, some malt the Indian corne, others barley, of which they make good Ale and such plenty thereof, few of the upper Planters drinke any water, but the better sort are well furnished with ... good English Beere."

The Planters were happy, the colony was growing, and more settlers were needed. In 1649, a pamphlet was published in London to encourage emigration to Virginia. The following were prominently listed among the attractions of the new colony:

"That they have six publick brewhouses, and most brew their own beer, strong and good."

'That they have ... plenty of victual, bread and good beer and housing, all of which the Englishman loves full dearly."

While the settlers of Virginia were still seeking to solve the problem of beer in Virginia, our Pilgrim fathers were negotiating that very point with the London Company which was responsible for planning the voyage of the Mayflower. The Pilgrims voiced their fear that the "drinking water would infect their bodies with sore sickness and grievous diseases."

It should be understood that in the 17th century beer was the universal beverage of Englishmen as well as most of Northern Europe. Common water supplies were usually contaminated. Although the science of hygiene was unknown, it was the source of frequent sickness, sometimes more fatal than driving under the influence.

The London company which chartered the Mayflower had first come to assure the Pilgrims that they would have to drink water, but that they would "have their meat, drink, apparel and full provisions out of the common stock of said colony."

One of the interesting side results of these negotiations was that a young man named John Alden was hired by the Company. John Alden, famous in the annals of love and romance, was a cooper taken aboard the voyage to look after the hogsheads of beer promised to the Pilgrims.

Apparently, however, he had seen Priscilla across the deck of the Mayflower. Happily, he decided to join the Pilgrim fathers rather than returning to England on the ship.

The Company's promise, however, to supply sufficient beer was not kept. The supplies of ale on the Mayflower proved insufficient for the voyage. As the Mayflower was navigating along the coast of Massachusetts heading south toward their destination at the mouth of the Hudson river, they ran out of beer.

It was because they ran out of beer that the Pilgrims stepped ashore at Plymouth Rock. The journal of one of the Pilgrim's records: "We could not now take time for further search or consideration, our victuals being much spent; especially our beer."

The result was that, much against their nature, our Pilgrim fathers and mothers "were hasted ashore and more to drink water."

Fortunately, the water at Plymouth was pure. Governor Bradford wrote that while it was "not so wholesome as the good beer" of London, it was "wholesome enough for us that can be content therewith."

Not everyone could "be content therewith and the colonists' demand for beer needed determined leaders to slake it."

John Winthrop, the future Governor of the Massachusetts Bay Colony, booked passage to the colony on the good ship "Lady Arbella," carrying not only the new charter of the Bay Colony, but also "42 Tonnes of Beere" (about 10,000 gallons). He thus assured that his arrival in the colony would be a time of happy memory.

Thus beer was there at the beginning of the nation, in the form of a lusty brew of ale, with sufficient alcohol to kill the bacteria in the water and make the drink safe, and sufficiently nutritious to refresh and embolden the fathers of the great new nation to be.

Ein Prosit der Gemutlichkeit!

Stalking Some Great Native Beers
in Denver

November 18, 1984

One cannot write a column about beer for very long time without friends asking, "OK, what beer is the best beer?"

I have noticed that this question most frequently comes from my wine drinking friends. My beer drinking friends already know what the best beer is: it's the next beer of course. That way they always have something to look forward to.

The fact is that among us beer lovers, your taste is as good as mine — probably better. So there is little use in my picking out the beer I like best. Indeed each of us may have his or her own favorite.

But there is always that next beer, and we do have to decide upon it. Shall we opt for the safety of the known and familiar brand? Or shall we try to introduce our taste buds to a little adventure?

An excellent opportunity to taste new beers is offered at "The Great American Beer Festival." Which is held in Denver each June in conjunction with the American Homebrewers Convention and the American Microbrewers Conference.

Why would anyone want to go to an American beer festival? Don Bradford, one of the organizers of the "The Great American Beer Festival," recently succinctly stated in

"Beer" magazine the general public awareness problem: "Think American beer and up comes conformity. The world over is aware of the distinctive contribution to world beer styles, the American pilsener. Derided in many circles, it nevertheless represents perfection in its style. However considering volume sold and drank, the talk that surrounds it, and the marketing campaign of each one, you'd think that's all that came out of American breweries."

What he is talking about are the beers most of us drink most of the time. Ninety-five percent of the beer consumed in America is of one single type. It includes Yuengling, Pabst, Iron City, Miller, Rolling Rock and almost all the media advertised brands.

What if every car tried to be a Chevy? That's what most of the American beer industry has tried to do. They have reached the mass production perfection at the cost of variety.

But is that all there is to beer? Heaven forfend.

There is a whole country full of variety — of other tastes in beer — out there. There is the real purpose of the Great American Beer Festival: to bring together all of the unknown, unsung, local beers of America in one place. The object is to make the "whole spectrum of the beer community" available and to "give people a chance to taste and compare what's brewing stateside.

I attended the Great American Beer festival last June. Three thousand families attended from all over the country. The walls of the convention hall were decked with banners. Beer booths lined two walls and extended out into the center of the hall. On a large stage, the Boulder Philharmonic Orchestra played classical and popular orchestral music while the sturdiest yeomen and yeowomen in the nation went from booth to booth sampling the best beers America has to offer.

At the festival there were 44 brewers who offered 76 different beers to try. It was a taste-treat sensation. There was real American stouts and porters; English style pale ales, bock beers, amber beers; brown beers and Vienna style darks. There were also cream ales, Scottish ales, festival ales, and an award winning Russian stout.

Each festival-goer was allowed to vote for his favorite. The best-liked beers were first place — Russian Imperial Stout by the Yakima Brewing and Malt Co. of Yakima, Wash. This is claimed to be the strongest draft beer in North America. Second place — Grant's Scottish Ale, made by the same company. This is a deep rich ale with a 5.6 percent alcohol by volume, but is available normally only on draft at the Yakima brew-pub.

Third place — New Amsterdam Amber Lager, made by the Old New York Brewing Co. The beer is a conscious imitation of Bass Ale, and a very successful one at that. It is available at several Centre County restaurants and taverns. Fourth place — Anchor Christmas Ale. When one tastes the products of the Anchor Brewing Co. of San Francisco, one experiences the real meaning of the words, "Go West, young man." Fifth place — Albany Amber Ale, by the William S. Newman Brewing Co. of Albany New York. This is a delightful English style ale that we hope will soon find its way south to Pennsylvania.

Sixth place — Matt's Premium Beer, made by F.X. Matt of Utica, New York. This smooth pilsener is generally available in Pennsylvania. Seventh place — Riley's Red Lion of Little Rock, Arkansas, is the astonishingly good tasting product of a brewer and a banker who have joined forces to bring back real ales to the Ozarks.

Eighth place — Sierra Nevada Pale Ale, of Chico, CA. This English style pale ale is kraeusened (primed for natural carbonation) and contains one pound of hops per barrel. Ninth place — Genessee Cream Ale. The one brewery which makes its best claims that it's "not like beer and not like ordinary ales, either. It's completely different." Tenth place — Redhook Ale, produced by the Independent Ale Brewery of Seattle. This beer claims to be to normal American lager "what Corton Charlemagne is to mountain red wine," whatever that means.

So now you know that lurking out there, in such unlikely places Yakima, Little Rock, Chico, and Albany, is a whole bunch of new beers to try. What's the best beer? Why, it's the next beer, of course.

Ein Prosit der Gemutlichkeit!

Porter: A Hearty Drink
with Strong History and Tradition

December 2, 1984

This is an article about love at a distance. For years, I have been reading about a legendary beer so famous that it became the inspiration of at least five generations of Englishmen bent on creating the greatest empire emanating from Europe since the age of Charlemagne.

It also became the favorite brew of the British Empire's most stalwart opponent, General and President George Washington. More than one battle and affair of state waited until the father of his country had satisfied his predilection for this particular brew.

I speak in reverent tones, of course, of porter.

Let me share with you, in abbreviated form, the account of porter which my illustrious predecessor and noble mentor, John Bickerdyke, penned and published in 1885. In his honored tome, "The Curiosities of Ale and Beer," he tells the following story.

In the early years of the 18th century, in the age of Tom Jones and the colonization of Penn's Woods, the lovers of malt beverages in London were accustomed to enjoying three classes of brews: ale, beer, and "twopenny," the latter being a short beer.

Many who preferred a more subtle combination of flavors would combine one of the three with another by ordering a half and half. "Others again — and these were the real connoisseurs of malt liquors — would call for a pot of 'three threads,'" which was a combination of all three. This was very time consuming, for the bartender would have to go to three different casks and through three distinct operations just to fill a single pint of beer. Though taste was honored, service declined.

"But the hour had come — and the man," wrote Bickerdyke. "One Ralph Harwood, whose name is too little known to an ungrateful posterity," brooded over the inconvenience occasioned by the calls for three threads. He, therefore, conceived of the idea of a drink which would combine in a single brew the several virtues of all three.

Harwood succeeded in concocting a marvelous brew which he called "Entire." The venerable Bickerdyke records: "It was tasted; it was approved; it became the fruitful parent of a mighty offspring, and from that day to this has gone on increasing in name and fame."

How the mighty brew received its name of "porter" lies hidden in the mists of legend. One story holds that Harwood's famous brew was early recommended to the strong-backed, hard-working porters of London as "a wholesome liquor, which enables the London porter-drinkers to undergo tasks that ten gin-drinkers would sink under."

Another theory is that the men Harwood sent round to his customers to introduce the new brew would announce their arrival with the cry, "Porter," meaning not the brew but its bearer. The name, so the legend goes, stuck to the brew as well as its bearer; it even gives its name to the famed "porterhouse" steak. In the tastes of 18th century London, porterhouse steak and porter beer crowned the perfect meal.

The fame of porter beer spread 'round the globe, and its praises were great. Porter has been called the "drink fit for the gods," likely being too potent for mere mortals.

The Oxford newspaper, The Student, recorded the reception given to porter by students at Oxford University in 1750:

"Let us not derogate from the merits of porter — a liquor entirely British — a liquor that is the strength of our nation, the scourge of our enemies, and which has given 'immortality' to aldermen. 'Tis with the highest satisfaction that we can inform our Oxford students that Isis herself has taken this divine liquor into her protection."

Such was the glory of porter in its day, and its enjoyment knew no bounds. President Washington's love of porter was legendary. In 1790 his secretary planned ahead for a prospective presidential visit, noting, "as the President means to visit the place in the recess of Congress, it is probable that there will be a large demand for Porter at that time."

Today, the legendary taste of porter is barely known. Departing from the ways of our forefathers, the lusty taste of porter is no longer the inspiration of the builders of nations and empires.

Local Availability

Every once in a great while — when the gods are asleep, the moon is full and the wind is right — some modern copies of the ancient porter find their way into Happy Valley.

The Fred Koch Brewery of Dunkirk, N.Y., sends forth into the world a brew which it calls "Jubilee Porter." It is lightened greatly to introduce Americans to a whiff of what the old porter tastes might have been like. In Centre County, this tasty brew is available at Centre Beverage distributors and Nello's Restaurant and Bar and is recommended as an introduction for your taste buds to the ancient glories of porter.

Also available locally (at Zeno's and Nittany Beverage in State College) is the product of the most renowned of present day English brewers, the Samuel Smith Brewery of Tadcaster, maker of "Taddy Porter." This deep rich brew is made to be served and drank at room temperature. When served cold, it has about as much taste as chilled coffee. But served at 60 degrees, it suggests the kind of Olympian revelry that once inspired both Oxford students and George Washington.

What must have been the original taste of this famous beer? In our weakened age which boasts — Yes! literally has the nerve to boast, "All you ever wanted in a beer and less" — there is the ghost of a memory of a beer so deep and strong and true that compared to it all the oceans of the globe are but water. As one Englishman exclaimed on drinking his first real porter:

> *And what this flood of deeper brown,*
> *Which a white foam does also crown,*
> *Less white than snow, more white than mortar?*
> *Oh, my soul! Can this be Porter?*

Joy of Christmas Spirits

December 16, 1984

There are some folks who say that Christmas is not what Christmas once was.

In the ancient days, a story was once passed through England that a savior had been born to redeem this dull and work filled world. We do not know whether all who heard believed the story. But we do know that just about everyone who heard it believed the very story itself to be a sufficient cause for joy and celebration.

Thus it is recorded that Christmas was "celebrated from early ages with feasting and hearty, boisterous merriment" To raise up the lowest spirits to the joy of the occasion in the bleakest month of winter, special Christmas ales were brewed. The joy of the Christmas story and the warmth of a Christmas ale were welcomed at every Yule-time hearth. The poet Marmion caught the spirit in his verse:

> *England was merry England then,*
> *Old Christmas brought his sports again*
> *'Twas Christmas broaches the mightiest ale*
> *'Twas Christmas told the merriest tale*
> *A Christmas gambol oft would cheer*
> *A poor man's hearth through half the year.*

The Wassail Bowl is best known to be associated with Christmas cheer. In ancient times the chief ingredients of Wassail were strong beer, sugar, spices and roasted apples. The following is a recipe for Wassail served in 1732 at Jesus College, Oxford as transcribed by the venerable Bickerdyke:

"Into the bowl is first placed half a pound of Lisbon sugar, on which is poured one pint of warm beer, a little nutmeg and ginger are then grated over the mixture, and four glasses of sherry and five pints of beer are added to it. It is then stirred, sweetened to taste and allowed to stand covered for two to three hours. Three or four slices of thin toast are then floated on the creaming mixture, and the Wassail bowl is ready." In another recipe this mixture is made hot, but not boiling, and is poured over roasted apples laid in the bowl.

Such a recipe must have been the inspiration for the following old carol which celebrates our theme:

Come help us to raise
Loud songs to the praise
Of good old England's pleasures
To the Christmas cheer
And the foaming Beer
And the buttery's solid treasures.

Merry olde England did not become merry on lagered beer nor even on the standard ales of today. Special holiday beers and Christmas ales were deep and manly draughts. So do not attempt to try the recipe above with Miller, Bud, or even Twelve Horse. To revive the Wassail and the joy of Christmas past, the ancient ales and beers must be rediscovered.

In the 19th century and up until Prohibition most of the 1500 breweries of America annually produced special Christmas and holiday ales and beers. The 14 years of Prohibition not only wiped out half of America's breweries, but also all but one or two of its holiday brews.

Special Christmas Brews

The times, however are catching up to the past. The brewing of Christmas ales and beers is once again spreading across the land. In 1974, the Anchor Brewing Company introduced the first new Christmas Ale in America since 1939. Every year since then Anchor has brewed a new and different Christmas Ale to cheer the hearts of San Franciscans. Nearer to home, the Fred Koch Brewery of Dankirk, NY brews a delighted "Holiday Beer." It is lighter than many Christmas ales, but deeper and fuller bodied than ordinary ales. This Holiday Beer is available at some Centre County distributors and restaurants.

Not much farther away but not yet available in Pennsylvania in Newman's Winter Ale, specially brewed for the holidays in Albany, NY.

Special Christmas imported beers are available in most large cities. They include Noche Buena from Mexico, and Aass Jule ol (pronounced Arse Yule Ale) from Norway. Noche Buena is brewed by Austrian immigrants who modeled it after the holiday brews of Imperial Vienna. It has been described as one of the best examples of "Teutonic nostalgia" for the colorful beers of the 19th century. It is a dark brown malty brew with a great blend of imported hops. Aass Jule ol is not really an ale' the word "ol" means beer in Norwegian. It has a dark, rich, malty flavor which seems to have the power to redeem the darkest day in December.

Across the country, microbrewers and regional brewers have been bringing out special Christmas brews which are not widely distributed. In Minnesota, August Schell makes an amber beer with deep taste which it calls "Xmas Beer." In Wisconsin, the Walter Brewing Co. of Eau Claire has been making a dark "Holiday Beer" since the 1880's. Walters also continues to market another brand called "Lithia Christmas Beer." In Colorado, the Boulder Brewing Co. began brewing a special Christmas Ale in 1979. It is a strong, dark ale flavored with fresh ginger root. Michael Lawrence, the brewmaster at Boulder, merrily informs us that "It is modeled after the mulled ales of 17th and 18th century England.

The West Coast, however has the largest number of Christmas Ales. In addition to Anchor of San Francisco, the award winning Yakima Brewing Co. of Washington State makes an annual holiday mulled ale of honey and spices which is described as Wassail. It is "Grant's Christmas Ale" which has a 6 percent to 7 percent alcohol content. Farther south the Sierra Nevada brewery of Chico makes "Celebration Ale" for the holidays. It has been described as a "classic winter ale in the English tradition."

Thus with the rediscovery in America of Christmas ales and holiday beers there is some small reason to hope that Christmas may once again be celebrated as Christmas once was. Just as on that first Christmas night the breath of the humblest stable animals warmed the crib of the child who came to bring joy to the world, so special Christmas ales and beers have traditionally been brewed to warm us to the joy of that blessed story.

Ein Prosit der Gemutlichkeit!

Put Down Your Old Standby Brew and Try Something New

December 30, 1984

If you are like most people, you have a favorite beer.

Perhaps you have been drinking it for years. It's familiar and you feel comfortable with it. It's available most places. Your mate can find it at the store. Nobody looks at you strange or exotic when you order it in public. When you walk into your favorite pub the bartender sets one in front of you before you even order it.

You feel that life is full of difficult decisions and your beer should be your friend.

But your favorite beer — and even your favorite friends can get boring on occasion. This is one of the sad facts of life.

However, a caring Providence had already foreseen this problem. It has provided for a growing availability of imported beers.

For many decades Americans were very happy with their regular beers. Up to the 1970s less than 1 percent of all the beers consumed in America were imported. By 1980, imported beers were still only about 3 percent of the market.

But suddenly last summer, American beer drinkers in droves said "I've had enough — I'm not going to take it anymore." Imports of other tastes in beer rose 31 percent last

July, 25 percent last August and 24 percent last September. During this same period, domestic consumption of American beers was down by about 1 percent.

In terms of actual numbers this means that about one bottle or can out of every case of beer sold in the United States was an imported beer. If this rate of growth continues, it might be that one beer in every three six-packs sold in 1985 will be made by craftsmen in faraway lands.

The most popular imports came from the Netherlands, Canada, and Germany. But other countries are competing to offer new tastes. The top 10 brewers of imported beers and their countries of origin were:

> Heineken (Netherlands)
> Molson (Canada)
> Beck's (Germany)
> Moosehead (Canada)
> Labaat (Canada)
> St. Pauli Girl (Germany)
> Dos Equis (Mexico)
> Guinness, Harp, Bass (Ireland/England)
> Okeefe, Old Vienna, Cinci (Canada)
> Foster's (Australia)

But they are just a few of the brands that are pleasing American beer palates. More than 400 beers are not available in America as importers are straining to introduce new brews. Most Centre County restaurants and taverns carry at least one import — usually Heineken or Molson — and usually several others. There are more than 100 imported beers available locally.

Finding the Right Import

Suppose that you are ready to meet new acquaintances and make new friends in beer. How should you go about it?

First, don't be nervous. You are not married to your old beer. Your old beer is a good friend and it will understand. That is what all the foam and bubbles are about.

Second go to your favorite pub or beer distributor and see what he has. Then ask him why he doesn't carry more. When he starts paying more attention to other customers, select a brand from among those that he does carry. Next time visit another pub or distributor to see what is carried elsewhere.

Third keep on the lookout for a beer called "Pilsner Urquell" you can try the "Imported Beer Taste Test No. 1" This test is designed to show that not all beers are the same.

Pilsner Urquell is probably the most famous beer in the world. It rates "five mugs" (the highest beer rating) in the judgment of the world's top beer experts. It was first made in Czechoslovakia in 1842 and it is the model or prototype of almost all American beers. Many a beer label has the word "pilseur" or "pilsner" or "pils" on it in honor of its descent from Pilsner Urquell. Miller Lite beer is one such beer which still refers to itself as a "Pilsner" on the label.

Pilsner Urquell is available at several Centre County pubs including Duffy's in Boalsburg, the Victorian Manor in Lemont; Dante's; the Deli; Hi-Way Pizza Shoppes; Zeno's; Café 210 West; Nello's; and the Brewery, all in State College.

Taste Test

So, now it is time to describe the "Imported Beer Taste Test No. 1."

First pour yourself a glass of an American light beer, such as Miller Lite. It should be poured so that a head forms. Lift the glass up to your nose and try to smell the hops and malt. (Do not expect much from the light beer.) Now take a good mouthful. Don't just gulp and swallow; swish it around in your mouth with your tongue. The idea is to taste it. Relax, then swallow without haste.

Enjoy for a minute or so the memory of the sensations in your mouth and on your tongue. A beer should have a "finish"; that is, a taste that lingers on after the beer has been swallowed. Good beer is meant to be drunk slowly.

Now, try the same procedure with the Pilsner Urquell. Then repeat tasting each until you get the taste and feel of each one as well as their distinctive differences.

The nice thing about this test is that you can't flunk it. If you don't taste any difference, or if you don't like it you can say, "This is a dumb test." You can then go back to your old favorite.

On the other hand if you can taste a big difference, and if you like it, you can say "I've just been impressed by my taste buds." You can then go to taste and compare other American favorites with the favorites of other lands.

In either event, you will have made a new acquaintance and you will have joined the millions of Americans savoring the best brews of other lands.

Ein Prosit der Gemutlichkeit!

Giving up the Rat Race
for a Great Glass of Beer

January 13, 1985

Matthew Reich is not the kind of a man who you would expect to find brewing beer. He received a degree in business administration from the University of Massachusetts.

He then started climbing the corporate ladder; first as an executive at CitiBank, next as lending officer and CitiCorp Leasing. Then came a career jump to Hearst Corp.'s International Circulation Distributors. He was well on his way to corporate status, wealth, and success. He was even a wine enthusiast, and taught a course or two on wine appreciation at the New School in New York. He did everything right.

Then fate magically intervened and at the age of 29 he left it all to brew beer. Now he is on his way to real wealth. Power, money, and status all pass away, but a really good beer is unforgettable.

It all happened quite simply as fate usually does. One day a friend came over to his home and innocently asked, "Hey why don't we try to make some beer?"

He and his friend went out to make a humble home brew. But up from their brew kettle wafted not only the spirit of a good beer, but also the spirit of American Excellence and Enterprise.

Reich recounts how, with the first sip of golden nectar, he and his friend had concocted, he was magically changed from a corporate status seeker into the quintessential Yankee entrepreneur: "It was so good and so much fun that I said, 'Why don't we sell it?'"

Reich found himself in a good place to think of being an entrepreneur and of making beer. "At one time," he noted, "New York was actually the capital of American beer making, producing more beer than either Milwaukee or St. Louis." At its height near the turn of the century, New York City had 121 breweries competing to produce distinctive European style brews for American tastes.

But the tradition had been lost. The last of the great New York breweries emptied its brew kettle and closed its doors in the Bicentennial year if 1976.

What had brought an end to the great New York brewing tradition? It was the race to standardization and corporate merger that had started after World War II. The large national advertising firms joined with the new media of television and radio to dictate national markets.

They demanded "national beers" for which to create an image. Every beer had to be lighter than the next one. The mass image of lightness drove the ancient types of deep tasting brews out of the market. It had affected not only New York. From about 750 breweries in America in the 1930's, only 50 were still brewing in the whole country by 1983. "It was the end of an era," observed Reich.

But Reich was undaunted. He knew what he had tasted and trusting his taste buds, he set out to recreate the great New York brewing tradition. After that first fateful home brew he spent the next two years planning. He studied the market and talked investors into putting up a quarter million dollars to finance his quest for a deep tasting beer in the old tradition.

He then searched out the nation's leading brewmaster, Dr. Joseph L. Owades, who is reputed to understand brewing almost as well as Anton Dreher of Vienna and Gabriel Sedlymayr of Munich, the greatest brewers of the 19th century. Together, Reich and Owades tested hundreds of recipes until they came up with a production quality beer suitable for the rebirth of a great brewing tradition.

Reich fittingly named his new brew "New Amsterdam." The first batch was brewed in Utica, New York on Aug. 26, 1982. It took only one day to brew it, but it had to be aged 35 days. It was a tough time of waiting says Reich.

"I was so worried. I kept thinking what if some guy throws the wrong switch and drains the tank?"

The wait was worth it. On Oct. 1, 1982, the beer was tasted, approved, and celebrated. The gap in history was closed and the Great New York Brewing Tradition was reborn. Reich packed cases of it into the drunk of his car and went from pub to tavern to restaurant to bar, introducing his old/new taste in beer.

New Amsterdam is not like the nationally advertised beers. It has deep, rich taste and body. Reich wanted to create a beer that was anything but light.

"Americans have been led up the garden path to lightness," he says, "To me, lightness is tastelessness. That is what my beer is all about — it's an antidote to tastelessness."

Reich's beer is what is called an "amber lager." It is very similar to Bass Ale and to the English style of pale ales, but it is not as bitter. It has a dense head of foam, which is common to beers made with real barley instead of less expensive grains. It is made from expensive two row barley instead of the cheaper six row variety. Its hops are a mix of Cascade hops from Washington State and Hallertauer hops from Germany. You will be able to taste the hops in every glass.

Local Availability

Obviously, some out there agree with Reich's philosophy and his taste buds. New Amsterdam was voted the best American lager at the 1983 and 1984 Great American Beer Festivals.

It is now distributed in 12 states, and is available locally at Duffy's in Boalsburg, Nellos and the Brewery in State College.

Reich left the corporate race for success in order to brew a quality beer. He succeeded in that now his success is our good fortune.

Ein Prosit der Gemutlichkeit!

Turning Search for a Different Brew
into the 'King of Beer'

January 27, 1985

Anheuser. Bush. Budweiser. The most successful names in American brewing history. It's an interesting story how they all got together.

In the middle of the 19th century a young brewery supplies salesman by the name of Adolphus Busch immigrated to America from Mainz, Germany. Traveling through St. Louis one day, he chanced to set his eyes upon a lovely young lady by the name of Lilly Anheuser.

The romance seemed to have all the earmarks of a modern soap opera. In fact, Lilly's father, Eberhard Anheuser, was a soap manufacturer.

In the 1850s Eberhard Anheuser had invested the profits of his soap factory in a small brewery venture in St. Louis which had been founded by Georg Schneider in 1852. By 1860 the Brewery had failed and Eberhard Anheuser was its largest creditor. He found himself with little choice but to buy up the interests of minority creditors. Reluctantly he became a brewer.

Fortunately, it was at this time that Adolphus Busch met Lilly. They were married in 1861, and Adolphus joined the company in 1864, first as a salesman, later as a partner, and finally as president.

Adolphus Busch was a perfectionist. After joining the firm he decided to make the perfect beer. So he and Lilly made a tour of Europe to study the great advances which were being made in brewing methods there. The goal was to produce a beer which would be "the very highest point known to the art of modern brewing."

Busch had a dream of producing a national beer, one that would transcend all local tastes. It would not be another dark or deep tasting beer. Such beer would have been only one among many in the America of the 1870s. To catch on among the public at that time, a national beer would have to be different. That is what Busch went to Europe to find.

Our story shifts across the Atlantic. Before the communists strung an iron curtain down the middle of Europe, that continent was about twice as big and twice as exciting as we think of it today. Right in the middle was the little country of Bohemia, which today is part of Czechoslovakia.

At one time the capital, Prague, was the cultural and geographic center of Europe. It had one of Europe's oldest universities and more importantly, one of its oldest and most splendid and innovative traditions of brewing beer. It was to this that Adolphus Busch was drawn like a magnet.

In the 1840s several breweries in Czechoslovakia had begun experimenting with a new style of beer which became known as the "pilsner" style. It was the result of a new method of fermentation and a new process of lagering the beer, or aging it, for long periods at cold temperatures. The result was a very light, clear beer where before almost all beers had been dark and deep-tasting. The most famous brewery to initiate this method was the Prazdroj Brewery in Pilsen, Czechoslovakia, which still makes Pilsner Urquell.

Several other breweries in Czechoslovakia were experimenting with the new methods. Busch traveled to the best of them. He found the perfect brew that he was looking for at the Budvar Brewery in a little known town called "Budejovice" (pronounced Bu-de-you-vit-sa) in the Czech language and called "Budweis" in the German language, since Bohemia at the time was part of the Austro-Hungarian Empire.

The beer of Budvar was a bright, clear brew which was very light in color and in body. It was said that one could hold a glass of it up to the sunlight and see a golden flame in the liquid beneath the foam. It was the quality of lightness that Busch seized upon. It was this quality that would distinguish Busch's beer from the others in America. He returned to America and refitted his brewery for the new fermenting and lagering process.

Busch presented the new style of beer to the public in St. Louis during America's Centennial celebration in 1876. The new beer was called Budweiser in honor of the little known town in Czechoslovakia where Adolphus Busch had found his inspiration.

The new beer was an instant success. Americans were thirsty from subduing a new continent, building ribbons of railroads, forging new steel mills, and taming the West. They wanted a light beer, a real thirst quencher, a quaffing beer for hardworking men and women.

Americans showed their gratitude to Adolphus Busch for the beer he had found in that little town of Budweis by buying more of his beer than any other in the world. By 1900

Busch was selling a million barrels of Budweiser per year. The Anheuser Busch Company produced more than 65 million barrels of beer last year. That is not only more than any other company in the world, but more than any other country in the world, including West Germany.

Adolphus and Lilly grew into the epitome of the dynastic brewing family. When the Busches celebrated their golden wedding anniversary in 1911 it was a world event. The following is from a newspaper report of the time:

"The Busches of St. Louis had a pleasant golden anniversary in California the other day. The ways of beer have been pleasant ways for them. The husband crowned the wife with a $200,000 diadem. The President of the United States sent a $20 gold piece. Col. Roosevelt sent a solid-gold loving cup and the Emperor of Germany sent a like gift. Presidents, ex-presidents, and emperors paid tribute to the man who made beer and made it pay."

When their first son was born there were fireworks and a gunfire salute at the brewery as though a prince had been born. Today August A. Busch III, the great-grandson of Adolphus reigns as the "King of Beer."

I haven't really told you much about the physical properties of Budweiser beer or how it tastes yet. We'll leave that to a later article. It's just the two most important ingredients in every beer are the spirit of the people who brew it and the spirit of the people for whom it is brewed.

Ein Prosit der Gemutlichkeit!

Bud Deserves 'King of Beers' Title

February 10, 1985

In my last column I gave some of the history and background of the Anheuser-Busch Co. This week let's talk about American beer with the focus on the physical characteristics of Budweiser and Michelob.

Ingredients. Under the Reinheitsgebot, or the German Purity Law of 1516, traditional European beers can contain only four ingredients: barley malt, hops, yeast, and water. Nothing else is permitted. Of the major American beers only Stroh's Erlanger and Hudepohl's Christian Moerlin of Cincinnati, Ohio can met just these purity requirements. All other major American beer contain chemical additives, different grains, or other ingredients that are not permitted.

Malt. Only malt made from barley is permitted under Reinheitsgebot. This is the most important area in which American beers violate the purity law. Budweiser contains about only 70 percent barley malt. The rest is rice. Most other beers contain corn.

Anheuser-Busch does not attempt to hide the fact that its beers contain rice. On the contrary, the fact is proudly proclaimed on the label. The company claims that rice "contributes to snappy taste, clarity, and brilliance of the beer." However true that may be, with rice in the beer, it cannot be exported to Bavaria.

But there is another aspect to barley malt that has to be taken into account. There are two types of barley: two row and six row. Two row barley malt is much better, as well as more expensive. Most American beer contains no two row barley malt. Budweiser contains a blend of two row and six row, while Michelob does not seem to convey the better qualities of the malt.

Busch beer contains six row barley and corn instead of rice, since corn is less expensive.

Hops. Information on hops is difficult to get on most American beers. It is known that Budweiser contains a blend of eight or nine varieties of hops, several of which are imported European varieties. However, Budweiser like most American beers is fairly lightly hopped, so little mention is made of the blended hops.

Yeast. One of the most expensive ingredients in beer is the yeast. Brewers must go to fantastic lengths to maintain the purity and continuity of their yeast culture since yeast is a bacteria that is in the air we breathe. The defining characteristic of Budweiser beer, according to Michael Jackson, the world authority on beer, "is a unique, delicate fruitiness deriving from 'apple esters' in the yeast which is used."

Brewing. Between mashing the malt and fermentation comes the brewing. This is a fairly standard process. The wort must be heated and brought to a rolling boil. Most breweries use a system of coils through which superheated steam flows. In 1912 the Stroh brewery converted back to direct flame after one of the family members became convinced that direct heating was better than the steam coils. Basically "fire brewed" beer means oil fired heat applied to the outside of the brew kettle rather than superheated steam forced through pipes in the bottom of the kettle.

Fermentation. After being brewed, the yeast is added, and the beer is fermented for a period of days. With Budweiser, this is usually up to six days.

Aging. The beer is then passed to lagering or aging tans to mature the flavor. This aging process is usually 14 days to 32 days. Budweiser beer is aged for 21 days. Michelob for 32 days. Many European beers are aged for up to 90 days, while many other American beers are aged only 14 days.

It is in the aging tanks that Budweiser's famed "beechwood aging" takes place. This phrase does not mean that the beer is aged in beechwood casks. Rather it refers to a process whereby beechwood chips are layered on the bottom of the aging tanks. The purpose of the beechwood chips is not to impart any taste or aroma to the beer, but to provide more surface for the fermenting yeast to cling to. Basically, it is a process to use the yeast more efficiently.

Krausening. This is a process designated to bring about natural carbonation of the beer. While the beer is aging, freshly fermenting beer is added causing secondary fermentation in the aging tanks. If this is done in pressurized tanks, the secondary fermentation naturally saturates the beer with carbon dioxide. Both I.C. Golden Lager and Budweiser are examples of kraeusened beer. If beer is not kraeusened in the aging process, carbon dioxide must be artificially injected into the beer before bottling or kegging.

Stephen Morris, author of "The Great Beer Trek" visited every American brewery and compared their brewing methods and their beers. He comes to three conclusions of interest here.

First, he concludes that "American beer is often maligned for its blandness and rarely for its many virtues." Among American brewers he says, "there is more attention paid to the traditions of brewing than a jaded public would suspect."

Second, he found that Americans know what they like, and they have historically liked a light thirst quenching, quaffing beer, which American brew masters have been quick to provide in clear, consistent, inexpensive abundance. This competition has bred a set of national brands which "have achieved levels of quality and consistency which make distinction next to impossible."

Finally, he concludes that Budweiser, self-dubbed "King of Beers," deserves its throne. "Among the nationals," Morris observes, "Bud has not been afraid to entrust its reputation to the beer drinker's palate. The company is proud of its brewing techniques as well as its quality control. Full bodied, more bitter than its national competitors and with a dry finish Bud can call its own, this is America's most reliable beer.

Ein Prosit der Gemutlichkeit!

Dark Beers:
Courage to Peer into a Glass Darkly

February 24, 1985

We Americans live in an age of enlightenment, lightness, and light.

The pursuit of enlightened self interest is our highest social value. We like light music and light reading, light entertainment and light conversation. We eat light cuisine and drink light beer. We even treat sex lightly. In a very secular sense, we worship the light of the world.

Our regular American beers reflect this predilection for lightness. Bud, Stroh's and Rolling Rock, for example, were originally brewed to be among the lightest beers in the world. But even the lightest in the world would not be good enough for us if a way could be found to make them even lighter.

The American brewing industry found a way, and brought out a new type of beer called "light" beer, such as Miller Lite, I.C. Light, and Natural Light. Not to be outdone Pabst came out with "Extra Light." The race to lightness soon escalated as Bud introduced "L.A." and the rest of the industry joined the race. It seemed that only nothing would be lighter than what was being offered. There were rumors of mergers with Perrier.

But the eyes grow weary in all this light, and the taste buds begin to atrophy. It sometimes seems that we are losing any sense in a plague of lightness.

But there is an antidote. There is a hope. One can see darkness at the end of the tunnel. For those who do not like a drink they can see through, for those with the courage to peer into a glass darkly, there are amber, brown and black beers of a multitude of styles.

As darkness descends let us briefly summarize the types of dark beers we might seek out to regain our senses and to reawaken the gratitude of our taste buds:

English Style Pale Ales. These are the beers closest to the type of beer our colonial forefathers drank. Pale ales are not pale; they are called pale only because they are pale in relation to most other English beers. They are actually amber in color, and they have enough taste to make you sit up and take notice. These beers include Bass Ale, John Courage, Watney's, Whitbread and Sam Smith's pale ale.

The Vienna Style Lagers are next on the list. These beers originated in Vienna, but today seem to come from every place but Vienna. These are amber-colored lagers similar to the English pale ales, but usually with a more biting flavor. They include Dos Equis from Mexico, Lutece from France, and Hacker-Pschorr Oktoberfest from Germany.

Munich Dark. This is the classic style of beer that made Munich the beer capital of the world about a century and a half ago. It includes Prior Double Dark from Philadelphia, Sau Miquel Dark from the Philippines, Heineken Dark, Beck's Dark, and Ausburger Dark.

Bock and Double-Bock. The origin of the name "bock" is lost in legend. Many believe that it comes from the kick of a billy goat. Indeed, one brand comes with a white billy goat on a string about the neck of each bottle. Such was the fame of bock beer that the Duke of Brunswick presented a barrel of it to Martin Luther to fortify his courage at the Diet of Worms. Apparently it worked. To the Assembly Luther reportedly declared: "Here I stand; I can do no other." You can spark your own reformation with a bottle of Aass Bok from Norway, or Ausburger Bock from Wisconsin. There are also the German double-bocks from Bavaria. You can always identify them by the fact they all end in "-ator." They include Salvator (originated by the Franciscan monks), Maximator, Optimator, Celebrator (the one with the billy goat), Delicator, Animator, and about a hundred others, all from Bavaria.

Next, there are the American microbrewery beers. The goal of American microbreweries is most often to brew darker-, deeper-tasting beers. Locally available is New Amsterdam Amber Lager, and a new one, Chesbay, made by Chesapeake Brewing Company from Virginia. This latter beer has a very strong taste of grain or malt. Pour it slowly to prevent the yeast at the bottom of the bottle from becoming stirred up.

Next are the Porters which I described at some length in a previous article. One can add Sierra Nevada porter and Thousand Oakes porter, both from California, to the list of nectars of the gods.

Stouts must be on any list of beer styles. These are deep, heavy, coffee-bitter brews. They include Guinness, of course, Mackeson Triple Stout and Cooper Stout.

Finally there are the **special English** brews so hard to come by, but well worth the fealty and homage of every Black

Knight. I speak of such specialty brews as Sam Smith's Nut Brown Ale and Oatmeal Stout, Watney's Stingo, Newcastle Brown Ale and McEwan's Scotch Ale. Coors has been licensed to brew George Killian's Irish Red Ale to darken the days of Westerners.

All these beers are as different from light beers as night from day. But beware! To enjoy their differences they should be drunk at a different temperature. Cold light beers are for the heat of the day. Dark beers are for the cool of night. They are made to be drunk about 20 degrees warmer than you would normally drink your Budweiser, Heineken or Rolling Rock Light. Drink light beers ice cold, at, say, 35 to 45 degrees Fahrenheit. Dark beers, on the other hand, taste best at 56 to 65 degrees Fahrenheit. I like mine at room temperature.

You may stumble around in the dark for a while until you grow accustomed to the differences in beers. But it's worth it. Someday you will be grateful that you developed the courage to face a beer as opaque as the future.

Ein Prosit der Gemutlichkeit!

Two Kinds of Beer in the World: English Ale, Everything Else

March 10, 1985

The world expert on beer, Michael Jackson, writes, "There are two kinds of beer in the world: The English kind and the kind everyone else drinks."

The beer available in Britain encompasses many differences between it and the modern style available in most nations. First, of course, English beer means ale as opposed to lager. Ale is top-fermented at a warm temperature, and served at a warm temperature, in the ancient style, before there was universal refrigeration.

But the ancient style of beer also refers to the fact that the "real ale" is "live" ale. That means that it has not been pasteurized, filtered, or chilled. It is brewed in the brew-pubs or small breweries in the vicinity and shipped quickly to its destination at a pub. There it rests until the excitement of the trip abates. Then the cask is tapped and its beer carefully brought to one's glass by mechanical or gravity flow — never gas injected pressure.

The difference in beers has other consequences too. Since ale is not pasteurized or filtered, it is often cloudy and opaque with bits and particles of grain and yeast.

Michael Jackson calls it "A tall, dark stranger of a beer." In his book, "The English Pub" he distinguishes English beer from the beers of all other nations. " In other lands," he writes, "beer too often glisters like gimcrack gold, all bright and shiny, and transparent; English beer has impenetrable depths."

The "impenetrable depth" of English beers is a subject which has inspired poets, novelists, literary giants, and even mass movements. Thomas Hardy once described the beer of Casterbridge in his novel "The Trumpet Major," in the following language:

"It was the most beautiful color that the eye of an artist in beer could desire; full in body yet brisk as a volcano; piquant, yet without a twang; luminous as an autumn sunset, free from streakiness of taste; but finally, rather heady. The masses worshipped it, the minor gentry loved it more than wine."

There are such beers in the world. A different experience that ties men to men in good fellowship and shared enjoyment. With wine everyone's taste is different, and the vintages change every year. But with beer one can realize the unity of shared experiences which storytellers dream about.

American Ales

In America such tastes are coming back again. In Albany, N.Y. a small brewer by the name of William S. Newman makes a traditional English draught ale which rivals its English models.

Newman apprenticed in England with Peter Austin, brewmaster of the Ringwood Brewery. There he learned the secrets of brewing cask-conditioned ales and brought them back to these shores. In 1982 he opened a new brewery in a former mattress warehouse.

Newman produces both a dark "winter ale," a lighter "amber ale," and a pale ale. All three are deep and heavy by American standards.

Newman's beer is a taste of old England. But since it is served "live" i.e. unpasteurized, it is only served on draught, and it does not travel very far from where it is made. But if you want to know what an English pub beer is like without going to England, you can find it in Albany.

Newman's beers are made with malted barley, English hops, water and yeast. It contains no additives and has a short shelf life. It is available in many of the pubs and restaurants in Albany, Troy, and Schenectady.

What can you do until you can get to Albany? There are a variety of imports from England which offer a whiff of the classic "live" taste.

First on any list is the pale ale brewed at Samuel Smith's Old Brewery in Tadcaster, England. This is England's proudest bottled pale ale.

Other English bottled pale ales are Bass Ale, John Courage Export, Charles Wells Bombardier Ale, Whitbread Ale, Fuller's London Ale and Watney's Red Barrel. These are the imported brands of England's famous "Burton Ales." They are not "live" but they are English.

Darker, heavier English ales include McEwan's Scotch Ale and Samuel Smith's famous Nut Brown Ale.

Most English ales are not meant for guzzling nor simply quenching thirst. One brewer of an English style beer insists that his beer "is the one beer to have when you are only having one." And another critic quipped of Newman's Pale Ale that is "was not what one looks for after mowing the lawn in August." "But," he says "this beer stands for something."

It may seem strange to talk about a beer that "stands for something." After all, a beer is just a beer, isn't it?

The idea of English ale is not only in what it is but in how it is enjoyed. English ales are meant to be drunk slowly with friends. In England, unlike the United States, most beer — more than 75 percent — is served on draught in pubs. People congregate and talk over the events of the day with a pint or two of deep tasting draught.

So the enjoyment of English ale is a different experience combining the deepest impression on one's taste buds with a social dimension of civility. Unlike wine, English ale, is first of all, the taste of good fellowship. Think of a taste that brings people together and you will be thinking of the secret of English ale.

Ein Prosit der Gemutlichkeit!

British Ales Invade Manhattan

March 24, 1985

A few years ago an Englishman, Richard Wrigley, visited New York and tasted the beer. He decided that the colonists had lost the Revolution.

So, like a modern general Burgoyne, he planned a new invasion to bring British culture back to New York. This time, however, the battle was not to be fought with flintlocks and muskets, but in the market place with an English pub and English Ales.

Wrigley returned to England to prepare an expeditionary force. Instead of conscripting Hessians as was done on England's first attempt, Wrigley purchased six brew kettles from the Black Forest and Bavaria. His real secret weapon, however, was a brewmaster from the Samuel Smith Brewery of Tadcaster.

The invasion arrived last year with Wrigley's return. He immediately established a beachhead on the West Side of Manhattan island. Wrigley and his cohort, Robert D'Adonna, commandeered a warehouse in the SoHo district and converted it into a three-tiered brew pub from whence to launch their strike at New York City's culture and taste buds.

The warehouse is a four-story plain brown building. It fronts on an old open marketplace across from the "Live Poultry Market." As one looks at it from the square it has the massiveness of an old armory. To the left is an ironwork fence with gold letters over the old grill majestically describing "The Manhattan Brewing Company."

Behind the fence is a black horse drawn wagon with intricate gold lettering with which the golden nectar of British ale will be delivered to other pubs throughout the city. To the right corner is a set of brown doors with a brown and gold wood plaque which identified it as the "Thompson Street Brewery." It must be only camouflage, for they are one and the same.

We entered the brown doors beside the plaque and walked up steps which spiral their way to the floors and tiers above. On the walls as we ascended were brightly painted barrel heads with the shields and trademarks of a multitude of English and European breweries.

Then we passed through a metal fire door and found ourselves on a sawdust covered floor confronting an entire wall of massive, highly polished copper kettles three stories high. Behind them on a raised platform is an impressive battery of dials and gauges for the brewmaster. Above them brightly polished copper steam pipes rise three stories to the rafters above. The big kettles are not being used to make beer yet, however; that is done elsewhere on the premises.

In front of the brew kettles (14,000 liter wort tuns and lauter tuns) are six long wooden tables with copper tops arranged in the fashion of a German beer hall. If you are going to sit down you will probably have to sit beside some other people already enjoying the beer and the food or still trying to decide which to enjoy first.

Across from the wall of copper kettles is a stand-up bar with marble pump handles and an engaging bartender with an encouragingly large beer belly. The pump handles are important. English ales do not take well to gas-injected pressure. The pumps are an indication that the beer is real ale. It is literally pumped by a mechanical lifting of the beer rather than a pushy gas in the cask.

Baskets of unshelled peanuts sit in front of every third or fourth person at the bar. They are unsalted because salt affects the taste of beer. The shells are husked onto the sawdust covering the floor. Above the bar two tiers of tables behind brass rails face the brew kettles.

From the marblehandled pumps flow live ales of legendary tastes. To be "live" means that the ale is not pasteurized or micro-filtered to kill the fermenting yeast or remove particles of malt. The difference between live beer and pasteurized beer is about the same as between fresh meat and meat that has been salted for storage.

One of Europe's most successful consumer campaigns, the Campaign for Real Ale (CAMRA), was organized to preserve England's live ales from the big beer companies who care more about long shelf life than fresh taste.

On the day we visited three types of ale were available: Original Pale Ale, Royal Amber Ale and Porter. We decided to start with the lightest.

The Pale Ale is golden in color but decidedly heavier than American Ale. It has a sweet palate, but is also well hopped. It can be described as the kind of beer one could sit with and talk about any subject — even politics and religion — and still feel mellow.

The Amber Ale is copper colored. It is the type known in England as Burton ale, after Burton-on-Trent. Its head is dense, and its flavors perfectly balanced. One can eat bratwurst or Irish stew with it and still feel that the beer is the main course. With it, a meal is not only the taking of nourishment but a civilizing occasion.

And then there is the Porter. Oh, the Porter. It is black, so black no light can pass through it when it is held up to the afternoon sunlight streaming through the windows. It has a tan head of the most exquisite foam which is so dense one's index finger itches to write one's initials in it. The taste is creamy smooth but bitter, with a rich taste like burnt coffee.

The experience of drinking English Ales invites conversation. Around us were students from Benjamin Cardozo School of Law, undergraduates from NY, Wall Street Brokers, a banker, and a variety of yuppies. They talked about the beer, the food, Irish guilt feelings, John Belushi, the New Right and the Old Left, religion in America, Rabbi Kahane and the philosophies of Republican and rainbows.

Will the invasion of English ales and the English pub succeed? Perhaps it might. There are plans to spread the beachhead of real ale into other Manhattan pubs, with the ale being majestically delivered in a horsedrawn wagon. Who knows, people may begin putting aside the drink they quaff simply to quench their thirst for brews to savor with good old fashioned conversation.

Paul Revere, get ready: The British are coming! The British are coming!

Ein Prosit der Gemutlichkeit!

Here's to the Great American Beer Festival

April 7, 1985

Munich in West Germany has its Oktober-fest scheduled for next September. Adamstown and Bernville will be celebrating the Seventh Annual Lancaster County Bier Fest and Bavarian Summer Festival in July. Milwaukee, Wisc. will kickoff Sommerfest at the end of June. But now is the time to start planning to attend the Great American Beer Festival in Denver, Colo., at the end of May.

The purpose of the Great American Beer Festival is to bring together all the best American beers in one place. This year the pride of the country's brewers will be brought together at the Regency Ballroom in Denver May 31 and June 1.

Beers will be available for tasting from America's Big-Six major brewers, 24 regional brewers, 21 microbrewers, two brewpubs, and three contract brewers.

These 56 brewers are planning to offer a total of 85 of their best brews. The varieties of beers will include: pale ales, bitters, red ales, altbiers, Pilsner-style light beers, Dortmunder-style lagers, Munich-style darks, Vienna-style ambers, bocks, and perhaps double bocks, San Francisco steam beer and maybe even a Russian Imperial-style stout — all made by American brewers.

The event is a grand opportunity to taste the variety of beers in America. Many beers from regional breweries and microbreweries are not available in Pennsylvania. Many people will simply never get the chance to visit Yakima, Wash., Little Rock, Ark., or Amana, Iowa, to taste the beers there. The festival is the best opportunity to taste the results of the brewer's art from across the entire continent.

The Great American Beer Festival is sponsored by the American Homebrewers Assoc. and the American Microbrewers Assoc. It is held each year as part of a week of events scheduled by these two organizations.

The week starts off May 28 with the American Homebrewers Assoc.'s National Homebrew Judges Training Program. This will be a day-long seminar on "flavor perception training." Its goal is to "provide a body of information that will contribute quality and continuity throughout the nation. Attendees will learn the fundamentals of tasting and judging beer and how to organize a competition."

May 28 is also the first day of the Seventh Annual National Homebrewers Conference. This conference brings together homebrewers from every state in the Union for homebrew competitions, seminars on better brewing techniques and the camaraderie of other homebrewers. The conference lasts for four days, and includes VIP tours of the Coors and Boulder breweries, lectures by specialists on the technical aspects of beer making and presentations on everything from the world beer styles to building a small pilot homebrewery.

Starting May 29, and running concurrently with the American Homebrewers Assoc. conference is the American Microbrewers Conference. Microbrewing is one of the fastest growing industries in America. As a result of the microbrewers, the total number of brewing companies in the U.S. rose from 44 in 1984 to 56 in 1985, an increase of 25 percent.

The microbrewers' conference will present the most current information on designing and developing beer types, looking at microbrewing variety around the world and reviewing the status of brewpub legislation in 50 states.

Both conferences will come together for luncheon speakers and evening events. Luncheon speakers will include Adolph Coors of Adolph Coors Co., speaking on the "Community of Brewers", David Bruce, emperor of the Firkin Empire of Brewpubs in London, speaking on brewpubs; and Byron Burch, author of "Quality Brewing," speaking on the myths surrounding homebrewing. Michael Jackson, a world beer expert from England, will be the host for "The Quintessential Beer Tasting," which will feature 12 internationally classic beers to be tasted with the expert.

On May 31, there will be a special presentation by Johannes Schulters of the Maisel Brewery and the Frankonian Brewing Museum, speaking on the 200 breweries and beer styles of Frankonia, West Germany.

You have got to like beer a lot to be interested in all this. But if you are, it is an opportunity to learn more than you ever thought there was to know about beer, as well as to have a very good time. The great seal of the American Homebrewers Assoc. says it all. Its symbol is a turkey and the motto says, "Relax, don't worry, have a homebrew."

If you enjoy people with a sense of humor, who can laugh at themselves and their predilections, go to Denver to spend a few days with people who make and enjoy beer.

Further information on The Great American Beer Festival and the conferences is available from the American Homebrewers Assoc., P.O. Box 287, Boulder, Colo., 80306, or by calling (303) 447-0816.

Ein Prosit der Gemutlichkeit!

Homebrewing Adds New Sparkle
to Old Trade

April 21, 1985

Everyone knows that homemade pies and home-cooked meals are usually a lot better than anything you can buy at the store. Wine enthusiasts, on the other hand, generally prefer store-bought products. But what about beer?

Recently I was given a most delightful opportunity to find out. I was invited to a meeting of the Happy Valley Homebrewers. This is a group of people — men and women, young and old — who have joined hundreds of other folks across the country brewing better quality beer at home.

Eight people were present with nine of their own homemade beers. The variety was impressive. Four of the members had brought: a porter, three amber ales, two steam beers, a sweet stout, a wheat bock beer and an extract.

Two of the amber ales by Gordon Law were better than anything I had yet bought commercially. The porter and wheat bock beer made by Cliff Newman were dark, deep and rich. They both had the kind of taste that lingered on enjoyably. Dave Jumper served a very creditable steam beer and porter, and Jay Whelan's dark bitters extract was a pleasure to sip.

It is truly encouraging to find such excellent beers being presented by homebrewers. For it has only been since 1979 that the hobby of homebrewing was legalized after almost half a century of legal exile.

The story of why homebrewing of beer was illegal for so long reads like something out of a Woody Allen movie. The brewing of beer – at home or otherwise – was, of course, illegal during the 13 years of Prohibition. When Prohibition ended in 1933, legislation was drafted to legalize the making of both beer and wine at home. The regulations specifically provided for "the home production of wine and/or beer." However, the clerk in charge of transcribing this sentence, perhaps while reaching for a glass of the first thing legalized, inadvertently left out the rest of the clause, "and/or beer." When the regulations were printed, only the home production of wine had been legalized.

For the next 36 years, no one ever got around to correcting the mistake. Finally, Sen. Alan Cranston, D-California, sponsored a bill that was signed by former president Jimmy Carter in 1979. The main provision of the new law reads as follows.

"Beer for Personal Family Use. Subject to regulation prescribed by the Secretary of the Treasury, any adult may, without payment of tax, produce beer for personal or family use and not for sale. The aggregate amount of beer exempt from tax under this subsection with respect to any household shall not exceed: (1) 200 gallon per calendar year if there are two or more adults in such household, or (2) 100 gallons per calendar years if there is only one adult in such household."

Since the passage of this law, a whole industry has grown to meeting the needs of homebrewers who know that they can make better beers at home.

For those interested in learning about homebrewing, there are now a national association, several magazines, a large number of books on the subject and beer-making supply stores that have sprung up around the nation.

The American Homebrewers Association publishes a magazine five times a year for homebrewers called "Zymurgy." The word "zymurgy" means the science of fermentation, and the magazine concentrates on news and articles about the making and appreciation of beer. A subscription comes as part of membership in the homebrewers association, which costs $17 per year. The address of "Zymurgy" and the association is Box 287, Boulder, Colo., 80306.

There is also the "Amateur Brewer," published by Fred Eckhardt. This is probably the most technical publication at a subscription price of $9 per year. It can be ordered from Eckhardt at Box 546, Portland, Ore., 92707.

There are too many recent books on homebrewing to report on all of them, but I can list a few.

Probably the most authoritative and most well written book is "The Complete Joy of Homebrewing" (Avon Books, 1984 paperback, $8.95) by Charlie Papzian. The author is president of the homebrewers association, and the humor and expertise he brings to this work make it understandable and precise for both the novice and the more experienced homebrewer.

William Mares has published a Vermonter's introduction to homebrewing in a book called "Making Beer" (Alfred A. Knopf, 1984 paperback, $7.95). Mares has a conversational, homey approach that many new homebrewers might appreciate.

There is also a local homebrewing supplies outlet. Newman's Homebrewing Supply in Port Matilda is carrying hops and malt and other supplies necessary to get started on your own adventure in home brewing.

There are a lot of misconceptions about homebrewing which we discussed at the Happy Valley Homebrewing meeting. Perhaps the most important ones are the ideas (1) that homebrewing might be too difficult for a novice, or (2) that homebrewing might not produce a good quality beer. I can speak on the basis of experience that the amateur brewers in Happy Valley can produce a homebrew of superb quality. They also seem enthusiastic about sharing their art with new members who, they say, can be producing their own fine brews in a short period of time.

Perhaps the day will come when the perfect accompaniment of a home-cooked meal will be a home-brewed beer.

Ein Prosit der Gemutlichkeit!

India Pale Ale Has History
of Pleasing Drinkers

May 5, 1985

In the 18th and 19th centuries the British Empire encircled the globe. It was said that, from East to West, the sun never set upon it. But the jewel of the Crown was India, and thereby hangs a story of poetry and beer.

There is a beer, made in America, which comes out of the legendary past of the British Raj in India. The beer is called India Pale Ale, or simply IPA, and it appears under the Ballantine trademark. On the label the following story is told:

"Discovered in the Spring of 1824 – purely by chance – when a keg of rare ale was opened after a sea voyage between England and Calcutta. The old sea captain and his crew first thought that the rocking of the ship had created this new, vigorous malt beverage. Actually its hearty flavor developed during the aging in wood."

That is, of course, quite true. But it is only half the story.

It was the custom and the regulation of their majesties, the kings and queens of England, to ensure to each man in their service his daily supply of beer. Men, they knew, could be induced to leave behind comfort, family, wife and home for service to the Crown. But the little bit of England which those men insisted on carrying with them, even to the farthest outposts of the realm, was their daily pint of ale.

Supplying the beer ration to the troops was no small challenge. Sea voyages in wooden sailing ships were slow, sometimes taking months to travel from England to outposts in India. Many times the beer, upon reaching its destination, was found to have gone bad.

The brewers took to trying different recipes in order to develop a stronger ale that could withstand the voyage. More hops were added to increase bitterness, and alcohol content was increased for stability. One of these recipes aged so well in the wooden casks that, as the label recounts, it became the legendary IPA.

IPA became a standard favorite wherever British subjects served their sovereign. It not only protected them against having to drink the foul water of many a colonial outpost, but also served as a taste and remembrance of home. Sometimes it was a small social occasion; other times, perhaps, even a ritual in which drinking IPA together with others from home served as a comforting reaffirmation of their identity amidst the seductions of a foreign culture.

Some idea of the important place of this beer can be found in the poetry of Rudyard Kipling. Kipling was the poet of the common British soldier in India, as well as the most famous bard of the empire. A brief glance through his "Barrack-Room Ballads" reveals that beer served as the background or main subject of a significant number of his poems.

In the hanging of Danny Deever, the sharing of beer together highlights the tragedy of Danny's execution. As Danny's soul leaves his body, a soldier ("Files-on-Parade") and his sergeant remark:

'I've drunk 'is beer a score of times,' said Files-on-Parade.
'E's drinkin's bitter beer alone,' The Colour-Sergeant said.

In the last verse, we find that beer provides the event upon which the day of Danny Deever's hanging will end:

Ho! the young recruits are shakin' an' they'll want their beer today
After hangin' Danny Deever in the mornin'

In his famous poem, "Gunga Din," beer is mentioned in the first line as an ordinary part of camp life from which the narrator begins: "You can talk 'o gin and beer when you're safely quartered here... " The poem then goes on to tell of the heroism of the legendary water-bearer, Gunga-Din.

When a young British soldier was denied his pint of beer and turned out of a pub it furnished the event for one of Kipling's most oft-recited poems during the two world wars. The poem is called "Tommy," which is the generic name for all British soldiers, much like "G.I. Joe" is for Americans. In the first stanza and refrain Tommy tells of the event:

I went into the public-'ouse to get a pint 'o beer
The publican 'e up an' sez, 'We serve no red-coats here!'
The girls be'ind the bar they laughed an' giggled fit to die
I outs into the street again an' to myself sez I:
O it's Tommy this, an' Tommy that an' 'Tommy, go away':
But it's 'Thank you, Mister Atkins,' when the band begins to play.

Tommy's further refrains about being denied his "pint 'o beer" express the universal feeling of every young man who has ever worn a uniform:

Then it's Tommy this, an' Tommy that, an' 'Tommy 'ows your soul?'
But it's 'Thin red line of 'eroes' when the drums begin to roll.
For it's 'Tommy this, an' Tommy that, an' 'Chuck him out, the brute!"
But it's 'Savior of 'is country,' when the guns begin to shoot.

Today the world is so much more complicated that the little things of yesteryear, like a "pint 'o beer," are no longer much noted. It seems that people do not feel in those ways any more. Thus, Ballantine's India Pale Ale has been referred to as an "anachronism." It is said that its taste harks back to a wholly different age. Even the English beer connoisseur, Michael Jackson, calls IPA, "a half-forgotten celebrity, thought by some to have retired, by others to be dead."

But Ballantine IPA survives. Its productions site has been moved several times due to brewery closings and buy outs. Presently it is being brewed by Falstaff in Fort Wayne, Ind. There seems to be just enough of the old-time spirit left to keep alive the brewing of this taste of long ago.

What is IPA? It is a classic of a beer. It is a highly hopped, aromatic, strong-tasting, bitter ale which is top-fermented and aged for six months in wood. Its alcohol level is 7 percent by volume. It seems to taste best if you close your eyes and imagine a torridly hot, sweaty, dusty day skirmishing with Afghani tribesmen in the Khyber Pass. In a word, it is, like its history, a bitter brew with a bite that makes it hard to forget.

Distribution of IPA is erratic. It seems to be available everywhere, but not regularly. Thus even finding some IPA may involve an imperial adventure. You'll just have to experience it for yourself, by Jove.

Ein Prosit der Gemutlichkeit!

To Enhance Taste of Beer, Pop its Bubbles

May 19, 1985

Have you ever sat watching bubbles rise from the bottom or sides of a glass of beer?

Perhaps watching these bubbles was your only point of cheer on the night you lost your first true love to the captain of the college football team. Or maybe you have been simply entranced by the magic of watching these bubbles come into existence, seemingly out of nowhere, and forming a stream of bubbles rising to the top of your beer.

To most people, these bubbles are a perfectly natural part of a beer, and are to be expected in every glass. In fact, some people would probably be disappointed if they did not see those happy strands of bubbles attaching themselves to the insides or bottoms of their glass and rising in bubbly processions to the head.

But get prepared to have your bubbles burst – those streams of bubbles are not really supposed to be there. They signify the presence of impurities and mean the glass is not really "beer clean."

Beer is one of the most complex and sensitive beverages a person can find. In the brewing and fermentation process, hundreds of compounds are formed that contribute to the taste of the beer. But those compounds are very sensitive and will react with any other impurities they encounter.

The problem is that many soaps, foods and other substances can leave a film on a glass even after it has been washed. Milk, cream, fruit juices, sugary soft drinks and even iced tea with sugar leave an oily or fatty film on a glass, and washing in soap does not necessarily remove it.

Soaps themselves often leave a film, and many dishwashing detergents today contain hand oils, fruit scents and a variety of other substances that also may remain on the glass even after rinsing.

Other substances that may remain on a glass are traces from lipsticks, sun tan oils, finger prints and other facial cosmetics. Lint from a drying towel, airborne kitchen grease and dust also can affect beer.

If traces of any of these substances remain on a glass after washing, any beer poured into that glass will begin to suffocate. The air will be drawn out of the beer, carbon dioxide gas will be induced to coagulate and those columns of bubbles will begin to form.

Of course, if it were simply a matter of bubbles forming, it would not be a cause for dismay. That would only mean that one had to drink one's beer a little faster before it went flat from the loss of too much carbon dioxide.

But the bubbles may also indicate two other changes in the beer itself. First, the presence of a film or other impurities will usually cause the head to collapse. A good head on a beer in a clean glass will leave a trail of "Brussels lace" on the inside of the glass as the beer is drunk. In a filmy glass, the head will noticeably decline or disappear, and the sides of the glass will not hold the traces of the history of that beer. Thus those initials one inscribed in the head when one poured it may not last to the bottom of the glass.

Second, the presence of a film or other impurities may cause a significant change in taste. Beer is sensitive, and it will react with any impurities to affect its flavor. A film of milk, soap, hand cream, lemon scent or sugar will react immediately with beer and change its taste.

Thus, those tell-tale bubbles clinging to the inside of a beer glass, or rising in a column from one point on the sides or bottom, may be a sign that the beer in one's glass is not the same as the beer in the bottle or tap from which it was poured.

Heavens to Murgatroy! What shall we do? The first rule is don't use your pilsener glasses for milk, your steins for flower arrangements or your mugs for iced tea. Isolate your beer glasses from glasses used for other things. Beer glasses for beer only.

The second rule is to clean your beer glasses and keep them clean. If your beer glasses or steins have been used for other beverages, it will only take a few minutes to make each one "beer clean." Try the following procedure:

First, wash each glass thoroughly with a good strong dishwashing detergent, preferably one that does not have any pine or lemon scents or any hand creams in it. Rinse well.

Next, fill your sink bowl with cold water. Now wash your glasses again, this time using salt like a cleanser to scour the glass clean. Pour lots of salt down the sides of each glass and scrub with a sponge, bottle brush or scrubber. Scrub hard to make sure the salt cuts away all traces of residues built up on the glass. Use lots of salt, and make sure that you scrub every nook and cranny in that stein.

Then rinse thoroughly again in the hottest water you can stand and let the glasses air dry. Do not wipe them dry with a towel. The towel may leave traces of soap from prior dryings or even lint on the glass.

Your beer glasses are now "beer clean." Store your beer glasses upside down to keep out dust or airborne kitchen grease.

Thereafter, wash beer glasses only with a special cleaner, such as "Beer Clean Glass Wash." You can buy "Beer Clean" and other cleaners in container sizes much larger than you want or need, at Jay Kay Distributors on North Atherton Street, State College.

What will all this get you, besides a spouse who thinks you are acting eccentric again? It will get you purity. Perhaps your only chance at it. Your head will stay up, and the initials in your foam will stand until the bottom of your stein; "Brussels lace" will grace the sides of each glass as you drink; the bubbles will stop forming along the sides and bottom; your beer will become clear and golden; and you will rest in the peaceful contemplation that the beer you are drinking is the same as the beer you poured.

Ein Prosit Der Gemutlichkeit!

'Tis the Season for Beer Fests

June 2, 1985

It's summertime and that means fun. Since fun and relaxation sometimes center upon the celebration of life and the enjoyment of beer, here are some of the summer beer events you may want to know about.

Lancaster County Bavarian Summer Festival

Close to home is the Lancaster County Bavarian Summer Festival, which begins June 29th. This event continues the tradition of the Lancaster County Bier Fest, now in its seventh year, and the Barnesville Oktoberfest. Both are now combined at the Gemutlichkeit Gartens in Adamstown.

The traditional Bier Fest parade, led by the grand marshal's horsedrawn wagon, will kick off from Adamstown at 1 p.m. Last year the grand marshal was Dick Yuengling of the Yuengling Brewery in Pottstown. When the parade arrives at the Gemutlichkeit Gartens, the first keg of beer will be ceremonially tapped and the entertainment will begin with Die Deutsche Blesskapelle, Walt Groller's Orchestra and Hans Hagemann on the accordion. Folk dances, including the "Official Chicken Dance" will be featured for the festivities.

On July 4, another full day of German fun is planned. The music will be the best in German and Austrian folk and dance music as well as polkas. The Happy Austrians will play from 2 to 6 p.m., and the Stratton Mountain Boys will dance, sing and yodel their favorite Austrian tunes from 7 p.m. to midnight.

Wiener schnitzel and all kinds of German sausages are planned to be washed down with abundant draughts of German style beer. In the evening, a sparkling, exploding fireworks display is promised to delight all.

The Gemutlichkeit Gartens are located on Route 272, just south of Reading. For more information, write to the Gemutlichkeit Gazette, Box 277, Adamstown, 19501.

The Milwaukee Summerfest

In 1961, Milwaukee Mayor Henry Maier visited Munich for the Oktoberfest. He liked it so much that he resolved to do the same in Milwaukee. He good-naturedly told the Mayor of Munich at the time: "You have good beer. But ours is better. You have a beautiful festival season, and a beautiful festival in Oktoberfest. Someday, though, our festival season will be better." Maier was not just talking through his hat.

When he returned to Milwaukee, he developed the idea and got it off the ground. The first Milwaukee Summerfest was held in 1968. Since then, it has grown into a major Midwestern event. Last year it featured Huey Lewis, James Taylor, the Everly Brothers and Linda Rondstadt, and attracted almost three quarters of a million people.

The Munich Oktoberfest is sponsored by Munich's seven breweries, and is a true beer festival. Milwaukee's Summerfest also is sponsored by her three main breweries: Pabst, Miller and Heileman (Old Style).

Last year when I attended, the main attractions were the entertainment, ethnic foods and beer. Wisconsin was settled by sturdy Germans, Poles and Swedes. It has little fear of beer, and people enjoy it abundantly from stands throughout the waterfront park area and at every restaurant in the park.

If you like American-style beer and good clean fun, the Milwaukee Summerfest leads off with a parade June 27 and lasts until July 7.

The Great British Beer Festival

The Great British Beer Festival is scheduled for August 11-18 in Brighton, England. This will be one of the major events of the year. It is sponsored by the Campaign for Real Ale (CAMRA), and will bring together at least 200 British ales and beers.

The festival will be in the exhibition halls behind the Metropole. It is my understanding that there will be enough atmosphere with the beer to make one wish that we had lost the War of 1812.

You can get more information, as well as order festival T-shirts, by writing to Campaign for Real Ale, 34 Alma Road, St. Albans, Hertfordshire, AL1 3BW, England.

Tours

"All About Beer" magazine is sponsoring a two-week tour of Europe for beer lovers. The tour, scheduled for Sept. 28 to Oct. 13th, will visit seven countries: Belgium, Germany, Austria, Switzerland, France, Lichtenstein and Holland.

The tour will encompass the original Oktoberfest in Munich, and the Great Belgian Oktoberfeesten near Brussels. There will be visits to breweries in ancient monasteries and modern mass production facilities. It also includes a Rhine-River cruise and a Black Forest journey, as well as a taste of Europe's finest brews.

For more information, write to Cole Travel Agency, Box 510, Fond du Lac, Wis., 54935, telephone (414) 921-1395.

Irish Festival of Good Beer

Where you are orange or green or just full of blarney, the Northern Ireland Tourist Board invites you to "come to a festival with a difference and soak up the atmosphere and the local brews." The Irish Festival of Good Beer is scheduled for June 20-22, at Hildan Brewery, Lisburn.

For more information, write to the Irish Festival of Good Beer, Hilden Brewery, Lisburn, County Antrim, BT27 4T4, Northern Ireland, or call (08462) 3863.

CAMRA Travel

If a European trip to search down exotic beers is your cup of bitters, you might contact CAMRA Travel. Its tour in March to the Spinamalt beer fair in Epinal, France, introduced the party to 700 beers and involved five brewery visits: to Hockfelden and Schiltigheim in Alsace, the Feldschlossen Brewery in Basle, the Ulm Brewery in Germany, and the Brasserie de Saint Sylvester in Lille, Belgium.

The next CAMRA tour is a one-week trip to sample the brews of Belgium. For those who are not familiar with Belgian beers, it should be said that Belgium is one of the top beer-producing and beer-consuming nations of the world. The trip costs 125 English pounds, which at today's exchange rates is a real bargain.

For more information, contact Joe Bates, CAMRA Travel, 34 Alma Road, St. Albans, Herts, AL1 3BW. England.

Oktoberfest

And there is the mother and father of all beer festivals – Munich's famous Oktoberfest, which begins in late September. There are probably few rooms left by now, and you will be well advised to begin planning your 1986 visit.

For more information, you can call the German Tourist Agency, 747 Third Avenue, New York, N.Y., 10017, telephone (212) 308-3300.

Ein Prosit der Gemutlichkeit!

English Group Saved Beer
from Distasteful Fate

June 16, 1985

Some people think of beer as only a drink. But there are others who think of it as a cause.

I have previously written of Fritz Maytag, who left the enjoyment of his Maytag washing machine fortune to others while he dedicated himself to saving a failing brewery.

He lost his marriage over it, ten years of his life and missed about 3,000 San Francisco sunsets, but he eventually succeeded in becoming a true craftsman of beers fit to be acclaimed among the world's finest.

I have also written of Matthew Reich, who left the corporate success ladder at Citi-Bank and Hearst to take the real beer tradition back to New York City.

But America is not the only land where top talent and dedication is attracted to hops and malt. Let me tell you how a few dedicated men, in defense of real ale, launched the most successful consumer movement in Europe.

The background of the story is depressingly familiar. By the 1960s in England, the marketing people, wielding their dreaded "bottom line," had seized control of the biggest companies in the beer industry. These "bottom-liners"

122

multiplied advertising and mergers like an uncontrollable cancer that gobbled up local breweries and their unique local brews. Closings, mergers, buy outs and bankruptcies occurred everywhere as the industry tried to concentrate into a few big companies with mass production.

The bottom-liners also dictated the new beers to be put out by the big companies in place of the brews they had driven out of the market. There were to be only a few national brands. All were to be characterized as bland, undistinguished, chilled, filtered, pasteurized and artificially carbonated beers, with low production costs, high profit margins and long shelf lives.

Michael Jackson, the English beer expert, described the situation: "The fate that had overtaken so many of life's pleasures seemed set to overtake beer, and to do so irreversibly. The distinctive was being wiped out by the bland."

But the bottom-liners were not to take over English habits as easily as they took over beer industry advertising, for the English take life's pleasures very seriously. Their beer is one of the small pleasures they take most seriously, and they enjoy it in their pubs and inns in copious abundance.

The average red-blooded English male drinks about a quart of beer a day, which is almost twice as much as the average red-blooded American male. Further, while most beer in America is drunk out of a can or bottle at home, almost three-quarters of all beer in England is served on tap for serious enjoyment in friendly neighborhood pubs.

There, beer is a civilizing drink and not a thirst quencher. Life without good beer in the neighborhood pub would be life without good conversation. England would not be England without it. Long ago Hilaire Belloc advised his fellow Englishmen, "When you have lost your inns, drown your empty selves, for you will have lost the last of England."

The average Englishman was not about to drown himself, nor to lose the last of England. It was clear, therefore, the threat of the marketing people would not be allowed to go unchallenged. The best was called for and the best came forth.

A young man by the name of Christopher Hutt left a lucrative job at Ford's marketing department in answer to the call. He wrote a book called "The Death of the English Pub." In it he boldly described the plans and goals behind the slice advertising of the marketing people.

Pubs were to be streamlined for quick service. Traditional live draught beer was to be phased out and replaced by cold tasteless pasteurized beers with lower handling and storage costs. Dartboards and conversation were not good for volume sales. They had to go.

Hutt exposed the goal of the marketing people to turn the pubs into places to get tanked up, like a service station, rather than to enjoy good fellowship and good conversation.

Hutt's book had immediate effect. All over England, like a vast Saxon conspiracy against a new set of Norman invaders, people got together to share information on where to find real ale and what pubs still served it.

At the same time, Frank Baillie published "The Beer Drinker's Companion," which was a guide to surviving local brews and the local pubs where they were served. It was an immediate success. The old-fashioned pubs found themselves filled to overflowing with Britons looking for good beer and good conversation.

Not long after Hutt's book exposed the threat to the English pubs, a few journalists met to plan a national movement to counter the big beer companies. They decided to form a group called CAMRA, "The Campaign for Real Ale."

They held the first national conference in 1972. The word moved slowly at first but then membership soared. In 1973, 1,400 members; by 1975, they had 30,000 members in chapters all over England.

The cry was taken up in the media and in every pub. Control of the market by big companies was not to deprive the average Englishman of his traditional pleasure. CAMRA published a monthly newsletter called "What's Brewing," which alerted citizens of every attempt by industry to bottom line local brews or to change local pubs.

CAMRA also came out with an annual "Good Beer Guide," which was sold faster than it could be printed. By the end of the decade, it was the biggest selling paperback in England, with sales of 100,000 copies a year.

Thanks to the work of Hutt, Baillie, and others, the public was alerted and was able to save England's three most esteemed institutions: the English pub, the unique variety of English ales, and simple conversation with neighbors in a friendly place.

Many small breweries that were being buried by advertising were rescued by the movement. There was a renaissance among new breweries. Home-brew pubs made a major comeback. The industry giants backed off and reintroduced some traditional live ales.

In 1976, the head of the National Consumer Council called CAMRA "the most successful consumer movement in

Europe." Today it is still going strong, keeping up the fight to preserve English ales and the English pub from the marketing people and their dreaded bottom line.

If one is planning a trip to England to try the beers, or if one is merely interested in experiencing some English civilization, CAMRA's monthly newspaper and regional guides are indispensable. One can subscribe to "What's Brewing" and obtain the "Good Beer Guide" by writing CAMRA, 34 Alma Road, St. Albans, Herts, AL1 3BW, England.

Ein Prosit der Gemutlichkeit!

For Summer Fun
Make Sure the Beer Fits the Occasion

June 30, 1985

It's summertime, and that means hot, sunny afternoons, picnics at the park, backyard barbecues and softball games. It also means special dinners served on the porch or patio, parties on the lawn and sipping a tall one in the cool of the evening.

Beer is a beverage that can be enjoyed with each one of these activities, and for most people it is, after water, summer's most popular refresher.

All beers are not the same, however, and some types of beer may go better with some activities than others. Similarly, different styles of beer may complement foods in different ways. So it may add considerably to the enjoyment of your summertime fun to match the right style of beer with the activity of the day, and to serve the right type of beer to complement the food to be served.

Let's, therefore, go through a day of summertime fun and talk about what beers might go best with your plans.

If you are not working on the lawn, playing baseball in the sun, hiking across country or otherwise strenuously enjoying the morning, the heat of the noonday sun will soon invite you to enjoy a cold refresher.

"Beer is an ideal thirst quencher, thanks to its balanced concentration and alcohol carbohydrate ratio," reports Food and Drug Administration physiologist Doralie Segal.

Of course, the ideal style of beer to quench a thirst on any hot day is the American-style pilsener. This includes the most popular brands in Pennsylvania: Yuengling, Straub, Rolling Rock, Schmidt's, Stoneys and Iron City, as well as the national brands: Bud, Miller, Stroh's, Pabst or Coors.

For lunch, one might plan, say, either a standard lunch of hamburgers and hot dogs or a special light lunch of salads and cold cuts.

The American-style pilsener does not do much for a hamburger or hot dog except to wash it down. For this type of lunch, one ought to look for a beer that will do a little more than swab the deck.

Two American beers that immediately come to mind are Ballantine's India Pale Ale and Genesee Twelve Horse Ale. One might also try a Canadian ale, such as Molson's Red or Labatt's. With any of these, one will know that there's more than just a burger or a dog in one's mouth.

For that light luncheon of pasta salad, greens, ceviche or cold cuts, one might suggest a lighter, smoother beer. Three beers suggest themselves for such a repast: Esquire from the Jones Brewing Co., Christian Moerline from Hudepohl and La Belle Strasbourgeois made by Fisher d' Alsace. Each of these is full bodied, but as light and smooth as silk, and will complement any light summer luncheon.

In the heat of a summer afternoon, what goes better than picnics, baseball and cold beer? Once again, the American pilsener hits the spot for most people. If your taste buds are up to it, why not try one of America's super premiums to fill your summer 'fridge or ice tub. I.C. Golden Lager, Michelob, Erlanger and Lowenbrau are definite steps up in pilsener beer enjoyment, and these super premiums certainly make it worthwhile to work up a thirst.

As the afternoon comes to an end, one's thoughts might turn to a relaxing evening with friends. If one is planning a pleasant evening dinner, one will want to begin with a beer to whet the appetite as well as to complement the appetizers.

The Northern beers of Scandinavia and the old Hanseatic cities of German suggest the perfect pre-dinner style of beer. They are generally brewed very dry and light with a highly hopped quality designed to stimulate the appetite. One might suggest Beck's or St. Pauli Girl from Bremen, Jever Pilsener from Friesland, Pincus Pils from Munster, Ringnes from Norway or Kalback from Sweden.

Then comes dinner and the opportunity to match the perfect beer with the piece de resistance.

With most red meats or Italian pasta with meat sauce, the near universal preference is for a Vienna-style amber or an English pale ale to match the full flavor. Try Amsterdam Amber from new York, Dos Equis Amber from Mexico or the pale ales of England, such as Bass Ale, John Courage or Whitbreat. If one is planning a special steak or roast beef dish, the Cabernet Savignon of English Ales is Samuel Smith Pale Ale, available locally at $42 a case.

With seafood and light meats such as veal and chicken which are served either plain or with rich sauces, one would suggest a Dortmunder such as D.A.B., the famous beers of Bavaria, such as Spaten, Dinkelacker or Furstenberg, or the Bohemian "Beer of kings," Pilsner Urquell.

After dessert and coffee, the dinner is over, but the mellow feeling that opens up to good conversation and true fellowship is usually just beginning.

One wants a beverage to complement the feeling. The drink must not itself become the center of attention, as a fine wine, a cognac or a liquor might be. Instead, one needs a beverage that plays like after-dinner music on one's good feelings, making one feel comfortable but not under pressure to perform or enjoy.

Porter. Bock. Two very different cultures had the same idea. Beers with flavors as deep as one's feelings for friends. Serve Augsburger Bock from Wisconsin, Celebrator Doppelbock from Germany or Aass Bok from Norway.

The English offer the famous Samuel Smith Taddy Porter, one of the deepest and truest malt beverages, available locally at $57 a case. For variety in deep, dark beer enjoyment, there are also McEwan's and McAndrew's Scotch Ales and Samuel Smith's Nut Brown Ale or Oatmeal Stout. These are all served best at 55 degrees F in pewter mugs and sipped slowly.

One enjoys the company of friends with such classic brews. Why? Because they open up a deeper appreciation of both the tragedies and comedies of life. As the poet, A.E. Hausman put it, "Malt does more than Milton can to justify God's ways to man."

Ein Prosit der Gemutlichkeit!

'Fun' Beers Basis for
Wine Merchant's Career Switch

July 14, 1985

Where do you go for the best beer in the world? Why, to the wine merchant, of course. The wine merchant in this case does not sell wine anymore; he imports beer. But his name is still "Merchant du Vin," which in French means "wine merchant." Thereby hangs an interesting tale of wine and beer marketing.

In the late 1960s, a young entrepreneur by the name of Charles Finkel made a name for himself in the wine business by introducing "boutique wines." Finkel scouted the small microscopic California wineries to corner the market on the best wines in California. Sending them back East, he introduced Americans to a new decade of wine appreciation and boosted the worldwide reputation of California wines.

He was so successful that someone bought his company, Bon Vin, and he went on to becomes the sales manager for the new Chateau Ste. Michelle winery in Washington. This winery was as outstanding as was Finkel's salesmanship, and Chateau Ste. Michelle became a major name in the U.S. wine market.

By the late 1970s, Finkel needed a new challenge. So he left Chateau Ste. Michelle to form a new company, Merchant du Vin, to import specialty French wines.

But then, all of a sudden, Charlie Finkel saw the light. It came in three flashes. The first was cosmic: "Next to water," he realized, "beer — not wine — was the most popular beverage on earth."

The second flash was personal: "I love beer," he recalled. "Even when I was in the wine business I drank it, particularly when I was in Europe buying wine."

The third flash put two and two together: "I know there is a consumer out there who is sophisticated and wants to taste the best beers the world has to offer."

So Finkel set out on a new adventure: to search the known world for the very best tastes in all styles of beer, and to bring them back to the American consumer.

Merchant du Vin became what is called a "contract brewer." Finkel approached breweries to purchase their rights to all or part of the American market in return for Finkel's merchandising. Through its distribution system, Merchant du Vin, then markets the beers throughout the United States.

Most of the brews carried by Merchant du Vin are local specialty beers that Finkel has discovered. These include such famous beers as Dortmunder Union Pils from Germany and Aass Bok from Norway.

Finkel also carries specialty American beers. One of the top beers in his line-up is Cold Spring Export from Minnesota. Except for a few Midwestern markets kept by the Cold Spring Brewery, it is Merchant du Vin that makes Cold Spring Export available to the rest of the country. Merchant du Vin also includes in its specialties Yuengling premium and porter.

But finding local specialty beers is not the only thing Merchant du Vin does. Some of its beers are the products of historical findings. Finkel and his staff research a particular style of beer and then locate a brewery to reconstruct the ancient type. Samuel Smith's Oatmeal Stout and Nut Brown Ale are two such historically reconstructed brews.

So far, Merchant du Vin has identified 31 types or styles of beer. In each category, it has located one or more outstanding examples to make available to Americans.

Merchant du Vin sets the strictest standards for the beers which bear its importing label. Any beer imported by Merchant du Vin must be "authentic." This means that it has to be naturally made, without any chemicals, additives or preservatives. Second, the beer must be an outstanding representative of its style.

As a result of these standards, Merchant du Vin's beers appear on just about every list of the top beers in the world.

Howard Hillman in his book, "The Gourmet Guide to Beer" (Washington Square Press, $5.95) lists tow Merchant du Vin imports among the top 11 beers in the world. These include Samuel Smith Old Brewery Pale Ale and Samuel Smith Taddy Porter.

Michael Jackson, the English beer connoisseur and author of "The World Guide to Beer" (Running Press, $9.95) and "The Pocket Guide to Beer" (G.P. mmmnam's, $5.95), lists two of Merchant du Vin's imports as among the top five beers in the world. His choices are Samuel Smith's Old Brewery Pale Ale and Lindeman's Lambic Kriek.

Charlie Finkel's approach to the marketing of beer is one of the best things that has ever happened to the beer market in the United States. It is an approach he happily brought with him from the wine industry. "We made wine fun for the public 10 years ago," he says, "and that's what we're doing now with beer."

His approach to sales is as much fun as the beer he imports. Most beer in the United States, he says, has been marketed on the "one-brand" approach. Each brewer has tried to make his beer taste as close as possible to whatever brand was most successful. Thus all American beers tended to taste alike.

But Finkel's approach is to sell variety. Finkel says that what Merchant du Vin is interested in doing "is teaching the consumer how much fun beer is by trying various styles of beer." Thus the emphasis is on opening up the consumer to new and pleasurable tastes.

Merchant du Vin does not only talk about educating the public about beer. Indeed, one of its most popular products is not beer, but its consumer-oriented newspaper, called "Alephanalia." It originated as a spoof, but it has continued as a major marketing item. Each issue carries extensive articles on several beers and beer styles. "Alephenalia" is free for the asking by writing to Merchant du Vin, 214 University Street, Seattle, Wash. 98101.

In West Germany, Holland, Belgium, America and England there are almost 2,000 breweries producing styles, varieties and tastes in beer as varied as the tastes in wine. The goal of Charlie Finkel and Merchant du Vin is to open us up to the fun of enjoying all of this variety.

Ein Prosit der Gemutlichkeit!

America Has History of Love for Alcohol

July 28, 1985

"There is nothing new under the sun," wrote the preacher Ecclesiastes 25 or 30 centuries ago. So when seemingly new problems arise, it is usually best to sit back, pour a tall mug of dark ale, and peruse the long history of mankind's many efforts to get from one day to the next.

These days the general public is worried about drunken driving and problem drinking among young people. State legislatures are considering proposals to make "happy hours" illegal, and there are local measures designed to stop beer deliveries to fraternities. In one state a law was enacted to regulate serving beer in pitchers.

But it seems that drunkenness was also a problem two centuries ago when the American Revolution was being won and a spanking new nation was being born. It may be instructive, therefore, to see how the founders of our country dealt with the problem.

Although ale and beer were the original drinks of the early colonists, by the latter part of the 18th century hard liquor in the form of rum, gin and brandy had become America's most popular drink. Imports flooded onto our revolutionary shores. As one writer of the period noted, "West India rum abounded."

After the war, in the heady atmosphere of freedom, the ever inventive Americans developed a taste for their own liquor in the form of whiskey and made it as popular as rum had been.

By the time George Washington was sworn in as our first president, drunkenness on hard liquor had become a major national problem among the sturdy yeomen and yeowomen of America. One citizen of the period wrote, "I cannot express my sense of the ruinous habits in the free use of distilled spirits." So attached were the frontiersmen of western Pennsylvania to their whiskey that attempts to tax it resulted in the first real test of strength for the new Republic — the "Whiskey Rebellion."

But the response of America's founding fathers was not to attempt to prohibit alcohol. On the contrary, our founders were clearheaded thinkers who acted with sense and moderation in all things.

First, of course, they sat down to discuss the problem over a few mugs of Philadelphia porter. Next, they studied the problem. Dr. Benjamin Rush, a founder of the temperance movement, signer of the Declaration of Independence and member of the medical faculty of the University of Pennsylvania, conducted research on the effects of alcohol on the human body.

He reported that heavy consumption of hard liquor had deleterious effects, but his findings on beer were quite different. Beers, he said, "contain a good deal of nourishment; hence we find many of the poor in Great Britain endure hard labor with no other food than a quart or three pints of beer with a few pounds of bread."

Similar conclusions were being reached elsewhere. The son-in-law of James Madison wrote to a Philadelphia newspaper in 1788 about his observations on the effects of spirituous liquors on "reapers and other laborers." He noted that these workers "enjoy more health and better spirits on beer..."

The idea gradually became prevalent that beer was the drink of health and moderation. Our founding fathers sat down, pour themselves another mug of Philadelphia porter, and decided that the sensible policy would be to encourage the manufacture and consumption of beer.

Massachusetts led the way in 1789 with a special Act of Assembly to encourage brewing. The preamble of that Act stated the reasons:

"WHEREAS, the manufacture of strong beer, ale and other malt liquors will promote the purposes of husbanding and commerce...; and

"WHEREAS, the wholesome qualities of malt liquors greatly recommend them to general use, as an important means of preserving the health of citizens of this Commonwealth..."

The Massachusetts Act thereupon exempted brewers of beer from "all taxes and duties of every kind," which was a very healthy inducement to the enjoyment of beer.

Nor was Massachusetts an isolated example. In 1792 New Hampshire adopted a law to encourage brewing by providing that every person building a brewery in that state would be "exempted from all taxes of every kind and nature that would be assessed under the authority of this State."

The 1790s were a time of good cheer in New England, and other parts of the country were not far behind in encouraging the manufacture and consumption of beer. A prominent Philadelphian, T. Coxe, noted happily in 1794 that, "Breweries are multiplying as their value is becoming manifest."

By 1799 it appeared that the policy of encouraging moderation was working. One J.B. Bordley, an agriculturist, reported, "In our large towns, beer is taking the place of diluted spirits, which is a reason why there is more sobriety than formerly."

In 1815 Thomas Jefferson took the position, "I have no doubt, either in a moral or economical view, of the desirableness to introduce a taste for malt liquors." Indeed, Jefferson boasted, "I am lately become a brewer for family use."

Stanley Baron, in his book "Brewed in America" (Little, Brown & Col, 1962), wrote that Thomas Jefferson symbolized an influential body of thought during our country's beginning. That thought held that beer "could bestow great advantages, both economical and social, on the country, and that it deserved every form of encouragement."

Of all things our founding fathers liked, they liked common sense, sobriety and beer the best.

Ein Prosit der Germutlichkeit!

Summer Dog Days Are Time for 'Washing Up the Wort Tun'

August 11, 1985

It's the dog days of summer. The term is over and half the town is away on vacation. The temperature is perfect, and the Sunday summer breezes on one's patio make one wish time would stop. In fact, it just about does stop for most people; they fall asleep before they even get halfway through the Sunday paper.

So it's the perfect time to write one of those "clean-up" articles. Through the year the clerical errors, the typographical errors, and the personal mistakes build up. One needs to correct one's mistakes and set the record straight; "washing up the wort tun," as they might say in the trade.

In one column this year a misplaced comma resulted in an editorial correction that compounded my mistake into downright error. There are only four — not five — ingredients in beer under the German Purity Law. These are: barley malt, hops, yeast and water. A comma had gotten itself inserted between the words barley and malt in a column last winter, and when the editor counted the items in the series, she counted five and changed the sentence to say that.

So if there are any people out there who noticed, please reprogram your memory banks. The Reinheitsgebot permits only four ingredients in pure beer: malted barley, hops, yeast and water.

Actually, this brings up a very interesting point. The exact wording of the German Purity Law of 1516, the "Reinheitsgebot," refers to only three permissible ingredients in beer: malted barley, hops and water. It makes no mention of yeast. Could this have been a clerical error or typo?

No, it wasn't. Back in 1516, no one ever saw a yeast cell. Yeast is a fungus that is as small as bacteria. Yeast floats in the air like germs. Back in 1516, no one knew what it was. The first yeast cell was not seen under a microscope until 1680 by the Dutch scientist, Anton Leeuwenhoek.

In early beer making, the wort was prepared, and the brewmaster would "pautre" (mutter magic formulas) over the tub. (Today, we say to "putter" around.) It would be by chance or magic that enough yeast in the air made it into the tub to cause fermentation. Of course, since these yeast cells thrive in grain and water, there would always be plenty of such yeasts in the air around a brewery.

Later brewers noticed a yellow or white substance in the dregs of the brew which they collected and added to the next brew. They linked it to the substance that made bread rise. But none knew what it was or how it worked.

Still later, of course, after the discoveries of Louis Pasteur in 1857, the workings of yeast were understood and scientific cultures could be separated and preserved for specific beer tastes. Today, the risk of contamination of a brew by wild yeasts is one of the biggest problems of quality control in brewing. It is a reason, for example, why bottom-fermenting lagers and top-fermenting ales are almost never made at the same brewery: the yeasts are different, and a brewer cannot afford to let one get mixed up with the other. The wrong yeast can get into the air and from there into the fermenting beer. A wild yeast can change the taste of a beer dramatically.

In another column, I had put together a paragraph which inaccurately conveyed the impression that Pasteur's yeast discoveries were used by the great Munich brewer, Anton Sedlmayr, in the 1820s. One astute reader was kind enough to point this out to me. I herewith wish to correct that impression: The accomplishments of Anton Sedlmayr in the 1820s in Munich were done without the help of Pasteur's discoveries. As mentioned above, Pasteur's research was not available until after 1857.

Another reader has written in to me to complain that I was not giving enough attention to Pennsylvania's outstanding brewing tradition. The reader is correct. I have not yet devoted the attention to the Pennsylvania brewing tradition which it deserves.

Actually, although certainly not neglecting Pennsylvania brews, I have concentrated on the beers of many other places on the theory that it's easier for people to recognize greatness in a stranger than in the hometown boy. The hometown beers are already pretty familiar and, as such, unremarkable. It's only when we have an appreciation of the state of the art elsewhere that we can appreciate how lucky we are.

Then there are the occasional confusions, omissions, or non sequiturs. Some of these sound great when you write them, but do not come through very well in print. Sometimes the editor crosses out a point I was trying to make. One learns to try to write more clearly.

In one column I had carefully crafted a joke into a column to compare trying new beers with meeting new friends. The editor let in the whole story about Providence seeing to it that there were many new beers to meet, but edited out the punch line that he leaves it up to you to find your own friends. If that does not sound funny to you, it may explain the editor's red ink through the punch line.

Finally, one of the humbling experiences of being a columnist is that the columnist does not get to write the headlines for his column. I always supply a suggested heading which tries to be interesting and to convey the content of the article. But the editor has a mind of her own, and I never know what flag my column might be flying when it appears in print. This leads to a great deal of caution. A joke, an exaggeration, a literary twist, may be taken seriously and end up as an embarrassing but eye-catching headline. This is simply an occupational hazard one learns to grin and bear.

I can only thank my editor and readers for their many kindnesses toward all the errors, mistakes, confusions, misspellings, and other assorted problems that creep into the drafts or printing of my columns. The people of Keystone County are pretty darn nice people.

Ein Prosit der Gemutlichkeit!

Penn State Alumni
Brew Award-Winning Beer

August 25, 1985

Becoming a distinguished alumnus can happen in more than one way but, Jim Kollar, Penn State '68, has found the best way of all. People all over the country are lifting their glasses to him.

Jim, of course, is brewing beer. And what a beer it is! Although his Chesbay Amber has been on the market for only a year, it is already winning national awards. It was just voted the Eighth Best Beer in the Nation at the Great American Beer Festival in Denver.

Jim Kollar didn't start out making beer. In fact, he's a veterinarian who owns a thriving animal hospital in Virginia Beach, Virginia. At Penn State in the '60s Jim studied pre-vet and played Penn State football. He was the star linebacker for the Nittany Lions in 1967, the year they went to the Gator Bowl.

At Penn State Jim met his wife, Marilou. Marilou was a Phi Beta Kappa honor student and now runs her own psychology clinic in Virginia Beach, overseeing about eight other psychologists. Marilou is one of Jim's four partners in the brewery. The other three are Jim's brother, Frank, and two friends, Lou and Rozalyn Peron.

Jim's first venture into the production of alcoholic beverages was literally a bust. Jim set out to make a batch of homemade sparkling burgundy. All twelve bottles exploded. It was lucky for us, though, because the next time he ventured into home production he began brewing beer.

Jim got really interested in homebrewing. He found that he could produce a beer at home that was infinitely superior to anything he could buy at the store. Soon he was producing it weekly in five-gallon quantities, filling his garage with cases of beer for himself and his friends.

America is a wonderful place. Neither a man nor a woman can do anything really well without thinking of how to sell it. Jim was no exception. After about five years of homebrewing, he itched to open a brewery and put his beer on the market.

Jim had learned from Joe Paterno that you can't do well at anything without a good coach and a lot of training. So Jim set out to "get in shape" for a brewery. In 1980, he attended the brewing course at the University of California at Davis. Then he toured microbreweries all around the country. Other microbreweries shared their successes and mistakes with Jim, and he was glad to listen.

By 1981 Jim convinced his partners that they had a winner. So they incorporated the Chesapeake Bay Brewing Company, and in 1982 started to build their own new brewery in a nearby industrial park. They worked 60 to 70 hours a week, in addition to their regular professions, to construct a very modern brick brewhouse.

All of the partners took an active part in the venture. Rozalyn was an industrial psychologist, so she began running label recognition studies to design the label for the brew. Marilou developed the marketing strategy. Jim, Frank and Lou concentrated on the problems of construction and assembly of the plant.

By 1983 the building was completed. The next jobs were to get the production team together and to formulate a production quality beer. It's one thing to make a few gallons of great homebrew; it's quite another thing to brew a great beer of absolutely consistent taste and quality.

Jim found the best brewmaster available. He was Wolfgang Roth from Bavaria, who had been brewing beer for 14 years — since he was 18 years old — and had his degree from the prestigious Ulm School of Brewing and Malting Science.

Jim and Wolfgang set off for Austria to formulate the perfect recipe for their beer. There they worked with Michael Braitinger of the famous Brauerei Muhlgrub until they had the exact combination of hops, malt types and yeasts.

Kollar had a pretty good idea of what kind of beer he wanted to brew. He wanted real beer taste. When you put that beer to your lips, you don't put advertising images in your mouth; you want the real taste of malt, the real taste of hops, and the work of a yeast that's earned its pay. Jim figured that for every light beer drinker who wanted "less" in his or her beer, there were dozens of Sylvester Stallones and Clint Eastwood-types out there who didn't feel comfortable with yellow fizz in their glass.

Jim and Wolfgang came home with the recipe for a deep amber brew. It has the manly qualities of a European brew, a certain bitterness to help one face the tragedies of life, a distinctive feel in the mouth and the sense of being substantial rather than being light.

Brewer's Digest says of the latter quality, that it's "a sense of being a food rather than just a highly carbonated malted beverage." It also quotes Michael Braitinger as saying, "Chesbay is making beer like it was brewed 100 years ago. I feel so lucky to help reincarnate that."

Chesbay Amber has no additives and it preserves its taste instead of its shelf life by not being pasteurized. Because it is an all-natural beer, you will notice a white sediment at the bottom of each bottle. That is your guarantee that the beer is brewed and bottled in the old style. The sediment is some of the yeast which has continued to float to the bottom of this lager after bottling. It means the beer is live — the way all beer once was. When you pour it, pour slowly to leave the sediment in the bottle.

Chesbay meets all the requirements of the German Purity Law, the Reinheitsgebot, which establishes the highest standards of brewing. It is about four percent alcohol by volume, and it uses three malt types, hops from Czechoslovakia, Germany and Yakima, and a Bavarian yeast culture.

For storing, keep your Chesbay at "cellar temperature." (That term by custom refers to an English cellar, which is normally 40 to 50 degrees Fahrenheit). The company's recommended serving temperature is 50 degrees Fahrenheit, although Jim Kollar says he likes his refrigerator-cold.

Just by coincidence, Chesbay comes in the same style of short 12-ounce bottles as our own local pride and joy, Straub's of St. Mary's. So local beer lovers should feel comfortable with a Chesbay in their hands.

No doubt you'll want to share the Penn State spirit with Jim and Marilou. Their beers are available locally at Nittany Beverage at $18.50 a case. At six-pack shops, look for the blue and green label Rozalyn designed — the one with the Chesapeake seagull on it.

Ein Prosit der Gemutlichkeit!

Beer Tasting:
Learning to Appreciate a Brewer's Taste

September 8, 1985

Beer is one of man's favorite beverages. It is brewed and served in almost every country in the world, and enjoyed at every level of society from the richest to the poorest. One of the reasons for this is that beer is not pretentious; a man can order his favorite brew without someone judging his place on the social scale. Beer is just meant to be enjoyed.

But a unique opportunity has come to present itself over the past few years. The high value of the dollar and the increasing sophistication of the American consumer has brought about the availability of the biggest selection of beers in decades. In the 1960s you were lucky if you could sample 50 imports from overseas; today you can sample about 500 brands.

Amidst this cornucopia of choice, the question is how to enjoy it. Obviously, there are differences in beers and the only way to learn some of those differences is to try them. For this purpose there has been invented the "Beer Tasting."

The "beer tasting" is not exactly like a wine tasting. At a wine tasting everyone is setting up his own taste to judge what the sun and the rain did to a grape one summer. But beer is much more of an art. What you taste in a beer is the taste a brewer intended to put there. So the object of a beer tasting is not so much to judge a taste, but to learn to appreciate another man's taste, namely the brewer.

So, how does one have a Beer Tasting? Probably the best type of beer tasting for a beginner is one where the goal is to learn to distinguish the different styles of beer from one another. Here are some guidelines for the would-be discriminating consumer to his or her own beer tasting.

The Quantity of Beer. Normally about six to nine beers is the right number to try in an evening. For a tasting one does not drink the whole bottle. Usually a third to a half bottle is sufficient. Thus, in a beer tasting of six to nine beers, one would be expected to consume only two or three full bottles per person.

Selecting the Beers. The kinds of beer selected for a tasting are important. One should not make the choice on the basis of country of origin, but on the basis of style. Thus, one should be sure to try a standard American pilsener. Next, one might try a North German lager, such as Beck's or DAB. Finally, one might try the cream of all pilseners, Pilsner Urquell from Czechoslovakia.

The next set of beers might include: 1) an English pale ale, such as Bass Ale; 2) a Vienese style amber lager, such as New Amsterdam; and 3) a deep amber such as Chesbay.

Finally, on the third level, one might try the dark beers. These might include the famous Pottsville Porter, made by Yuengling; the very rich Samuel Smith Nut Brown Ale, and, of course, a Guinness Stout.

There are, of course, many other styles left over for another beer tasting; Bocks and Doppel Bocks, Canadian-style lagers, wheat beers, Lambics, Belgian Abbey Ales, Irish Red Ales, and a host of other styles. If you like your first beer tasting, there will still be a lot of styles left for many more tastings.

Order of Tasting. Always start with the beers which are lightest in color and lightest in taste, and proceed to the darker, heavier and stronger brews.

What Food to Serve. The best food to serve with a serious beer tasting are cheeses and breads. You should not serve pretzels or potato chips or peanuts. Salts and the oils in these foods will affect the tastes of the beers very much.

What Glasses to Use. You want a glass to hold three to four ounces of beer with enough room for the head to form. Six-ounce juice glasses, wine glasses, or 6-ounce pilsener-type glasses such as those used at many bars with bottled beer would be the best, but regular tumblers will work just fine, too. One should try to have beer-clean glasses, and a separate, dry glass for each style of beer.

What Temperature to Serve At. This is important for serious beer tasting. To drink a pale ale or a Guinness Stout at ice cold temperature is as much of a waste as drinking cold coffee or eating warm ice cream. Pilseners, lagers and light beers are made to be drank at about 40 degree Fahrenheit. Most dark beers, ales, pale ales, porters, stouts, bocks and doppelbocks are best served at 50 to 60 degree Fahrenheit.

What to Look for in a Beer. In tasting a beer, look for five basic things: appearance, head, bouquet, taste and finish.

Appearance. When you pour your beer, take a look at it. Color, clarity, translucency and bubbly character can each be noted. The color of beer is normally determined by the degree to which the barley malt is roasted. While usually the clearest beers are the most popular, the deepest tasting beers are not clear. Clarity often reflects simply the degree of filtration. So, appearance is a balancing of pleasing appearance with depth and balance of taste.

Head. The crown of the brewer's art and the crown of every glass of beer is its head. The perfect head is as thick as whipped cream, with bubbles so small you can barely see them. But, again, it is not only the head that makes a beer, but a perfect balance of qualities.

Bouquet. There are two aromas to look for in a beer. The first is the aroma of the barley malt. This is a heavy, sweeter, wet-grain smell. The second aroma is the bitter smell of the hops.

Taste. Next, drink some. Take a good drink, and swish it around your mouth. Let it flow over all sides of your tongue. Taste the beer as it hits the front of your tongue and as it tastes in the other parts of your mouth. Then swallow.

Finish. After the swallow comes one of the main pleasures of good beer. The finish. It is the pleasant after-taste of the hops and malt. The finish is a physical phenomenon that confirms your memory of the beer. It is the reason good beer is made to be drunk slowly.

Visit your distributor or six-pack shop and buy some varieties. Invite some friends over and compare some tastes. With the addition of several excellent cheeses, the "Beer Tasting and Cheese Party" has been born.

Ein Prosit der Gemutlichkeit!

Spirit of Cincinnati Brewing
Available in Centre County

September 22, 1985

A new beer has come to Centre County, brewed in the spirit of Cincinnati, Ohio. It is called Christian Moerlein, made by the Hudepohl Brewing Company. This year Hudepohl is celebrating its 100th anniversary.

Hudepohl was founded in 1885 when Ludwig Hudepohl II and a partner bought the old Koehler Brewery on Buckeye Street. The company produced Buckeye beer, and later Hudepohl, reaching production of 40,000 barrels by 1890.

At that time, Cincinnati was considered to be one of the beer capitals in the world. The quality of Cincinnati beers was recognized everywhere, and Cincinnatians drank beer at a record-breaking per capita average of 320 pints a year for every man, woman and child in the city.

Beer was a very essential part of the social life of the city. In 1890, there were 1,810 taverns in Cincinnati which was a ration of about one tavern for every 40 families. It was the custom in those far off times for most of these to serve a free lunch each day. The majority of folk ate in the taverns each day and, just as in England or Germany at the same period, taverns were the places where most social, political and business activity occurred. The slogan, "There is no free lunch," was not true in Cincinnati until Prohibition.

In addition to the taverns, Cincinnati also had the most amazing beer gardens in the world. Cincinnati is surrounded by hills; it is said that the town lies in the center of a "huge amphitheater." At different points on the rim of these hills there were built about a half dozen huge beer gardens. To get to them, one would ride up the side of the hills on steep inclined planes. Here is a description of these beer gardens from the Hamilton County historical records.

"At the summer of these planes are immense beer gardens with mammoth buildings, where on stifling summer nights the city hive swarms out, thousands upon thousands of all classes and nationalities, who thus come together and alike yield to the potent influences of music and lager." The orchestras and bands played Bach, Mozart, Beethoven and Wagner, and the popular songs and tunes of the period all evening long.

One of these beer gardens on Mount Adams was said to be the largest in the world and absolutely "unequalled in splendor." One description reads: "Viewed from the city the long lines of a hundred lights, in places rising tier about tier... made the place appear an illuminated palace in the skies."

The beer gardens were considered to be an important prop to family stability. It is recorded that the population of the city would "resort on Sunday afternoons, with their wives and children, to the beer gardens on the hill tops, where there is music, green arbors, kindly skies and soft airs. All classes... with their families to the toddling infant thus mingle in calm, peaceful reception." As many as 8,000 people might attend evening concerts at a single beer garden.

Such customs fit in not only with the city's social life, but also with a brilliant cultural life of unrivaled excellence. Henry Wadsworth Longfellow had dubbed Cincinnati "The Queen

City of the West;" visitors from Europe acclaimed it the "Paris of America;" and in this century Winston Churchill described it as "the most beautiful of the inland cities of the Union."

It was in this spirit of strong community, strong family, strong culture and local pride, that the beers of Cincinnati were brewed. Prohibition period destroyed some of the social life of the city, but not its spirit. After Prohibition nine breweries reopened, and "Prosits" once more echoed through the town as the people celebrated together again.

Hudepohl reopened in 1933, and by the 1940s had become the central brewer for Cincinnati and the whole state. Almost all of Hudepohl's 2.2 million-barrel production was drunk by community conscious Ohioans.

In the late 1970s Hudepohl, which is still owned by the same family, decided that Budweiser, Miller and Stroh could have the mass market for lowest common denominator beer. Hudepohl would begin to shift attention to the super premium market.

The first fruit of this decision was Christian Moerlein (pronounced more-line), a definitely super premium beer. Christian Moerlein is the first American beer to pass "Reinheitsgebot." This is the German Purity Law of 1516 which is still enforced in Bavaria. No beer can be sold there unless it is pure, that is, made from only barley malt, water, hops and yeast. Christian Moerlein is made in the tradition of all Bavarian Beers, and was certified in 1983 to be pure enough to be marketed in Germany. Only one other American beer, Erlanger, made by Stroh's, has been so certified. Most other American beers are made with rice or corn grains rather than all barley, or contain chemical additives.

Christian Moerlein has a clean, crisp taste, the kind you might imagine that Cincinnatians would have enjoyed on hot summer nights in those hilltop beer gardens. It is brewed the same way as the finest German lagers, and has a definite malty taste and the fine aroma of choice hops. It is one American beer that can proudly stand beside the German imports.

Christian Moerlein is made with the most expensive two-row barley, and a combination of Yakima-Idaho and Hallertauer hops. The beer is fermented for 14 days and lagered for 42 days. It has an alcohol content of four percent by weight, and about five percent by volume.

One of the special things I like about Christian Moerlein is the label. It's gold and black on a cream background and show a charming 19th century liberated woman with a flowery hat in the old art-deco style. How do I know she's liberated? That's easy: She looks like the pictures of my grandmother and great aunts at the turn of the century. Women back in those days, at least women from the old country, were definitely liberated. My grandmother considered absolutely no man to be her equal, least of all the poor blokes who married: 1: here, and 2: her daughters.

In addition to Christian Moerlein, Hudepohl also makes a special Oktoberfest beer, which is available for a month in the fall, and a spring bock beer, available in the early spring. The latter are not available in Centre County yet, but will one day, we hope, grace our seasonal tables.

Ein Prosit der Germutlichkeit!

Oktoberfest is the Season
for Toasting to Good Fellowship

October 6, 1985

This is the time of year when the thoughts of all true lovers of beer, festivity and good fellowship turn to Munich in Bavaria: For this is the season of "Oktoberfest."

There is nothing like Oktoberfest anywhere in the world. Oktoberfest is when an entire city and an entire province get together to have a good time. Muncheners have been doing it for 175 years.

It all began in 1810 when Crown Prince Ludwig of Bavaria became engaged to Princess Therese of Saxony. A great October wedding was planned, and all of Munich was excited about the coming royal celebration.

Of course, there were lots of royal weddings in the 19th century, and this one might have turned out no more memorable than any of the others. But it so happened that there was a young coachman in Munich who had an idea. This young man was also a sergeant in the national guard, and while on duty one weekend he suggested to his major that the royal wedding be celebrated with a horse race.

Now if you had an idea like that today, you would probably have to organize a multi-million dollar political action committee, collect petitions, and lobby the harness-racing commission just to get anyone in the governor's mansion, let alone the White House, to even consider the idea. But times were different in 1810; in those days a good idea was a good idea no matter from whom it came.

Thus it was that the major took the sergeant's idea to the king, who approved it and gave the order. The race was scheduled for the wedding day. A large meadow on the western edge of town was selected for the race track. In honor of the crown princess, the meadow was named the Theresienweise, which means, "Therese's meadow."

The race on that blessed day was a great success. And the winner of the race was — you guessed it — the very same young coachman-sergeant who had suggested having the race in the first place!

Now the people of Munich are not thoughtless about their good times. If they like something, they remember to do it again. Thus, the Muncheners then and there decided to have a celebration on Therese's meadow every year. The Muncheners also have lots of children.

The farmers from the surrounding villages liked to come to the horse races, so they soon scheduled their "Central Agricultural Show" and rifle shooting to be held at the same time each year. Of course, these added to the crowds of hungry, thirsty people at the races, and soon caterers set up tents and hired bands to serve them food and drink. By 1818 merry-go-rounds, folk-dancing, carnivals, and shows of all kinds were added.

A few years later the horse races were abandoned and perhaps Therese's wedding was forgotten, but the celebration was now an annual event in the life of Munich. Each year it begins on the third weekend in September and lasts 16 days.

I have attended the Oktoberfest twice. Each year it is opened with a huge parade led by the lord mayor of Munich. The entire city joins in the parade and when it reaches Therese's meadow, the lord mayor ceremonially taps the first keg of beer to the cheers of his city. The celebration then begins with a quarter of a million voices raising their stein in the famous Oktoberfest toast: "Ein Prosit der Gemutlichkeit!" that is, "A toast to good fellowship!"

Therese's meadow is no small field. It is about the size of University Park campus. On one side is set up a fairway with the best roller coaster I have ever ridden, and carnival rides of all sorts. Next comes the streets of food concessions, with every kind of pastry, sausage and tasty dish. These are really delightful if you like good food: they are not all sugary food nor all deep fried, but the finest foods of a whole city of food lovers. It is as though all the prize winners in the food contests at the Grange Fair were cooking up their best.

All along the way through the fairway, carnivals and concession streets are round, kiosk-like stands. At these anyone can walk up to buy brandy, schnapps or cordials.

But the real "raison d'etre" of Oktoberfest are the streets of beer halls. About a dozen temporary buildings, each about the size of the indoor sports facility on the Penn State campus, and each capable of seating about 6,000 people, are erected for Oktoberfest.

Each of the halls is brightly painted, with flags and shields of all sorts in the rafters. Around the sides and rear of each hall are special areas reserved by Munich's businesses and institutions. I remembered passing the IBM and McDonald's areas, each about the size of the Autoport restaurant. On the left side of each hall are the open kitchens, with thousands of half-chickens on revolving spits and my favorite, pork shanks, called "haxon." There are also sausages, large Bavarian pretzels, and the hugest radishes you ever saw, all being prepared by a corps of alternately hard-working and happily toasting cooks.

Old women in brightly colored Bavarian dirndls carry huge baskets of bread, or a dozen liters of beer, or magnificent trays piled high with plates and food, down the long rows of tables to serve the singing, talking, laughing Muncheners.

In the center of all this activity is a raised band stand, and on it is a 10 to 20 piece band. The music is "oompah," the songs are friendly, and everybody joins in singing. For certain Munchener favorites, everybody at the long tables locks arms with the person on both sides and the rows of people rock from side to side while singing a "heimatlied" or folk song.

And all of this is to celebrate the spirit of Munich: beer. The symbol of Munich is a little monk with a beer stein, who is the original munchkin; for Munich had its beginnings in the monastery founded there in 1102 A.D. That monastery did two things well: it brewed beer and it prayed that the people of Munich would always be happy. By all accounts its beers have been enjoyed and its prayers have been answered for 800 years or more.

The Oktoberfest is sponsored by the breweries of Munich. There are six of them, and one or more of each of the great beer halls at Oktoberfest is their responsibility. The six breweries are: Augustiner, Hacker-Pschorr, H.B. (Hofbrau), Lowenbraw, Spaten and Paulaner. Their symbols are as much identified with the city of Munich as the city's own seal with the munchkin on it.

Although today is the last day of Oktoberfest, it is only now that the famous Oktoberfest beers are arriving in

America. These beers have been brewed traditionally the previous spring and are called "Marzen" beers. They are amber in color, and brewed deeper, darker and stronger than the normal German beer.

I have found three Oktoberfest beers so far this year. Pletcher's Beer Distributor in Bellefonte is carrying Paulaner Oktoberfest beer delivered straight from Munich. W.R. Hickey Beer Distributor in State College is carrying Wurzburger Oktoberfest beer from another Bavarian city, Wurzburg. In Washington, D.C., recently I was able to try some Spaten Oktoberfest from Munich. Of the three, Spaten is the strongest and hoppiest; Paulaner the lightest. But somewhere out there is Hofbrau, Augustinerbrau, Lowenbrau and a Hacker-Pschorrbrau Oktoberfest yet to be tried this year.

If you love good fellowship you will love Oktoberfest, and if you like beer you'll have to try Oktoberfest beer.

Ein Prosit der Gemutlichkeit!

Adolph Coors and the
History of a Rocky Mountain Lager

October 20, 1985

The year was 1847. At that time one of the most important and powerful nations in Europe was a country which no longer exists. It once covered much of what we know today as East Germany, as well as most of the northern and western half of Poland. The nation was called Prussia and the ambition of its people affected most of the next hundred years of European and American history.

In that year Adolph Coors was born in the Prussian town of Barmen, now renamed Wuppetal. His parents were as poor as church mice but at the age of 13 young Coors was lucky enough to get a contract of apprenticeship as a printer's assistant.

In those days education was not an easy thing to come by. For most young people, the only way to receive an education was to become an "apprentice." Basically, what that entailed was buying oneself into indentured service in return for learning a trade.

Young Adolph Coors might have ended up printing advertising flyers for the rest of his life except that in 1862, when Adolph was 15, his parents moved to Dortmund. There they were able to secure a new apprenticeship for their bright young son, this time at the Henry Wenker Brewery.

However, the joy of learning a new trade was overshadowed by the death of both of his parents that same year. This meant that he not only had to complete his apprenticeship duties each day but to support himself too. It also meant that he had to earn enough to pay his apprenticeship fees. As an apprentice, a young man not only had to work to learn, but to pay for the privilege of doing so.

So during the day he worked to learn as a brewer's assistant while at night, to earn money, he worked as the brewery bookkeeper. Despite the death of his parents he kept his word and completed his apprenticeship contract. At the age of 18 he took off to learn more of brewing by working in other breweries in Prussia.

At the age of 21, young Coors had to decide between seeking adventure in the wars of Europe, or seeking adventure in the wild, wild American West of the New World.

It is hard for us today to imagine the lure of excitement that the American West exerted on the imaginations of young Central European men in the 19th century. Gunfights with outlaws, Indian wars, stark desert and mountain landscapes, new towns and the chance to create something out of nothing at all filled young minds with boundless sense of adventure.

In 1868 young Coors made his way to the port of Hamburg to leave for America. He was too poor in money to be able to buy a steamship ticket. But he was rich enough in spirit to sneak onto a ship as a stowaway. He was caught on the high seas, but he was able to talk the captain into letting him pay for his passage by working after he landed. For the whole next year he worked as a bricklayer, stonecutter, fireman and laborer to pay off the shipping line for his passage over.

By 1869 he was out of debt and immediately headed west again. He found himself as the foreman at the Strenger Brewery in Chicago until 1872. In that year the wanderlust got into him again, so he went to work for the railroad and ended up in Denver, Colo.

Young Coors had saved his money back in Chicago and upon arrival in Denver, he went looking for an opportunity to get into business. He was soon able to join with a partner in a new bottling business. By 1873, he was selling "bottled beer, ale porter, cider, imported and domestic wines and cider water." The bottling business was a financial success, but it was not as much fun as he had known when he was brewing beer.

One day young Coors took a walk near Golden, Colo., where he first saw the beautiful, clear, cool water of the Rocky Mountain springs in the vicinity. Now, to a brewer, pure water is the first ingredient of pure beer. Coors also saw an abandoned tannery nearby which could be turned into a brewery.

He had found a beginning and he started dreaming. What he needed next was someone to believe in him and his dreams. In Denver there was a very successful ice cream parlor owner by the name of Jacob Schueler who knew that the best investment in the world was a bright young man with a sense of adventure, a love of hard work, and a dream. Schueler raised $18,000 to add to Coors' savings of $2,000 and suddenly the dream had come true. At the age of 26 young Adolph Coors had his own brewery. Within a year he was turning a profit.

Coors brought over from his apprenticeship in Europe the knowledge of how to make the wonderful light lager beers which had been developed in Czechoslovakia in 1842. He brewed a cold, pure fresh style of beer, fitted perfectly to the crisp, dry air of the American west.

Coors' Banquet Lager is considered by Michael Jackson, the author of "The Pocket Guide to Beer" and the "World Guide to Beer," as "the ultimate U.S. beer in terms of its light, clean, refreshing character." Stephen Morris, author of "The Great Beer Trek," says that Coors beer is regarded by many "as the ultimate American quaffing experience."

Coors beer has always had a certain mystique. This mystique is owed to three facts. First, Coors is a pure beer with no artificial additives. Although it cannot meet the requirements of Germany's Reinheitsgebot, because it contains rice in addition to barley malt, it is an all-natural beer. Coors adds rice to its beers, just as Budweiser does, because rice makes the beer clearer and lighter. Coors ferments its beer eight days, and ages it for 45 days, which is one of the longest aging periods in the industry. Coors bouquet comes from its combination of American Cluster, Cascade and German Hallertau hops.

The second reason for Coors' mystique is that, unlike most other American beers, it is not pasteurized. Coors pioneered the development of a super-fine filtration process which makes possible what Michael Jackson calls "the remarkable fresh taste of Coors." Although it does not have to be refrigerated, the fresh taste of Coors is best insured by keeping it cool and by drinking it within 60 days of leaving the brewery.

The third reason for Coors' mystique is its western background. A single visit to Denver and a hike in the Rocky Mountains are enough to show why Coors is the preferred taste of America's west. It is perfectly suited to the cool, dry air of the mile-high city and the snow capped mountains of the Rockies.

Ein Prosit der Gemutlichkeit!

Challenge and Tradition at Blitz-Weinhard

November 3, 1985

It was 1975 and all across America the bicentennial celebration of the opening battles of the American Revolution was in full swing. But even as the stories were being retold of the first stirring battles of the colonists against the British Empire, newer marketing empires were planning an attack on one of America's oldest independent brewers.

The Blitz-Weinhard brewery had been the easy favorite of Oregon beer drinkers since Territorial days. But on the 200th anniversary of the beginnings of the War of American Independence, the imperial marketers of the two industry giants — Anheuser-Busch and Miller Brewing Company — had targeted Oregon for a massive invasion.

Redcoated marketing men and women were poring over media maps of the state of Oregon trying to decide on the best places to attack the local taste buds. Millions of dollars were being assembled. Radio stations and newspapers all across the state were selling out all the time and space they had to the invading brands. When everything was prepared, battalions of advertising images more powerful than Hessian regiments were poised to march across the state to conquer and subdue local taste.

Fred Wessinger, the president of Blitz-Weinhard and great-grandson of Henry Weinhard, the company's founder, heard of the assembling invasion. Fred and his brothers had just completed pulling the company back together in 1974 by buying up the last odds and ends of stock. Now they were facing the challenge of their lives to determine whether the old-time tastes and spirit of American independence could survive.

In early 1975 Fred was sitting in his office pondering all this and thinking of his great-grandfather. What would Henry have done, he wondered, as he poured himself a tall, cool white-capped glass of memories.

History records that Henry Weinhard had emigrated to America from Germany. He didn't stay long in the built-up cities of the East. The Old World spirit which motivated America's toughest pioneers kept him walking as far to the west as he could go. In 1856 he arrived at Fort Vancouver in the Oregon Territory with his German Brewmaster's certificates and a copper brew kettle in his hand.

Henry knew he had ended up in the right place. Fort Vancouver was bustling with the toughest men in the world – soldiers, loggers, trappers and hardy pioneers of the kind who crossed a continent to make America great. They were thirsty – and they loved Henry's beer.

Henry brewed at Fort Vancouver until 1862 when the soldiers were all called away to fight and die on Civil War battlefields like Antietam and Gettysburg. Then he moved the brewery across the Columbia River to Portland where the fame of his beer had already spread.

Sitting in his office in early 1975 Fred Wessinger was thinking of these and other stories of his great granddad, but one story in particular kept coming to mind. There was an old legend of Henry's "other brew." It seems that Henry had always made two beers — one for the general public, and a second, secret brew that he made only to serve to his friends and employees. It was called his own "private reserve."

"That's it!" Fred thought. "Whatever is going to happen will happen, but I'm bringing back Henry's private reserve." Fred immediately called his brewmaster, Jack Daniel (that's his real name, honest), into his office.

"I've decided to revive a tradition," he told him. Fred asked him to prepare a new beer to serve employees and guests to see them through the hard times ahead. "I want an old-time traditional brew, like Henry had at the turn of the century," Fred said. And then he put his money where his mouth was: brewing beer. Daniel explained, "Henry believed in making beer in small quantities taking a lot more time than anyone does today and sparing no expense when it came to selecting raw materials.

"So I decided to use these principles and combine them with modern technology to make the kind of beer Henry would make if he were here."

Daniel worked on that beer for the next 22 months. It was a brewmaster's dream come true to have absolute freedom to brew a perfect beer without regard for cost. Daniel experimented with the most costly ingredients, and the longest and most varied aging times. Each experimental batch was "babied through."

Finally in late 1976 Daniel presented his result as the finest product of the brewer's art. It was tasted, and everyone knew that the tradition had been reborn. A spark from the past, no matter how small it may have seemed at the time, had been rekindled.

The new beer was definitely needed to raise the spirits of Fred and the employees. The invasion of the marketers was at its worst phase. Under the media onslaught the sale of Blitz beer was on its way to plummeting from one-third of the market to less than a tenth.

The idea of Henry's private reserve had originally been simple: to have a special beer to cheer up employees and guests. But by a fortuitous turn of events it turned out to save the brewery.

It seems that the employees liked the new beer so much that they also wanted to enjoy it after work. Many of them used to have a beer at Jake's bar across the street before they went home. So they took a couple of cases over to Jake's to have available for public sale.

Jake's manager, Doug Schmick, tried the beer and was "wildly enthusiastic." He was convinced it was the best beer in America. He told the owner of Jake's, who started carrying Henry's private reserve at his other restaurant in Seattle.

Word about the new beer spread quickly. Bud Clark of the Hollow Goose Tavern wanted some, and then other bar owners were calling for it. Soon Fred Wessinger was driving all over town in a station wagon delivering cases on special request.

Suddenly he realized that he stumbled onto the answer to the invasion. People wanted a better beer. They were only trying the new invasion brands in their quest for a real quality brew.

It had all started out as a simple bow to an old company tradition. Within a few years, "Private Reserve" was accounting for 60 percent of the entire company's sale and Henry's was fast becoming the best-selling super-premium on the West Coast.

Next time: Henry Weinhard's Private Reserve: Product and Philosophy.

Ein Prosit der Gemutlichkeit!

'Henry's:' A Beer from the Past

November 17, 1985

We live in an age that loves newness. The most popular commodity in the world is what we call "the news." We love new cars, new clothes, new movies, new hit songs, and even new life styles. We love change and we worship what is advanced, progressive, and forward-looking.

Imagine, then, a company which believes that it is "better to look to the qualities of the past rather than the trends of the present." One would not probably expect too much of such a company, especially if it described its major product as "a deliberate step backward."

But there is such a company and its product and philosophy have been an amazing success. It is the Blitz-Weinhard Brewing Company of Portland, Oregon and its major product is a beer called Henry Weinhard's Private Reserve, which most people simply call "Henry's." In my last column I recounted the story of how "Henry's" came to be a commercial beer almost by accident. In this column, the attention is on how "Henry's" is actually made and the idea behind it.

"Henry's" is a very special beer, brewed to be of absolute top-quality. It is hand-made in the old 19th century manner, with attention given to quality and quality only.

When "Henry's" is brewed, the brew kettle is filled with about 1,020 barrels of wort, which is only about 75 percent of the kettle's capacity. After brewing, the bottom 620 barrels are drawn off and discarded, leaving only the top 400 barrels to complete the brewing process. This is done to assure absolute consistency of flavor.

One of the amazing things about "Henry's" is that it is made in such small batches of only 400 barrels each. The amount of "Henry's" produced in an entire year is less than the amount of beer produced by Anheuser-Busch in a week.

After brewing, "Henry's" is fermented and aged six full weeks, a period of time that is two or three times the usual aging period for American beers. As each batch is being aged, it is watched every day; the company says that the brewmaster "babies" each batch through.

It must be remembered that beer is not a collection of chemicals — it is alive. There are more than 800 biological compounds in fermenting beer, each undergoing biological change. It is keeping all these living, growing, developing things in rein that means a consistently perfect beer.

Each batch of "Henry's" is separately bottled and each bottling is numbered on the label. It is very much like noting the vintage of a wine. Besides assuring the quality of each batch, the numbered bottles have become popular with bottle collectors.

The ingredients in Henry Weinhard's Private Reserve as as special as the brewing method. Although corn adjunct is used, the barley used is the expensive two-row type. This barley is richer and smoother than the less expensive six-row barley used in most beers.

Some years ago cuttings from Germany's finest hops of the Hallertau region were imported to America and replanted in Oregon and Washington state where they are now called Cascade hops. The Cascade hops of America are now as acclaimed as their parents from Hallertau. There are more Cascade hops used in "Henry's" than in any other beer, according to the brewery.

The result is a beer very similar to the light, dry beers of northern Germany. It is described by Howard Hillman in "The Gourmet Guide to Beer" as "a premium beer with a golden hue. Floral, citric hops obvious to the nose. Malty palate dips in the mid-taste: Hop finish."

Michael Jackson, author of "The Pocket Guide to Beer" and "The World Guide to Beer," says that Blitz-Weinhard is "the leader of the new wave of super-premium beers."

What is the philosophy that has made this beer from the past into one of the beers of the future? This is how the company understands itself and its product:

"Over the past two generations or so, beer in America has gone through a substantial change. At one time we had available to us a great number of products, offering a wide variety of flavor and differences to suit the various tastes and interests of the individual drinker. Today — perhaps as a result of requirements of mass-production and low cost — we have available only a few brands of beer. And these tend to be so similar that even brewing experts have difficulty in discerning one from another.

"Concerned about this trend, we asked ourselves, if, instead of continuing on this too-well-worn path, we might find a method of brewing beer as it once was. Our goal was to produce the finest traditional premium product possible, without concern for volume, time, or even cost.

"As a model for our efforts, we studied the methods used by our founder, master-brewer Henry Weinhard, in producing an exceptional beer he had reserved for the enjoyment of special guests and friends.

"We made every effort to follow as closely as possible the slower and more painstaking techniques of the Nineteenth Century and to avoid the mechanical processes of today."

"Henry's" is not available on the East Coast yet. To my knowledge, it has made it only as far as Houston and Denver. I have had the pleasure of drinking it in Denver, where its clear, crisp, well-hopped flavor was enjoyed by many at the Great American Beer Festival.

Encouraged by its brush with the past, Blitz-Weinhard has entered the market with a new-old ale. The company's policy is to stick to the "fringes of the market" and "to supply something on the unique side."

The new ale is an Irish-style ale, dubbed "a premium light ale." It is described as having "an inordinate amount of hops," in order to give it an exceptionally desired hoppy taste and finish.

If any readers are going west, they might encounter these two special treats from Oregon. They might even bring back samples for their friends.

Ein Prosit der Gemutlichkeit!

Yule Ales Add to Advent

December 1, 1985

'Tis Advent, that holy time of the year when we begin to prepare ourselves for the coming of the Infant. In ancient days this time of year was exciting in a much different way than excitement is generally experienced today.

Nowadays, it seems, excitement is experienced as something that is thrilling because it is new, unknown, risky, sexy and dangerous. Today's young people seem to look for excitement at the edge of life.

But the ancient excitement of Christmas was something quite different. Christmas wasn't something which happened at the edge of life, but something that happened at the heart of life. It wasn't a search for something new and dangerous. On the contrary, Christmas was as predictable as clockwork, and as familiar as one's most favorite feeling. Each year Christmas came on exactly the same day, and everyone tried very hard to do the same things in the same way they had done them in the past.

To today's young people that might sound boring. And yet ... and yet ... in those days it had seemed so very exciting. To me, Christmas had always seemed like a challenge without equal. It was an adventure in time. Every year people tried to see if they could rekindle and pass down the same feeling that had been felt on that first Christmas morn.

They all knew and believed with childlike simplicity that something wonderful had happened on that hallowed night almost 2,000 years ago. They believed that hearts had been opened and changed in a way that had never happened before. They naively believed through all the years since then that the original joy had been rekindled again and again each and every year at Christmas, just as it had been experienced on that first blessed eve.

Oh, the excitement of it all! Each year they wondered: Could it happen again? Would it? Could the magic still work? The anticipation grew to the highest levels of expectation and awe: If they did all the same things, heard the same stories, ate the same foods, drank the same drinks, rejoined in the same ways, would they again feel the excitement of their own first Christmas when they were children? Did they still have it in them to unlock all that joy one more time?

The wonder of it! Could their joy be great enough to renew again for one more year the tremendous joy of that first blessed eve in the year One, when the time of our time began? And so, on the 4th day after the winter solstice, when they were absolutely sure that the sun had begun to rise again in the heavens, they celebrated Christmas.

In ancient days everyone had worked so hard to make it happen again each year. They bought presents which they believed would bring out each person's most childlike joy. They baked Christmas cakes and cookies, worked for weeks to prepare festive decorations for every room and window, searched out old recipes for Christmas goose or turkey stuffing, hung mistletoe in their hallways, hauled in the Yule logs, and brushed up on the ancient Christmas stories and carols to tell over again to their children and themselves. Old fights were ended, debts forgiven and friendships renewed in this season.

One of the smallest and least significant contributions to the annual challenge to rekindle the ancient joy was made by the brewers of Europe and early America. In those days everyone felt the obligation to contribute whatever they could to the annual renewal of the community's joy. Each year the brewers made their small contribution by brewing special Christmas ales and holiday beers for the season.

The ancient tradition is undergoing a rebirth in America. Since the early 1970s, when there were only one or two remaining Christmas ales available in America, both small and large brewers are taking up the challenge to deepen the joy of the Christmas season by bringing out special seasonal brews.

Christmas ales and holiday beers are normally brewed deeper and darker than beers for other seasons. At Christmas time, one was expected to sip slowly to enjoy the deep contentment of the season and the memories of childlike joy.

As I write this column in advance of the season, most Christmas ales and holiday beers have not yet come on the market. But here are some names you might look for to taste the challenge of Christmas past:

Aass Jule 01 (pronounced "Arse Yule Ale") from Norway. This is a special, rich, malty, dark lager developed specially for the winter holiday season.

Noche Buena Cervesa Especial from the Montezuma Brewery in Mexico. This is a Marzen-style brew in the old tradition of the Austro-Hungarian Empire. This is a dark brown, medium-bodied beer with a delicate malt taste.

Anchor Christmas Ale. This is a special ale brewed to a different recipe each year. It is always a real ale, brewed especially dark, heavy and hoppy for the season.

Newman's Winter Ale. This is brewed in Ithaca, New York, as a "winter warmer," and is a real ale, truly dark and different.

Sierra Nevada Celebration Ale. This is brewed in Chico, California, by two of the most traditional-minded, dedicated microbrewers in America.

Boulder Christmas Ale, made by the "second largest brewery in the Rockies," but nonetheless a very small microbrewer. It is modeled after 17th and 18th century English mulled ales.

F.X. Matt's Traditional Season's Best from Utica, New York. This is an amber, Vienna-style holiday special made by true craftsmen. It is trucked right through Pennsylvania to Washington, D.C., Virginia and Colorado, but is not marketed here in the Keystone State. Perhaps we must be more sincere this year in extending holiday greetings to our neighbors in the empire state.

Some other Christmas ales and holiday beers one might encounter in one's travels are: Hudepohol's Christmas Beer from Cincinnati; August Schell's Xmas Beer from New Ulm, Minn.; Fred Koch Holiday Beer from Dunkirk, N.Y. (The Koch Brewery was recently purchased by Genessee); and Grant's Christmas Ale from Yakima, Wash.

It is hoped that the Spirit of Christmases past will inspire many more brewers to introduce new Christmas ales and holiday beers in 1985 to reawaken the ancient joy of the season. And it is hoped that we all should imbibe them in the spirit in which they are brewed.

Ein Prosit der Gemutlichkeit!

The Joy of Beer Brewing

December 15, 1985

Drinking beer is one thing — brewing it is another. Have you ever wondered about how a brewer feels about brewing beer? Is it a special craft, or is it only a job? Recently Fritz Maytag, president of the Anchor Brewing Company, wrote an article about his feelings which was published in "Zymurgy," the magazine of the American Homebrewers Association.

Maytag, you may recall from one of my columns about a year ago, was the heir to the Maytag washing machine fortune. He could have become anything he wanted, from a millionaire playboy to a financial empire builder.

Instead he bought a small brewery and set out to become a craftsman. No one can become a craftsman with money. So Fritz worked 16 hours a day, seven days a week for a dozen years to be changed into that. Finally he succeeded in crafting some of the finest and most appreciated beers in the world — Anchor Steam Beer, Liberty Ale, and Anchor Christmas Ale. In that time, he also allowed his work to craft him.

I thought you might like to know what it's like to work in a business where the bottom liners only control the cost parameters in order to let the spirit and heart live and grow. The following is excerpted from Maytag's article.

The Joy of Brewing

"Nearly any day (or night — I love the nights) of the year when I stroll through the brewery, I find something that has never failed to bring joy and a special feeling of awe. I am speaking of a vat filled with actively fermenting beer. Always when I see it I stop and look and wonder. Always I lean over and take a gentle sniff. Sometimes I blow the foam away — as I learned to do long ago from some forgotten brewer — to see the appearance of the wort. I watch the foam come slowly back, covering the little round window I made.

"I look out over the whole batch, gradually adjusting my sense of time to that of the fermenting beer; watching for changes, watching for movement, watching foam bubbles form and burst, watching the dark swirls slowly accumulate and move toward the outer edges.

"What in the world is going on here? Who am I to have caused this to happen? How many billions of billions of yeast cells are living here? How marvelous that in this vat is something so far beyond the human brain's ability to number or comprehend. And most of all, how wonderful that this will become beer.

"It will move out into the world of people. Each glass will have a little foam on top, just like this fermenter. This beer is alive, and will bring a special mysterious happiness into many people's lives.

"I am sure I have spent many more hours looking through a microscope at fermenting beer than any other brewery owner in the world. I have watched and watched and watched. I have looked and looked at yeast cells dividing and budding, at bacteria in all their horrible splendor and multiple shapes, at wild yeast, at hop resins and all that protein, at all those tiny things so small that they jump around from being bumped by Mr. Brown's moving molecules.

"The first time I did this, early in my brewing career, I was terrified by all the bacteria I saw. How could we ever get rid of them? How to clean up this beer? How could we get a pure and healthy yeast to thrive here? Before I learned about putting a little caustic soda in the drop of beer to clean out the protein, I thought everything that moved was bacteria. God knows even after adding the caustic soda in those days there was plenty of movement. Have you seen this? The unbelievable life force in one single drop of "old fashioned" beer?

"Gradually over time our beer became cleaner and cleaner. Nowadays looking for bacteria is like looking for a needle in a haystack. How proud I am of that. How well I remember the long rods, the short rods, the fat rods, the cocci in all their many groupings. How close I felt to Pasteur late one night in the lab when I realized that the drawings in his great work are absolutely accurate. How proud I was as I began to understand from personal experience something of the courage and discipline and patience and effort required by the great pioneers like Koch and Pasteur.

"From the first time I ever contemplated a batch of fermenting beer, I have been thrilled by the thought that all those billions of yeast cells are making a magical drink for people. In my early days, our one fermenter held the equivalent of about 20,000 glasses of beer. I would stand there wondering who the people were who would drink it. Where would they be? What would they be doing?

"Nowadays our fermenters hold twice that much beer. And as I stand beside one, watching the living changes on the surface, I try to imagine 40,000 people each drinking a glass. Think of the full moons, the hard work finished proudly, the sadness and happiness.

"I am very proud to know that this will be good beer. It is clean, the yeast is thriving. All those people will drink it because they choose to. And with any luck it will bring a bit of happiness into each life. I am very proud to think that this brew will be a part of all those lives, a magical part. I can barely begin to get my mind around this joy.

"I leave the fermenting room. If it's daytime there is a bustle of people working — someone here to see me, or I have somewhere to go. The brewery is alive around me, and all the people who work for me and with me. The phone is ringing, there is a tour in the tap-room.

"If it is nighttime, the copper kettles are glowing under the lights, the brewery is quiet, I think of all the many, many people working together who have built this company, all the years, all the agony and joy. How proud we all are.

"But I have a special joy that I have tried to describe, but which I can never really share with anyone. It is waiting for me any time I go into that fermenting room. The beer is alive there in the vat, we are old friends, and we know what we are up to. That is the joy of brewing."

Permission to reprint Fritz Maytag's article was kindly given by "Zymurgy," the journal of the American Homebrewer's Association.

Saranac 1888 Unveiling
'A Taste Imported from the Past'

December 29, 1985

What happens when the good try to get better? They often end up best of all.

In 1984 Matt's Premium Beer, brewed by the F.X. Matt Brewing Company of Utica, New York, was voted the best pilsener lager at the Great American Beer Festival.

But Matt's did not rest on its laurels. Over the following year it developed a new super-premium beer to offer the discriminating public. On May 29, 1985, Matt's unveiled a brew designed as the perfect beer: Saranac 1888. F.X. Matt II, president of the company, says that "Saranac 1888 is brewed to our ideal of what a classic beer should be."

The brewery calls it a "taste imported from the past."

The beer is the third major American beer brewed by a national or regional brewer — instead of a microbrewer — to meet the standards of "Reinheitsgebot." The "Reinheitsgebot," or German Purity Law of 1516, strictly limits the ingredients which may be found in pure beers. Except for some microbreweries, only Stroh's Erlanger and Hudepohl's Christian Moerlein brands are similarly brewed to meet the strictest standard in the world.

Both Erlanger and Christian Moerlein have been submitted to Bavarian authorities, and have been certified as "Reinheitsgebot." Officials at Matt's have indicated to me that they also intend to submit samples of Saranac 1888 for Bavarian "Reinheitsgebot" testing and certification.

Saranac 1888 is an all-malt lager. This means that it contains no other cereal grains as "adjuncts" to the barley malt. Almost all other American beers use cheaper grains such as corn grits and rice in place of some of the barley malt. Under "Reinheitsgebot," the use of such adjuncts renders the beer "impure." Beers containing any other cereals besides barley malt cannot be sold in Bavaria.

In addition to being an all-barley-malt brew, Saranac 1888 is made exclusively from two-row barley malt of the Klages variety. Two-row barley is much smoother and also much more expensive than the more commonly used six-row barley.

By comparison, Michelob uses only 80 percent of the two-row barley and 20 percent of the less expensive adjuncts. Budweiser beer has only 70 percent barley malt of both two-row and six-row varieties and 30 percent adjuncts.

If you like a strong taste of hops, Saranac 1888 is one beer you will have to try. It contains copious quantities of both Cascade hops from the Yakima Valley of Washington, and the original Hallertauer hops from the Hallertau region of Germany. Both of these hops are highly aromatic and give the beer a definitely hoppy character.

Saranac 1888 is fermented for one whole week, and then aged, or lagered, for six weeks. That is a very respectable lagering period, since most American beers are lagered for only about two to four weeks.

Three weeks into the lagering period, Saranac 1888 is "kraeusened." This means that some freshly fermented wort is added to the already half-lagered wort. This brings about a second fermentation, and adds considerably to the smoothness of the beer as its natural carbonation. The kraeusening procedure is similar to the procedure used to make champagne naturally bubbly.

It is interesting to compare the three "Reinheitsgebot" beers. Christian Moerlein is much smoother and has a less pronounced taste, more like the beers of northern Germany. Stroh's Erlanger is in the middle. In Saranac 1888 the flavor of the hops and malt is strongest of the three.

Saranac 1888 is named to commemorate the year of the founding of the F.X. Matt Brewing Company in 1888. In that same year the legendary Adirondack and St. Lawrence railroad began winding its way from Utica to Montreal. Saranac is a small town along the rail line near Lake Placid, N.Y.

The packaging of the beer features a hand-tinted photograph of a railroad crew, and the six-pack carriers contain historical anecdotes and folklore of the region.

One of the anecdotes tells the tale of a railroad track foreman who discovered a most effective incentive to encourage his men to work quickly. It was up to the foreman to get the workers to lay track as fast as possible. One foreman came upon this method. At the point where the previous day's work ended, he would pace off the distance of a good day's work, plus a little more. He'd mark the spot with a barrel of beer and tell his men "when you reach it, you can have it." Not only did the men routinely make the distance, but they often finished early!

Saranac 1888 is definitely an American brew designed to compete with the imports. It is intended to evoke the earlier standards of American brewing.

"I guess we're a bit stubborn and demanding," says F.X. Matt II, "just like the men who built the railway and logged the Adirondacks. People respect those attitudes and I think they'll recognize it when they find a product, especially a beer, that reflects those qualities."

Apparently none of the Centre County beer distributors carry Saranac 1888 locally, but Midstate Distributors in Williamsport often have it in stock.

Ein Prosit der Gemutlichkeit!

The Best Beers in the World

January 12, 1986

Not long ago (last summer, actually) I got out of my car in the parking lot to go food shopping when a young man stopped me.

"You're Ben Novak, aren't you?"

"Yes," I said.

"You write on beer, right?"

"Yes," I replied, wondering what came next.

"I just came back from a trip out west, and I brought back a few six-packs of Anchor Steam Beer. I'd like to drop some off for you. Will you be home this afternoon?"

"Stake your life on it," I replied.

"I'll stop by later," he said, and we went on.

About half an hour after I got home from shopping the same young man walked up to my house carrying four bottles of the celebrated California copper-colored nectar.

I chalked it up as another example of an old Penn State tradition: sharing the best you can find with a friend who will appreciate it with you. It was the kind of thing fraternity brothers used to do for each other when I was a student. That was a pretty wonderful tradition, I thought, as I poured a mug of the foaming beer.

Thinking of the tradition of sharing the best, it occurred to me to write a column about the best beers in the world. These are the kind of beers worth sharing with a friend, if your friendship is good enough to share over a beer.

Some time ago, the world expert on beer, Michael Jackson, made a list of the five best beers in the world. Jackson is the author of the "World Guide to Beer" and the "Pocket Guide to Beer." Despite the credentials, it's a heck of a good list, and a good place to start. Here are his choices, with my descriptions.

Pilsner Urquell

This is the one beer that appears on every list of the greatest beers in the world. In 1842 the first pilsener beer was made by the Prazdroj Brewery in Pilsen, Czechoslovakia. It rapidly became the standard of the world. All American beers have tried to copy it but never equaled its complex tastes. The Czechs say that it has a golden color which refracts a special spark or flame when it is held up to the light. Pilsner Urquell has a light, fruity bouquet and a strong dose of Saaz hops, which are undisputedly the finest tasting hops in the world. Pilsner Urquell is aged for three months in six miles of caves cut into the sandy rock underneath the town of Pilsen. There it is lagered in oak barrels which impart a flavor unreproducible in any other beer. It is available at several restaurants in Centre County and at Nittany Beverage.

Samuel Smith Taddy Porter

Porter was George Washington's favorite kind of beer and it is also mine. It takes getting used to, though. This is an especially dark, thick, heavy, malty brew with a full range of tastes that only bloom at slightly below room temperature, at about 60 degrees Fahrenheit. While this temperature discourages many American palates, porter is the perfect answer to driving safety; it is a manly brew meant to be drunk slowly, savoring every sip, and accompanied by bracing conversation among friends. The only places in Centre County which serve it are Zeno's and Duffy's Tavern in Boalsburg.

Lambic Kriek

The Belgians are more devoted to brewing beer than even the Germans or the Czechs. This is the champagne of beers. It comes in a bottle with both a cap and wine cork, and it pours and tastes like pink champagne. This beer is an ale made with the wild yeasts of the Senne Valley and mixed with wild cherries. This beer is really an aperitif. Most people, including myself, would never have imagined a beer of this type. But it's real, and it's one of the greats. This is not available in Centre County but can be special ordered through Nittany Beverage.

Paulaner Salvator

The "-ator" at the end of its name gives this beer away as a doppelbock. It is a lager beer made with more deeply roasted malt. It is traditionally brewed as a special beer drunk only in the spring. It is a dark brew, heavier than pilsener, and with a decidedly bittersweet aftertaste. It is the most welcome warmer on the first days of spring while sitting at the outdoor cafe. This is available in State College at the Brewery, Hi-Way Pizza, and Zeno's. In Bellefonte it is carried by Pletcher's Distributors.

Anchor Steam Beer

This is America's finest contribution to the legends of brewing. It is an amber or copper-colored beer which is made with a lager yeast but at ale temperatures. It has a creamy head, and a very strong fruity bouquet. Anchor Steam has a complex of fragrant esters which balance with its all-malt body and bitter Cascade hops to provide a symphony of taste with every swallow. This beer is not yet available in Centre County, but can be found in most East Cost cities.

There are many other lists of beers, some with 10 or 20 beers listed, but few would quibble with Jackson's choices. So, if your New Year's resolutions included the deepening of friendship, share any of these with a friend.

Ein Prosit der Gemutlichkeit!

A Revolutionary Beer Lager
Result of Six Generations of Brewing

January 26, 1986

Sometimes tradition means a lot more than money, and Jim Koch of Boston is living proof of it.

Until a year ago, Koch (who pronounces his name as "Cook") was a member of a super-prestigious management company called the Boston Consulting Group. He had a fantastic office overlooking Boston harbor on the 31st floor of the Exchange, a home in Cambridge, an annual salary of over a quarter of a million dollars, and three degrees from Harvard (BA, MBA, and JD). What more could a man like that want? The Boston Globe called him "the picture of yuppie success."

Then he left it all to brew beer. It was a family tradition.

It seems that Jim's family has one of the longest lines of brewmasters in the United States. His great-great grandfather had come to America from Bavaria as a brewmaster in the 1840s. Ever since then every first son for five generations had become a brewmaster.

"I was the first oldest son in 150 who had not become a brewer," Koch reflected. Less than two years ago he decided that the tradition could not be allowed to lapse in his, the sixth, generation.

So, in his 35th year Jim left the Boston Consulting Group and formed his own company: The Boston Brewing Company. From his own savings as well as loans from relatives and friends he raised enough capital to get into the business.

To get started on his own as a brewer, Koch first had to have a distinctively special beer to offer. He set off to find one by going back through his family records from the late 19th century. That was the great age of brewing when American beers were winning gold medals all over the world. There he found a recipe developed in St. Louis by his great-great-grandfather, Louis Koch, in the 1870s.

It was just what he needed. It called for two-row summer barley, expensive Hallertau and Tettnang hops, and a complex, time-consuming process that includes old-fashioned krausening and dry-hopping. It takes 45 days to brew, ferment, and age it.

Koch doesn't have his own microbrewery yet. To get started he teamed up the best master brewer in the country with one of the best regional brewers in America. "My beer calls for a level of personal attention that the giants can't match," Koch says. So he chose Joseph Owades as his master brewer, and the Pittsburgh Brewing Company as the brewery to make his beer.

Owades is nationally known as the brewer who created the award-winning New Amsterdam Amber Lager as well as the first light beer in America. Pittsburgh Brewing Company, the brewer of IC Golden Lager, impressed Koch as having the skills and patience necessary to brew his old-fashioned kind of beer.

The first brewing took place last spring and Samuel Adams Boston Lager was fittingly introduced to Boston on Patriot's Day, April 12, where it was an immediate success.

Koch is old-fashioned in more ways than one. In addition to brewing an old-fashioned beer, he also believes that you don't need advertising to sell a good product. Koch relies totally on word-of-mouth and personal contact. To introduce the beer he took his old Boston Consulting Group briefcase, added cold packs, and filled it with five or six bottles of Samuel Adams. He then took off in his station wagon to visit restaurants and taverns to offer a taste to their proprietors.

"The response was tremendous," says Koch. "Nineteen of the first 20 that I approached said they would carry my beer." By last summer more than 110 restaurants in Boston carried it.

Samuel Adams Boston Lager also gained immediate acceptance at the Great American Beer Festival. Last June, just two months after it was introduced, it was voted the best beer in America by the 4,000 Festival-goers in Denver.

With the marketing success already attained (without spending a penny on media advertising), Koch is already planning to open his own brewery in Boston. He has taken over the old Haffenreffer brewery, which closed in 1965, and hopes to complete refitting it for brewing by September. That will restore to Boston a link with its own brewing tradition. It will also mean that the sixth generation of Kochs will succeed in continuing the family tradition. And Jim Koch's eldest son is watching with intense interest to see if he can take his place brewing Samuel Adams Lager in the seventh generation.

Samuel Adams Lager is definitely a distinctive beer. It has an all-malt body, and a complex taste that is similar to the symphony of tastes found in Pilsner Urquell. To demonstrate the quality of his beer, Jim Koch pours a bottle of it into a glass to form a good head. Then he sets the cap from the bottle on top of the head, where it sits while he talks. "That is the type of thick head they got in the old days," Koch says. "It looks like whipped cream and acts like egg whites, as my father used to say." Jim guarantees that you can write your initials in the foam and they'll still be there when you finish the glass.

It's an old-fashioned beer carrying on an old tradition. It's now available in Massachusetts, Connecticut, New Hampshire, Maine, and Rhode Island. And it has just recently been released in Pennsylvania through several Pittsburgh beer distributors. It's a good reason to take in an early Pirates game this year.

Ein Prosit der Gemutlichkeit!

Yuengling Beer: The Pearl of Pottsville

February 9, 1986

It seems to be part of the eternal nature of man to take for granted the things which are close to home and to assume that the best things always come from far away. But the world is a big place and, for the most of the rest of the world, it is we who are far away. Sometimes, therefore, it pays to look around us and check out whether some of the things we take for granted are really quite special.

Some of the most humble yet rewarding treasures which we in Centre County enjoy, but which are not available in most of the rest of the country, are the dark brown, golden and amber beers of D.G. Yuengling and Sons, America's oldest brewery, located just a few counties to the east of us, in Pottsville.

Yuengling beers are unheralded and unsung in our area. Centre County is located in a no-man's land — just outside of the major Yuengling marketing area, but too close to realize how much it is appreciated elsewhere.

In All About Beer magazine recently the editor reported on the thrill of receiving some Yuengling Pilsner and Yuengling Porter to taste at their California offices: "It's a real thrill for a beer lover to get the opportunity to taste a highly regarded regional domestic brew that's been unavailable in this area," he wrote. "It's an even bigger thrill when the beer is every bit as good as some of the beer lover's acquaintances have assured him that it is."

The report concluded, "Yuengling is one of our finest breweries. It deserves all the regional support that it can get."

But the All About Beer editors are not the only source of Yuengling's fame. James Robertson, in the "Connoisseur's Guide to Beer," reported on 550 American beers rated by a specially selected taste panel. Yuengling Pilsner was rated in the top 5 percent, scoring higher than 522 other beers in the selection.

Charlie Finkel of Merchant du Vin has also selected Yuengling as one of America's classiest domestic brews to market nationally to the high-priced yuppie market along with Minnesota's world-famed Cold Spring Export.

These are just three examples of the acclaim that Yuengling beers have earned among the experts. These are the folks who live far away and do not take such things for granted.

But there is another group of "experts" whose opinion is perhaps even more to be valued. They are the descendants of never-say-die Molly Maguires and wizened old-country Slovak miners, the survivors of Eckley and the Lattimer Massacre. They are the legends of my youth: Jim Thorpe, the football players of "Shamokin Joe," the miners of Pennsylvania's hard coal region, the toughest men in the world.

These men knew four things well: They knew their endurance, they knew their work, they knew their women, and they knew their beer. David G. Yuengling knew them, and he brewed exactly the beer they wanted. They have been drinking it and keeping both themselves and the Yuengling

Brewery afloat for 157 years. That is an expertise not to be lightly dismissed.

One gets a feel for this beer by driving on a visit to the Yuengling Brewery. The drive is best experienced by taking Route 45 east to Lewisburg, then Route 15 south to Sunbury. This part of the trip is scenic and pastoral.

But the real experience starts shortly after one crosses the Susquehanna and heads toward Shamokin on Route 61. The country gets noticeably tougher. Men moved the earth here. The Miller, Bud and Stroh's signs begin to disappear from the tavern windows. In their place is a longer word to which a tougher breed responds — "Yuengling."

Pottsville is a beautiful town set in a valley. Just a few blocks from downtown, on a street with very stately Victorian homes — much like Linn Street in Bellefonte — is the Yuengling Brewery.

The brewery is a picturesque, turn-of-the-century, red brick, Victorian structure. It has been featured by the brewery on many of the labels and posters as the quintessential, romantic brewery. It is entered on the Pennsylvania Inventory of Historic Places.

And it is historic. The gleaming stainless steel brew kettle is covered overhead by a skylight of stained glass windows. The walls around the brewing room are covered with murals of men making barrels and women washing bottles for the brewery. Suddenly one's mind stops racing: This is a place where there is reverence for time and pride in the work of one's hands.

The Yuengling Brewery is a family concern, passed on from generation to generation since David G. Yuengling arrived from the kingdom of Wurtemburg and built a brewery in 1829. The brewery has been managed for several decades by the elder Dick Yuengling. Last year his 42-year-old son, Richard, the fifth generation, took over the active management.

Yuengling's philosophy is that "each brewing company should try to have a beer that shows its particular character. A brewer can produce any beer he wants to. We feel we have the beer that we like, and the beer that the people of this region like. It's just us."

Yuengling makes three beers. The flagship brand is Yuengling Premium. Howard Hillman in "The Gourmet Guide to Beer" describes it as "Pale gold liquid, sweetish, pine forest nose, tart and slightly gassy with a citric aftertaste." The staff at All About Beer say that it is "an exceptionally distinctive and characterful pilsner."

Yuengling's second brand is "The Celebrated Pottsville Porter." Michael Jackson, the world expert on beer, and author of "The World Guide to Beer," notes that Yuengling Porter "is accorded cult status by followers in three states and the District of Columbia."

Yuengling's porter is not a real ale porter. It uses a lager yeast, but is brewed with a specially roasted malt which gives it its darker color and heavier flavor. Yakima hops are used.

Yuengling's third brand is Lord Chesterfield Ale. Once again this is a lager, but it is specially brewed to offer the old time taste reminiscent of a heartier thirst. It is a dry beer, with a flowery background, and a very sharp hop assertiveness. This is a beer of character.

Yuengling doesn't do much in the way of advertising. It doesn't pay burly men a lot of money to make its beer look macho. It's just there, in Eastern Pennsylvania, where 140,000 barrels a year are drunk by the loyal sons of the Molly Maguires and the coal miners.

At the All About Beer headquarters in California they are lucky to be able to get a six pack carried out west on a plane. Their comment: "Too bad it's not distributed in a wider area." But we are lucky here in Centre County, where the Yuengling market area is right beside us. Locally it is available from Centre Beverage which guarantees that it is fresh from the brewery and never sits with them longer than a month. Best of all, it's less than $8 a case.

Ein Prosit der Gemutlichkeit!

Scientists Become Brewers

February 23, 1986

The brewing of beer is a joy and an art. It is attracting people from just about every portion of the American spectrum, from rich playboys to Boston Brahmins. But two of the most interesting and most successful of America's microbrewers have come from the academic world.

Randolph "Stick" Ware received his Ph.D. in experimental nuclear physics from the University of Colorado in 1974. He served as a research associate with the Joint Institute for Laboratory Astrophysics for several years, and then became an advisor to the U.S. Congress as a science fellow with the U.S. Office of Technology Assessment. His prime duty there was a report to Congress on space station feasibility. Currently he is the manager of the University NAVSTAR Consortium. The NAVSTAR Consortium is a joint project of Harvard, Princeton, Columbia, M.I.T., Yale, Cal Tech., University of Texas (Austin), and the University of Colorado to develop a Global Positioning Space Satellite. He is on the physics department faculty of the University of Colorado.

David G. Hummer is an astrophysicist of world-wide reputation. Born in Manheim in 1934, Hummer is a fellow at the Joint Institute for Laboratory Astrophysics; on the editorial board of Computer Physics Communications; a senior fellow at University College, London; a consultant to the Los Alamos Laboratory for Astrophysics; and, most recently, the recipient of the Alexander von Humboldt Senior Scientist Award from the University of Munich, West Germany. He is world famous for his research on the "Hubble Constant." Along with Ware, he is also a professor of physics at the University of Colorado.

The academic and scientific credentials of these men are impressive. However, their scientific studies are not their whole lives. Each plays music professionally. Stick Ware plays electric guitar in a rock band which has performed for as many as 14,000 people in Denver's largest auditoriums. Dave Hummer played saxophone in jazz bands in Philadelphia and Cambridge, England, but his current interest is baroque and classical music played on medieval instruments.

Both Hummer and Ware are also farmers. Twenty miles north of Boulder they have a farm on which they raise their own food, including chickens and goats, and grow and can their own vegetables and herbs. Making cheese is a favorite pastime, and Ware has made a local reputation for making cheese with naturally seasoned bacteria, an ancient method of cheese production which he went to Mexico to study a few years ago.

Ware and Hummer are interesting men. But what makes them interesting to us is that they have also made time to found America's premier microbrewery, the Boulder Brewery of Boulder, Colorado.

Ware and Hummer got together in the early 1970s. When Hummer did his studies in England in the 1960s he had developed a real love of English ale. At the University of Colorado, he ran into Ware who was deeply into homebrewing at that point. It was a friendship made in

Heaven as they set out on a quest to brew the best of the English ales.

For Ware and Hummer, everything they do must be done to perfection. Their homebrewed beer was no exception and people noticed. Soon their friends were suggesting that they wished it were available to buy regularly. "Why not?" Ware and Hummer said, and by 1979 they had applied for and received their federal license to brew beer commercially.

The original brewery was a farmhouse on their goat farm. They scrounged junk yards for stainless steel food processing vessels and other equipment until they had what they needed to brew beer. The first beer for public consumption left the goat farm brewery on July 3, 1980.

In 1980, they produced 170 barrels on weekends, but, they realized, "we could have sold twice as much." In 1981, they doubled production, and doubled again the next year. The same English ale that Dave Hummer loved was also proving to be one of Colorado's most sought after tastes.

In about 1981, Ware was talking about the brewery with a friend in a ski equipment store. A stockbroker by the name of Jerry Smart overheard the conversation. He walked up to Ware, gave him his business card, and said, "If you ever need help with financing, give me a call."

It wasn't long before the demand for Boulder beer exceeded the capacity of their make-shift, goat farm brewery. So one day Ware decided to give the stockbroker a call.

Jerry Smart was true to his word. Within a year or so, he was able to float a $2 million stock offering. An entirely new brewery was built, designed on English principles. Beverage World magazine calls the architecture "absolutely divine."

The new brewery facility opened up in 1985. Production is now up to 4,000 cases per month, with a goal of 6,000 cases.

Jerry Smart is now president of Boulder Brewery and enjoying brewing more than he ever enjoyed the stock market. Stick Ware and Dave Hummer are the two moving forces of the board of directors. Together, these three have put together the inspiration, the financing, and the nuts and bolts of America's largest and most successful microbrewery.

Next: The beers of Boulder Beer.

Ein Prosit der Gemutlichkeit!

Boulder Beers Product of Quality and Idealism

March 9, 1986

There are some people in America who believe that all important change begins with having power. Young "idealists" today seem to believe that the world would be a better place if only they were given the power to tell everybody else what to do.

But fortunately there are others who do not believe that real change ever comes from power or wealth. On the contrary, they believe that meaningful change really begins with the individual.

This is the kind of change that people in the microbrewery movement across the country are betting on. William Coors, president of Coors brewing company, said it this way to the National Microbrewers' conference last summer:

"Anyone has the right and the privilege to get into the brewing business, but they don't have any guarantee of success. The success comes only to those who are willing to take less for their efforts. I suppose that most of you have already concluded that the wages of the microbrewer aren't the most fantastic. We work for the love and the fascination of our labor more than anything."

When Jerry Smart left his secure stockbroking firm to become president of Boulder Brewing, he was prepared for a tough, competitive struggle to survive in the world of small business. What he was not prepared for was the attitude of caring that is changing a whole segment of American industry and a whole part of peoples' lives.

When he first came to the Boulder Brewery Jerry recalled that his greatest surprise was "how many people loved the brewery, loved the beer, and wanted to be involved." He reported to All About Beer editor Dan Bradford his discovery that, "Deep down, a lot of people think there's a little bit of history being written, and they want to be a part of it."

How does a brewery change the world? It doesn't. It opens up people to the experience of time well spent. Some beers are not for drinking quickly to slake a thirst. Some beers just encourage people to sit back, slowly sip, and open up to the pleasurable experience of a good conversation. Only when one is willing to take the time is it possible to enjoy true taste and good fellowship. Jerry Smart found that good beer is an "opportunity to participate with other people."

The Boulder Brewery, as I reported in my last column, was founded by two University of Colorado physicists to bring to America the true goodness of the real, live ales of England. With those ales not only does there come a different taste, but also a different pace of life and style of enjoyment. It is for this that the ales of Boulder are brewed.

The people at Boulder brew three types of ale. All are made from only four ingredients: water, barley, yeast, and hops. The hops are Cascade and Hallertau, and the barley is all two-row. But by using both barley malt as well as roasted unmalted barley, and by varying the roasting and the hops, three very distinct styles of beer are made.

The first type is the classic English Burton ale, often called "bitters." This is the type of beer most commonly drunk in

England and the colonies at the time of the American revolution. Michael Jackson, author of the "Pocket Guide to Beer," describes Boulder's pale ale as having "a fruity nose, an aperitif dryness, and a roundness of body that is malty without being at all heavy."

"Decanted into a glass," says the Brewery, "this ale glows with a warm, amber color. The thick, small-bubbled head releases an arousing hop bouquet that invites sipping."

Boulder's second brew is a porter. Again, this is a classic porter in the English tradition. It is made with the same four ingredients, but both roasted barley as well as roasted barley malt are used. It is dark chocolate brown in color, and the deep taste of the roasted malt exudes elegance. The Brewery says that, "this is the ideal beer for slow savoring." With this brew, you can enjoy the true type of porter George Washington was so fond of.

The third Boulder brew is its seasonal Christmas Stout. This dark ale, specially brewed only for the Christmas season, has a nut-like flavor. This year the brewery produced only 1,100 cases, half of which were reserved before the beer was finished brewing. Next year, says the brewmaster, Michael Lawrence, they will plan for a much higher production.

All Boulder beers are handmade, non-pasteurized, non-filtered, and naturally carbonated. They resonate with richness meant for slow savoring.

Boulder ale and porter are now available in Eastern Pennsylvania through only four distributors: Pat Deon Beverages in Fairless Hills (Levittown) and Bristol; Montgomeryville Beer and Soda in Montgomeryville, and Cold Spring Beverages in Yardley.

Ein Prosit der Gemutlichkeit!

Michael Jackson: The Bard of Beer

March 23, 1986

"I recall a world famous editor telling a trainee that it doesn't take much skill to write an interesting story about war in an exotic land; the true journalist is the one who can find something fascinating and revealing under his nose."

"Well, what's usually under my nose is a glass of beer."

That is one of the explanations Michael Jackson gives to friends about how he became a writer on the subject of beer, and eventually the world expert on beer. I have often quoted Michael Jackson in this column, and I would like to tell you a little about his fascinating career.

Jackson is a pudgy Englishman who started off as a journalist in London. At one time he was a freelance writer, but quickly graduated to the position of editor of a British business magazine which specially covered marketing and media. As editor of that journal, he developed a reputation for his insightful articles about the press. As a result he was asked to do a regular television show called "What the Papers Say."

This brought him directly into news coverage as well as investigative reporting, and he was offered the chance to write his own newspaper column which was a hard-hitting commentary. Once again, this led him back to television where he became the anchorman and writer of a show covering world news. It was called "World in Action," and the program took him all around the world to cover breaking news.

All that action served to keep Jackson hungry and thirsty and he used the opportunity of traveling for news to also sample and learn to appreciate the cuisines, wines, and beers of the world. Being an unusual Englishman, Jackson actually noticed what we was eating and drinking.

True to his own journalistic ethos of seeing the "fascinating and revealing" in what was under his nose, Jackson began writing about food and restaurants. As in everything he does, Jackson achieved expertise in a full range of European newspapers and magazines.

He won several food writing and connoisseur awards, including the coveted Literary Medal of the German Academy of Gastronomy.

In the early 1970s the biggest and most successful consumer movement in Europe erupted in England. It was the Campaign for Real Ale, known best by its acronym, "CAMRA." This was a grass roots movement by the British to preserve their classic pubs and to preserve the tradition of real, live ales from being replaced by pasteurized, long-shelf-life, bland beer.

Michael Jackson made a major contribution to that movement with his first book on beer. It was called, "The English Pub — A Unique Social Phenomenon." The book is a beautifully illustrated, coffee-table type book on the great tradition of the English pub. It has been described as "a thoughtful, well-researched, witty treatise on one of Britain's nobler contributions to civilization."

Having sampled the beers of the world in his travels, Jackson also noted the lack of competent books on the subject. His next book, therefore, was called, "The World Guide to Beer," which immediately established him as the world authority on the subject.

"The World Guide to Beer" is written in Jackson's usual delightfully witty and erudite style. It is one of the first books of beer to discuss the subject by style instead of simply country of origin. This is critically important to Jackson: "The ability to distinguish styles is first base," he insists. The book covers almost all you might want to know about beer: how it is made, the story of its ingredients, the styles of beer throughout the world, and the anecdotes and history which make it interesting and readable.

His "World Guide to Beer" has been translated into at least five languages, and has sold more than 300,000 copies to a thirsty public.

Jackson's goal, and according to the London Times, his special accomplishment, has been to have "elevated beer to the status of wine — deservedly." Thus, to help the discriminating beer drinker he has also published a handy book called "The Pocket Guide to Beer." This book is very similar to the many pocket guides on wine which are available everywhere. In his book, Jackson gives thumbnail descriptions and ratings for the beers of 40 countries.

Jackson's great skill is an encyclopedic knowledge of beer, combined with a delightfully understated English wit. If one cares about beer, one will certainly enjoy and learn from Jackson's books. Beyond doubt, they are the standards in the field.

Ein Prosit der Gemutlichkeit!

Sierra Nevada Brewers Get Their Start Scrounging in Junkyards

April 6, 1986

A month or so ago I had a chance to visit San Francisco. High on my list of priorities was to sample some of the beers of the local microbreweries of California. One of the ones I wanted to sample fresh while close to the brewery was that of the Sierra Nevada Brewing Company of Chico, California, which claims to be the "oldest surviving microbrewery in America."

The story of the Sierra Nevada Brewing Company began in 1969 when Ken Grossman was 13 years old. In the summer of '69 Ken's next door neighbor taught him how to brew beer. Ken became fascinated and his parents, instead of treating the new interest as "forbidden fruit," encouraged his interest.

At college Ken studied chemistry and biology and continued to brew beer. After he graduated he opened a wine and homebrewing equipment store and was able to become even more involved in his own homebrewing.

In 1978 Ken heard of the opening of the first microbrewery in the United States. Although Jack McAuliffe's New Albion Brewery eventually failed, it was an inspiration to Ken. "If McAuliffe could open a brewery, so could I," he decided.

So Ken got together with a young man by the name of Paul Camusi. Ken had met Paul through Ken's brother who was an international amateur bike racer. Paul was a college student at the time, but he liked bike racing too much to get excited about studies, and he liked the idea of brewing good beer even more than bike racing. He shared the dream and enthusiasm of Ken about starting their own commercial brewery.

Ken sold out his wine and homebrew equipment store and invested the proceeds in starting a brewery. His parents knew Ken was serious, and that this was no flash in the pan. With a total of $110,000 Ken and Paul began building a brewery from scratch.

To buy new brewery equipment would have cost close to a million dollars. Their capital was nowhere near enough to do that, so they were determined to make their own. They scrounged junk and used equipment yards around the state to assemble the equipment that Ken could convert to brewery use. Their malt storage silo was originally a creamery vessel. The stainless steel brew kettle is made from a piece of equipment of unknown origin which they found in a San Francisco scrap yard. In less than a year they had put together a brewery system that worked, and they began brewing.

The dream of brewing was not just to own a brewery. It was the dream of producing, for the enjoyment of other people, ales and beers which were unavailable on the American market. America is the land of light lagers of Germanic origin. Ken and Paul wanted to make available the heavier, tastier, maltier ales, porters, and stouts of English and Colonial derivation.

One of the joys of talking to people like Ken Grossman is the dedication to perfection that he exudes. To make an English ale in America will not be identical to the ales of England. The barley is different from England's, just as today's strains of barley are not the same as the barley of a century ago. Similarly, the hops are not precisely the same, nor is the water and the yeast. Since these are the only four ingredients in ale, the slightest change in one changes the character of the entire brew.

What Ken and Paul sought to achieve, therefore, was the perfect American version of the traditional ales of England. This means that their goal was to adapt the English brewing method to bring out the very best of the American strains of barley and hops.

Switching over from homebrewing to large scale commercial is no easy task. Ken and Paul dumped 14 brewings down the drain before they produced the one that they could be proud to market to the public.

"Ours is a classic brew," says Grossman. "It isn't the type of beer you drink a lot of at a time. It's a connoisseur's ale."

"We have no intention of competing with the big breweries. Our goal is to be distinctive."

Ein Prosit der Gemutlichkeit!

Sierra Nevada Ales Brewed in the West

April 20, 1986

In my last column I wrote about the history of Ken Grossman and Paul Camusi who started the Sierra Nevada Brewing Company from scratch. That company is now the oldest surviving microbrewery in the United States, and Ken and Paul are the deans of America's microbrewery movement.

The products of Sierra Nevada are ales. This is significant. In colonial times, and up to the 1850s ales were the only kind of beer available in America. But with the perfection of the lager type of brewing in Pilsen, Czechoslovakia in 1842, the pale lagers gradually displaced ales in most of Europe and the Americas.

On the entire East Cost today, I am aware of only one brewery which still has the capacity to brew true ales. That is the Schmidt's Brewery in Philadelphia which makes McSorely's Cream Ale for the famous McSorely's Tavern in New York City. All the other so-called ales including, for example, Genessee Cream Ale and Chesterfield Ale, are really maltier and more heavily hopped lagers.

The difference between ales and lagers is in one of the four ingredients and in the temperatures at which they are brewed. Ales are "top-fermenting" beers brewed at warmer temperatures, while "bottom-fermenting" lagers are brewed at temperatures just about freezing. What this means is that during fermentation ale yeasts rise to the top of the fermenting beer, while a lager yeast sinks to the bottom.

Lagers and ales cannot both be produced in the same brewery building because of the problem of one yeast contaminating the other. As a result many breweries which once had separate breweries for the production of lagers and ales — such as Yuengling in Pottsville — have consolidated into a single building and today produce only lagers.

When we talk about the products of Sierra Nevada, therefore, we are talking about a different kind of beer than that to which we are normally accustomed. Sierra Nevada makes five ales.

Sierra Nevada Pale Ale. If you like English ales, such as Bass Ale or Whitbread, you will find that America can produce a worthy competitor. Sierra Nevada Pale Ale is a Burton-type, copper colored ale similar to the beers of America at the time of the revolution. It has a good, malty body, a fine billowing head, and a wonderful, unusual, delightful floral bouquet and taste. In 1983, it was voted the best beer at the Great American Beer Festival in Denver. If you are looking for a beer with complex flavors that you would want to savor, this is it.

Sierra Nevada Porter. The difference between pale ale, porter, and stout is in the heating of the barley. For pale ale, heat is used to halt germination and to begin carmelization of the grains. For porter, the barley is roasted until it acquires a taste like "burnt coffee." Some of this is added to different pale and crystal malts, and one has classic "three threads." The blend of hops and roasted barley in a fresh glass of Sierra Nevada Porter is enough to convince one that George Washington's favorite beer has been recreated with a flourish.

Sierra Nevada Stout. One adds to the pale, crystal and roasted barley malt, even deeper roasted barley to achieve a stout. The difference is an even heartier brew with what has been described as a "burnt chocolate" taste. This is the kind of beer you can spend a whole evening with. "It has substance," says one stout lover in Chico, "it gives you something to chew on."

Celebration Ale. This is Ken's and Paul's annual Christmas present. Sierra Nevada Celebration Ale is modeled after the mulled ales of 17th-century England. It is a copper-colored ale, with much more pale and crystal malt, and a marvelous fruity taste, huge hop aroma, and a long, long aftertaste.

Big Foot Barley Wine. This is produced in very small quantities but once a year. Barley wine is an unusual beer to be found in America. It is fermented to achieve a 10.5 percent (by weight) alcohol content, and has a deep vinous quality. This is one of the few brews which ages well.

Summerfest Beer. This is still an ale, but is brewed to the lighter in color, lighter in body, and lighter in alcohol (only 3.8 percent by weight) than the other brews in the line. But it is still a beer with taste and character. It contains the rare Saaz hops from Czechoslovakia, as well as Hallertau, to make its bouquet and aroma even lighter.

Ken and Paul have just purchased an entire German Brewhouse which they plan to reassemble in Chico to boost production to 10,000 barrels per year. They are also planning a pub and garden to enjoy their best in.

Ken Grossman and Paul Camusi have created a new reason to heed the sage advice of our elders, "Go West, young man."

Ein Prosit der Gemutlichkeit!

Homebrewing Can Create Gourmet Beer

May 4, 1986

There is an old and wise saying to the effect that "Charity begins at home." To that saying there is proverbially attached a practical corollary which holds that "Good beer also begins at home."

The connection between these two realities is deeply embedded in the history of our beloved Commonwealth. For, at the very time that William Penn was laying out plans for the City of Brotherly Love, he was at the same time constructing the first homebrewing facilities in Pennsylvania on his own estate at Pennsbury.

"Our drink has been beer and punch," Penn wrote in 1685, "and malt drink begins to be common, especially at the ordinaries and the houses of the more substantial people."

Now, 201 years after Penn wrote those words while sipping a homebrew on his veranda, you can also begin brewing beer at home, and in the process help to revive one of Pennsylvania's oldest crafts.

The brewing of beer at home was stifled for almost half a century by a tangle of federal regulations left over from Prohibition. But in 1979 the regulations were lifted, and the ancient craft of homebrewing has been slowly reviving.

Supplies for homebrewers, both amateurs and craftsmen, are now available in downtown State College at a special department of the College Avenue Market at 206 West College

Avenue. These supplies include all one would need to brew one's own beers and ales at home: malt and malt extracts; hops (including Hallertauer, Cascades, Brewer's Gold and English Fuggles); yeasts; fermenters; caps, and all the other accoutrements of homebrewing.

The brewing supplies department of the College Avenue Market is the joint inspiration of Cliff Newman of Port Matilda and Reed Van Der Berghe of State College.

A few years ago Cliff Newman had begun selling brewing supplies when the Dandelion Market closed. "There was no other source locally for malt or hops or equipment," he says. So he opened his own brewing supplies store in his house. He found that there was a growing local market. So this winter he moved his supplies into the College Avenue Market in order to be able to serve his customers better.

Cliff believes in brewing beer at home. In fact, one could call him an evangelist on the subject. He publishes a newsletter which he sends to his customers for free. He is also the founder and president of the "Happy Valley Homebrewers," which is a club created for men and women who want to share the art of brewing with one another, which is associated with the American Homebrewers Association. The newsletter Cliff publishes also doubles as the club newsletter.

Cliff is also a published author on the subject of beer. He has published four articles on homebrewing in "Zymurgy," the national magazine for homebrewers.

Reed Van Der Berghe is the cooking genius behind the gourmet food counter — called "Copacetic Cuisine" — at the College Avenue Market. Reed was stationed with the 36th Tactical Air Squadron in Bitburg, West Germany, in 1980, where he learned the true delight of pure, fresh, well-made

214

German beer. When he came back to the U.S., his taste buds could not get reacclimatized to the American standard beers. So he began looking to brew his own gourmet beer to match his gourmet foods.

Cliff and Reed have also gotten together to offer courses in homebrewing. The first course consisted of one class a week for four weeks. In contained 16 men and women, and began April 3. The participants have learned all about the ingredients of beer and have brewed their own beer with Cliff and Reed over the last month. Another course is planned to begin this coming week. There is a sign up sheet at the College Avenue Market, or call Reed at 238-6300 for details.

With Reed and Cliff one encounters a mutual admiration of craftsmanship. Reed says, "Cliff Newman makes homebrewing sound as exciting as I can make gourmet cooking class sound." Cliff says it all poetically: "We are craftsmen in a hobby whose canvas is the beer mug." The cost of the course is set to cover only the cost of the ingredients used in the beer the participants will brew. The poetry is free.

For Cliff, homebrewing is a hobby and a vocation and a personal love. In addition to teaching the course, he plans to spend every Saturday from noon to 5 p.m. at the College Avenue Market answering questions on homebrewing. Cliff will assemble a personalized homebrewing kit for any person who wants to begin homebrewing, and will spend all the time one needs to answer questions on his favorite subject.

It's always rare to find people more interested in their craft than in simply trying to sell something. But Cliff is one of those guys who cares more about what he does than what he gets out of it.

It kind of makes you think that we are still living in Penn's Woods.

Ein Prosit der Gemutlichkeit!

Wheat Beer: Champagne of the North

May 18, 1986

When it comes to appreciating the sense of taste, the French are among the world's experts. Good wine, they say, is best enjoyed in peace, and nary a wine critic I know would disagree. But good beer is worth fighting for.

"An army travels on its stomach," Napoleon insisted. So, in 1805, after conquering Italy and Egypt and defeating just about every other army in Europe, Le Grand Armee invaded Prussia and triumphantly entered its capital, Berlin. There the conquering hero and his brave troops found a new reason for winning wars: They were given their first taste of the wheat beer of Prussia — Berliner Weisse.

"Le Champagne du Nord" — the "Champagne of the North," they called it, and it is said that they enjoyed it in copious quantities.

Wheat beer is such a delight to the palate that it is the one exception made to Bavaria's centuries-old "Reinheitsgebot" or Purity Law of 1516. That law specifies that beer may be made with only four ingredients: barley malt, water, yeast, and hops. But the famous wheat beers are the exception which prove the rule. In making wheat beer the barley malt is replaced in large part with malt made from wheat instead. In most wheat beers, 50 to 75 percent of the malt is wheat.

Unlike most German beers which are lagers, wheat beer is an ale. That means that it is made from the type of yeast (saccharomyces cerevisiae) which rises to the top during fermentation. Most of the other beers of Germany as well as America are made with bottom fermenting yeast (saccharomyces carlsbergensis).

As a result of the top-fermenting process, wheat beers are brewed at a warm temperature (up to 68 degrees Fahrenheit). In the old days the beer was buried in the warm earth to mature. As a result of its ingredients and brewing process, wheat beers are very high in carbonation, have a very high malt-aromatic, and are only lightly hopped.

Since Germany has a northern and a southern part which compete with each other in all things, there are, of course, two basic, competing styles of wheat beers. The first style is Berliner-Weisse (pronounced vie-se). Berliner Weisse is a "weak beer." It has a lower alcohol content of about 2.5 percent. It has a high amount of lactic acid and vitamin B2. In Berliner Weisse, the wort is not fully cooked, and the amino acids from the grains are not removed. Berliner Weisse, therefore, has a very sour, acidic taste.

During fermentation, lactobacillus is added, causing a second fermentation. This results in yeast being present in the beer when it is bottled, and the beer is conditioned in the bottle. When Berliner-Weisse is purchased, it should have a sediment on the bottom of the bottle, which is the yeast.

Berliner Weisse is best enjoyed in a very large, champagne-type glass, big enough to hold 12 ounces of beer plus a good and lively head. Because of the acidic nature of the beer, the Berliners usually add a drop of raspberry syrup or essence of woodruff. With the raspberry syrup the drink is called a "Berliner Weisse mit Schuss." One can purchase the raspberry syrup locally at the Cheese Shoppe on Calder Way in State College. With a drop of essence of woodruff Berliner Weisse becomes a "Waldmeister."

Berliner Weisse is carried by Pletcher's Distributors in Bellefonte. However, you don't have to order a whole case to enjoy it. "Berliner Weisse mit Schuss" is available at Duffy's Tavern in Boalsburg. If you stop in and ask for one, be prepared to feel like a member of Napoleon's Old Guard. The drink will come in a very large stemmed glass, it will be the color of pink champagne, and it will have a light, frothy, sweet-and-sour taste that just might convert you from a grape-y effervescence to "Le Champagne du Nord."

The wheat beers of Bavaria constitute the other style of wheat beers in Germany, most commonly called "Weizenbier." Like Berliner Weisse, Bavarian wheat beers are top-fermented, only lightly hopped, and very malty, very fruity, and very refreshing. But, unlike the Northern wheat beers, the Southern ones are higher in alcohol (3.5 to 5.0 percent) and are tangy rather than acidic.

Bavarian Weizenbier is usually drunk out of a tall glass — 10 to 12 inches high — which widens slightly at the top. The idea is to allow the great Weizenbier foam to form a head at least two inches thick at the top. Instead of a drop of fruit syrup, the South Germans usually add a slice of lemon to bring out the fruity tang of a Weizenbier.

Weizenbeirs, like Berliner Weisse, are considered to be among the best refreshments and thirst quenchers. Hikers, bicyclists, and just about everyone in Germany enjoys wheat beers in the summer. A favorite drink combination available everywhere in the summer is the "Russ," made from half wheat beer and half lemon soda.

I had my first wheat beer in a very old rathskeller in Stuttgart. There the Dinkelacker Brewery had made it a city specialty. The Dinkelacker brand of wheat beer — Weizenkrone — is now available in Centre County, at Pletcher's Distributors in Bellefonte.

In the 18th century, wheat beers were considered such a joy and delight that kings insisted on it. King Frederick William of Prussia, known as "the soldier's king," even had his son — Frederick the Great — trained as a master brewer in order to assure the continuity of the kingly craft.

Ein Prosit der Gemutlichkeit!

A Vacation Guide to Beers

June 1, 1986

Memorial Day has just passed us by, and summer vacation time is upon us. The students have already left for summer jobs and summer beaches and soon, most Centre Countians will be making vacation travel plans to see America by car, boat, bus, and plane.

Since vacation is a time to get away and enjoy new sights and do something different for a while, one of the things some Centre County vacationers might enjoy is a tip or two on special local brews to look for which are not available here.

Of course, there are several regional breweries whose beers are available in stores throughout the region they serve. Travelers should have no trouble spotting these. But there are a large number of small, dedicated brewers who have brought out specialty beers which you might not have heard of. These are the microbrewers of America who have felt that the time had come to reintroduce the old brewing styles, as well as to discover and brew some new ones. So in your travels, here are some of the small breweries and beer labels especially to look for from East to West:

Maine — Two microbreweries have opened in the first Prohibition State. In Westbrook the D.L. Geary Brewing Company is producing Geary's Ale. In the state capital, brewmaster Timothy O'Rourke is brewing up Portland Lager for the new John Morgan Brewing Company of Portland.

Massachusetts — One of the best beers I've tasted is Samuel Adams Boston Lager. Although made in Pittsburgh at the Iron City Brewery, it is only marketed in Boston. If you are up that way be sure to try it.

New York — A few years ago it looked like the brewing tradition was dead in New York. But it has come back to life with super character. In Albany the William S. Newman Brewing Company is producing traditional style English ales. These are truly different ales, which take some getting used to. But if you're up that way, they're worth a try. In addition to the availability of all the imports, there are three new microbreweries. The ales of the Manhattan Brewery are available only at its brewpub at 42 Thompson Street. No true ale lover should miss the Manhattan brewery's superb British ales, porters, and stouts.

Over in Brooklyn, one of the newest microbrewery beers is M.W. Brenner's Amber Light beer brewed by the Monarch Brewing Company.

New Amsterdam Amber Lager was the very first New York microbrewery. It has opened its own brewpub in midtown Manhattan. New Amsterdam was available for a while in Centre County, but presently is not available. So if you get to New York, be sure to enjoy one.

Pennsylvania — The first microbrewer in Pennsylvania is the Dock Street Brewery in Philadelphia. I have read notices of its opening, but I have not yet located a bottle of its beer. It you find it in Philadelphia, try to bring back a few samples for your friends.

New Jersey — The Vernon Valley Brewery in Vernon, N.J. is one of the newest breweries on the East Coast. It was constructed as part of the Great Gorge Resort which features a summer amusement park, winter ski area, and 1,000 condominiums. The resort built the brewery as part of its plan to provide its customers with "a quality experience." An entire brewery was imported from Germany, together with a German brewmaster. The brew, Vernon Valley Brew, is available to the resort's 300,000 yearly visitors.

Washington, D.C. — The old Heurich Brewery has been reborn as Washington's first micro. The beer was introduced in May 1986 to a popular reception. Only 20 years ago, the Heurich Brewery stood on the site of the Kennedy Center.

Virginia — Penn State's own Jim Kollar is brewing Chesbay Amber and Gold in Virginia Beach. Although both are available in Centre County, stop in and say hello to Jim and his wife and enjoy their special brews if you are down that way.

Arkansas — The Riley-Lyon Brewery in Tumwater brews a lovely amber called Riley's Red Lion which is popular in Washington, D.C. and a lighter brew called White Tail lager which is most popular in Arkansas. This is the first southern microbrewery.

Texas — The second southern brewery is the Reinheitsgebot Brewery of Plano. It brews a lager which is growing in popularity called Collin County Pure Gold and a dark, sweet beer called Collin County Black Gold. Both are distinctive lagers which are worth looking for if you are in the area.

Over the next two columns, we'll be covering the rest of the country. Most of the Midwest and West will be covered in the next column. In the third and final column of this vacation microbreweries guide, we'll take stock of the brewer's boom in California, Washington, Alaska, and Hawaii.

Ein Prosit der Gemutlichkeit!

Brewery Hopping Across the Upper Midwest

June 15, 1986

In this column I continue our vacation guide to specialty microbreweries in the U.S. In my last column I listed breweries in the eastern and southern half of the country. In this column, we pick up in the upper Midwest and cover all the western states except California, Washington, Alaska, and Hawaii. These will be covered in our third column completing our summer vacation brewery guide.

Michigan — This Kalamazoo Brewing Company is brewing a light ale called "Bell's Beer," and an all-grain darker ale called Great Lakes Amber.

Wisconsin — Wisconsin, settled by Germans, Poles, and Swedes, is a beer drinker's New World. In Milwaukee, the Sprecher Brewery is a newly announced micro which should be producing a brew by now. The Vienna Brewing Company is also reported to be marketing a contract brew called Vienna Lager in the Milwaukee area.

In Eau Claire, the Hibernia Brewing Company has taken over the old Walter Brewery and has added a huge beer garden and a variety of new tastes. Hibernia kicked off its production with a dark wheat beer at the Great American Beer Festival last year. Hibernia is also contract brewing for the Newman Brewery, the Vienna Brewing Company, and several others.

In Madison, the Capitol Brewing Company has planned a 24,000 barrel brewery to begin brewing specialty beers in the home of the University of Wisconsin. It is supposed to be bringing out a tasty brew by this summer.

In Monroe, the Joseph Huber Brewing Company has been sold to one of the most respected men in the brewing industry, William Smith, former president of Pabst. One should expect a fine beer from Monroe in addition to its famous Augsburger.

Minnesota — Two small breweries in Minnesota merit your visit if you are in the area. The first is the August Schell Brewery in New Ulm. A friend brought me back a bottle of Schell Pils which was, in my humble opinion, even better than Pilsner Urquell. I hope to visit New Ulm this summer and will plan to report.

The second is the Cold Spring Brewery of Cold Spring. These are Minnesota's equivalents of the Yuengling and Straub Breweries here in Pennsylvania. Both Schell and Cold Spring are specialty beers marketed in selected national markets by Merchant du Vin.

In St. Paul, the Summit Brewing Company is offering Summit Extra Pale Ale, a dark porter, and a German-style lager to thirsty Minnesotans.

Iowa — Three microbreweries are competing for the tastes of Iowans. Two of these are in Amana, the site of the famous Amana Colony.

The Cold Spring Brewing Company is reviving the beers brewed by the Lutheran Church called the Community of True Inspiration in the Amana Colony. The True Inspirationists brewed a beer called "Gemeinde Brau," which undoubtedly contributed to their spirits. The brew is being revived according to the old recipe.

The True Inspirationists must have made quite an impact, as Amana also boasts a second brewery — which is quite a bit for a small Midwestern farming town. But true inspiration knows no bounds. Thus the Millstream Brewing Company of Amana is also brewing beer for thirsty Iowans in the vicinity. Their new brewery is on line to brew 5,000 barrels a year of "Schild Brau Pils" and "Millstream Lager." These will be marketed in Amana, Cedar Rapids, and Iowa City.

Over in Dubuque, Iowa, a group of five Milwaukee businessmen have purchased the old Dubuque Star Brewery and have completely refitted it as the Rhomberg Brewing Company. It is now brewing what it calls "Ultra Premium" beers under the names of Rhomberg and Rhomberg Classic Pale. Both are all-malt Old European-style specialties.

Colorado — The Boulder Brewing Company is one of the most impressive and most successful of the micros. It produces real ales, and models them as close as possible to their English counterparts. The Extra Pale Ale, Boulder Porter, and Boulder Stout are wonderful beer experiences you should not miss if you are in the Boulder area.

Montana — In the sparse population of Montana, one would hardly expect a market for a new brewery and a new beer. But the Montanans were thirsty for a new taste. Montana Beverage, Ltd. of Helena brews a Dortmund-style light lager which is Kessler Beer. The name of the beer is a revival of the Old Kessler Brewery of Helena, which was founded in 1865.

Idaho — In Caldwell the Snake River Brewing Company is brewing a sweet-tasting amber lager with aromatic hops.

Oregon — The Widmer Brewing Company of Portland is specializing in Altbier, an ancient German style of ale. This particular alt-beer is styled after the breweries of Dusseldorf.

Also in Portland, the Columbia River Brewing Company has just celebrated its first anniversary. It brews a specialty called Bridgeport Ale and has just introduced two new regulars: Golden Ale and a stout. It also plans to produce four seasonal brews, beginning this year with St. Paddy's Red Ale.

Ein Prosit der Gemutlichkeit!

Microbrewery Ventures Offer
Variety of Top Flight Beer

June 29, 1986

This is the third of three columns reviewing the microbrewing scene across the United States. In the first column (June 2), the microbrewing specialities of the northeastern and southern states were listed. In the second column (June 16) the microbreweries of the Midwest and West, including Oregon, were listed.

California and Washington are the greatest beer states in the Union when it comes to new microbrewery ventures and varieties of beer. Herewith the California and Washington microbrewery review.

California — The Palo Alto Brewing Company of Mountainview is getting excellent reviews on its London Real Ale. This brewery is listed as the first malt-extract brewery in the United States.

The Sierra Nevada Brewery of Chico is undoubtedly, along with Anchor and Boulder, one of the superlative brews in America. Its product line includes Pale Ale, Porter, Stout, Celebration Ale, and Summer Beer. A friend just brought me a six-pack back from California, and I vouch once more for the joy of Sierra Nevada.

Also in Chico, the award-winning homebrewer, DeWayne Lee Saxton, has gone commercial with Saxton's English-style Pilsner.

In Modesto the Stanislaus Brewing Company is brewing St. Stan Amber Alt and St. Stan's Dark. Their altbiers have a unique niche.

The Thousand Oaks Brewing Company in Berkeley is a national prize winning at the Great American Beer Festival. Its Cable Car Classic Lager, Golden Gate Malt Liquor and Golden Bean Dark Malt Liquor are specialties not to be missed if you are in Berkeley.

In Santa Rosa, a paradisiacal city about an hour north of San Francisco, the Excelsior Brewing Company has revived the defunct but once revered Acme label. Excelsior will be specializing in a tart wheat beer. We discussed German wheat beers in an earlier article this year, and are looking forward to tasting this new American entry.

California brewpubs making their own special beer to sell on premises include the Hopland Brewery in Mendocino and Buffalo Bills Brewpub in Hayward. There is also a new brewpub in Petaluma, and several others slated to start brewing under California's new brewpub law.

Of course, in San Francisco one can savor the perfection of Fritz Maytag's Anchor Steam Beer and Liberty Ale, and Old Foghorn Barley Wine.

Washington — This state is the first state to encourage innovation with the brewpub. Most states have a "three tiered" system for regulating beer sales. The three tiers are: brewer, distributor, and retailer. In most states, such as Pennsylvania, a brewer cannot sell his beer to the public, but must sell it to a distributor. A distributor can sell only beer by the case to the public, while only a retail license holder can sell you a glass of beer. This is why the beer is always free when you visit a Pennsylvania brewery; they are not allowed to sell it by the glass.

In the old days, beer used to be brewed on the premises. Every tavern brewed its own beer just like it baked its own bread. To get back to the old-fashioned fresh beer, Washington and many other states have passed amendments to their laws allowing a special license for beer which is made and sold on premises. These are the new brewpubs, making their own distinctive beers and selling them in their own taverns. Herewith a list of Washington's brews and brewpubs:

In Seattle, the Independent Ale Brewery leads the way with the Belgian-style Redhorn Ale. Also produced on premises are Ballard Bitter and Blackhook Porter.

Not far away, in Rolling Bay, the Kemper Brewing Company brews a special lager called Thomas Kemper.

In Monroe the Kuefner Brewing Company brews a bottle conditioned lager called Kuefnerbrau.

To the west of Seattle is Hales Ale, Ltd., in Coleville, making English style ales in the wild Northwest.

To the south of the state is the Hart Brewing Company, whose Pyramid Ale has achieved, despite the presence of so many other brewers, a cult following.

Finally, in the heart of the hop growing belt is the Yakima Brewing and Malting Company. Its ales have won prizes at the Great American Beer Festival, and its styles are more varied than anywhere else. Grant's Scottish Style Ale, Imperial Russian Ale, India Pale Ale, and Christmas Ale are worth a special detour if you are in the Northwest.

This year the American Microbrewers Conference has been moved from Denver for the first time to be held instead in the real capital of microbrewing — Seattle. It will be held this September, and offers the chance for America's microbrewers to see the cutting edge of brewing science.

Alaska — The Chinook Brewing Company in Douglas plans to be brewing by this September.

Hawaii — The 50th State is joining the microbrewery revolution with two new breweries. The first is the Pacific Brewing Company on the island Of Maui. The second is the Koolau Brewery in Honolulu.

That completes our American Microbrewery summer vacation guide. Whether you are able to visit any of these and try their specialties or not, it is hoped that this review will give some idea of the interest in brewing across the country, and the great variety of beers becoming available to the American palate.

Ein Prosit der Gemutlichkeit!

A Beer for the Festival

July 13, 1986

Today is the last day of the Central Pennsylvania Festival of the Arts. The body is tired, but the mind and spirit are still exhilarated by the presence of so much art and, what is more, the presence of so many people who appreciate it. For art is not only a source of private experiences which can be personally bought and collected. Art is also, and perhaps more importantly, a public celebration, a sharing of spirit, an act of community.

In the midst of so many art exhibits, and so many stages with artists performing, it is easy to take ourselves for granted. But take a look at some pictures of the festival some day, and notice how the crowds of people catch your eye. For the whole festival is itself a work of art, and its spirit is expressed best through the people who come and fill the streets.

Today many of us will be making our last stroll through the exhibits, making our last minute decisions on purchases, and getting ready to leave for home with another year's worth of happy memories of the festival. For the exhibitors it's been a long but happy week. Now they begin taking their booths down and packing themselves up to leave for many a distant place.

By midafternoon, the festival will have become a completed work of art. However, for the real student of art, it is only then, in the late afternoon or evening of the last day, that the festival can truly be appreciated. Just as an object of art is most enjoyed after it is finished and the artist is gone, so the festival can only be really appreciated when it is over or the crowds are gone.

In order to enjoy the festival itself as art, one needs but a quiet time of recollection and a good tankard of ale. Then one can summon up again the best of the sights and sounds and smells and tastes and feelings of the festival week. One can savor each one, turning it over carefully in one's mind, converting what might have been only a momentary thrill into a lasting impression. After all, isn't that what art is – the converting of something momentary, like a fleeting smile on an old woman's face – into something lasting, like the Mona Lisa?

So, late this afternoon or evening, sit down to really enjoy the festival. Create out of all its bright colors and wondrous events a work of art in your own soul where you can keep it and savor it for a lifetime.

What kind of beer would you put in that tankard to brew up a whole week of otherwise passing memories into something timeless? For me, a beer is not just a beer anymore then art is just art. One looks for character. What remains is not what is consumed, but what is savored.

When one thinks of brews to invite savoring and reflection, one thinks first of the style of ales perfected in those blessed Isles of the North Sea.

Reflect on Britain's Bass Ale for a moment — the brilliant copper color, the deep taste of the malt, the bite of the hops of Kent. It stirs the imagination. One can think of St. Paul's Cathedral, Westminster Abbey, Canterbury and Buckingham. One summons up the dreams and memories of a whole civilization distilled into a gleaming glass with a white head. One's own experiences of the week are placed into perspective by the brew: We are but the heirs of an ancient Anglo-Saxon civilization at an arts and crafts fair in a small country town in the middle of Penn's Woods.

And if the brew of Burton is not deep enough, consider Guinness Extra Stout. Here is an unsurpassed sipping beer. Its dark-roasted barley and heavily hopped bitterness invite your tongue to linger with it a long time and then savor it for its flavors long after each sip has been swallowed. Guinness, like the Arts Festival itself, is made to be enjoyed long after it has been consumed.

Taverns which care about their Guinness serve it both warm and chilled. The English and Irish drink it warm, where its flavors unfold like the petals of a flower in the sun. If poured properly, a Guinness head can fill nine-tenths of the glass. One drinks it very slowly, waiting for that large head to reassemble itself back into liquid form. It leaves time for memories to come back, and for tastes and sounds and smells to be recalled from the past; for experiences to be reassembled, and then for the events and the ale to be slowly savored and digested.

One's best evening of the whole festival, if one really takes the time to enjoy it, is the evening after it is all over, when one takes the time with oneself to make the festival last. This is the time you spend with your own thoughts and feelings, letting them wander through your soul until they find a place to settle down there.

All it takes is some time to reflect and some good English ale.

Ein Prosit der Gemutlichkeit!

America's Top-Selling Imported Beers

July 27, 1986

American taste in beer continues to become more cosmopolitan. Another 10 percent increase in consumption of imported beers by Americans was recorded last year, and it marked the 18th successive year of import sales increases. Today, one beer out of every case — one in 24 — is an import.

What are the most popular imports? The names on the list of the Top 10 haven't changed since last year, although the positions of some have changed.

Heineken continues to be America's favorite import. The story goes that in the 1880s a man by the name of Van Munching was a bartender on the ocean liner on which the owner of Heineken used to travel. On the long voyage he was able to talk Heineken into giving him the American distribution rights. It was a great selection. Van Munching set up the best import distributing network in America, and has held it for decades. Today Heineken has more than 36 percent of the entire import market, which means that more than one beer out of every three imported beer drinkers says, when he orders a beer, "Come to think of it, I'll have a Heineken."

Canada is America's next largest source of imports. It holds three of the top 10 spots on the most popular imports list. One out of every four imported beers comes from Canada. Molson holds the No. 2 spot with Molson Golden

234

and Molson Ale. In the No. 4 spot is Moosehead, and Labatt's holds down seventh position in the Top 10.

The Germans brew America's next most popular imports. Germany holds two positions in the Top 10. Becks is America's third most popular imported beer, and St. Pauli Girl from Bremen is in sixth place.

The Mexicans brew the fourth most popular beers in America, and last year Mexican beers recorded their greatest increase in popularity. Dos Equis continues a rather stable position on the list at eighth place in the Tp 10 (seventh last year). But Corona Light, a product of Cerveceria Modelo, Mexico's largest brewer, recorded another year of 300 percent sales increases, and moved from 10th spot to fifth in the Top 10. This is a rather phenomenal growth for a single brand of beer, and is all the more spectacular in that Corona is only available in 26 western states. For those traveling west who might like to try Corona, it is a very light, non-filling beer which goes wonderfully well with Mexican food.

The Netherlands which, with Heineken, is American's largest beer importer, also managed to capture ninth place with Amstel Light, another beer successfully marketed by Van Munching.

Rounding out the list in the 10th place from the land down under is Foster's Lager from Australia. The Aussies are some of the best beer drinkers in the world, and their beer is deserving of their affections and loyalties.

All of the beers on the Top 10 list are lager beers, golden in color (except for Dos Equis) and largely reflective of America's penchant for light, refreshing beers, though with more character than America's standard pilseners.

But with 400 beers now being imported, and with the accent on a wider choice of brewing styles, the Top 10 do not necessarily tell the whole story. So it might be worth while to look at the Second 10 most popular imports. Here is where the variety in styles begins to show a little more.

Although Britain is in fifth place when it comes to total amount of imports, its variety of brands lands it only at the top of the Second 10. Bass Ale, representative of Britain's most popular style of pale ale, is being advertised as the "Spirit of the Empire," and comes in as 11th in import sales in America. If we could count just this one style — pale ale — instead of just the brand — Bass — Britain would rate much higher in the Top 10.

Another brew from the North Atlantic, Guinness Stout, is Ireland-England's other distinct brewing style to make the list. Guinness Stout is a heavy, dark ale made with thick, roasted malt. Distinctly different from all the other brews in the Top 20, Guinness comes in 15th.

Between Britain's 11th and 15th positions come three more light lagers from around the world. Carta Blanca, another popular lager from Mexico, is 12th, Dortmunder, a distinctive light style from Germany, is 13th, and Grolsh, a very smooth lager from the Netherlands is 14th.

The Japanese have brewed a very popular lager entry with one of the prettiest labels in brewing. Kirin is the 16th most popular import. The Japanese also hold the 19th position in the Top 20 with Sapporo.

Canada's fourth entry in the Top 20 is O'Keefe, at 17th. San Miguel, from the Philippines, calling itself "The Classic Beer of the Pacific," is 18th. Finally, the fourth Mexican beer in the Top 20 is Tecate. This is the classic Mexican brew served with a lime wedge and the rim lined with salt.

That list again of the top 20 among America's 400 imports is as follows:

Heineken, Netherlands
Molson, Canada
Becks, Germany
Moosehead, Canada
Corona, Mexico
St. Pauli Girl, Germany
Labatt, Canada
Dos Equis, Mexico
Amstel Light, Netherlands
Foster's Lager, Australia
Bass, United Kingdom
Carta Blanca, Mexico
Dortmunde, Germany
Grolsh, Netherlands
Guinness, United Kingdom
Kirin, Japan
O'Keefe, Canada
San Miguel, Philippines
Sapporo, Japan
Tecate, Mexico

Ein Prosit der Gemutlichkeit!

Brewer Follows in Footsteps
of His Famous Ancestor

August 10, 1986

One of the special joys of living in Centre County is being able to walk slowly, lovingly, and often across the campus of Penn State and to enter into the spirit of the founders and of the 125 classes or generations of students who have graduated since that first class in 1861. There is a special attitude toward life, a reverence for the past, and an appreciation of creativity and courage which one can almost soak up amidst the older buildings on campus.

One can stand, for example, near the top of the mall and look to the left and right at Burrowes and Sparks buildings. Around the tops of each building are inscribed the greatest names of our civilization as it was known to the founders of Penn State spirit.

One was meant to stop and meditate upon them and upon the people who inscribed them there. Magelan, Longfellow, Shakespeare, Wagner, Socrates, Charles Dickens, Alexander Hamilton, Kant, Mozart, John Marshall, Dante, Hippocrates, Virgil, Roger Bacon, Copernicus. These are just a few of the names which were chiseled in Penn State stone for future generations.

There are many other names rimming both of these buildings — enough for more than the four years it takes a student to graduate. Enough to meditate upon as an alumnus for a lifetime.

There is one name on the list which may not be as well known to many, but whose life — and whose progeny — may well be deserving of a little more acknowledgement in this hurried world of ours. Inscribed over the southwest portico of Sparks Building, facing West Halls, is prominently placed the name of F.D. Pastorius.

Francis Daniel Pastorius was one of the great founders of the spirit of Pennsylvania, indeed fit to be listed among the great men who bequeathed to us our culture, values, and self-esteem.

Pastorius was one of those supremely deep and active men of the Age of Discovery. He traveled to every country of Europe, and studied at many of its greatest universities. He spoke seven languages fluently and wrote prodigiously. One of the things he wrote was the first encyclopedia ever compiled — long before Diderot.

But it was his driving quest to find congenial people among whom honor, courage, strength, and conviviality reigned, which made him great. He wrote: "I applied my greatest industry and efforts, at all times and places, solely to find out where and among what people and nations true devotion, the knowledge and fear of God, might best be met with and acquired. I reasoned thus within myself," he went on, "whether it were not better to teach the learning which I had received... to the new-founde American people of Pennsylvania."

For Pastorius thought was deed, and he arrived in Pennsylvania in August 1683, where he was specially greeted by William Penn himself. He may have shared a beer with

Penn from the first brewery in Pennsylvania which Penn was building. He secured the rights to 25,000 acres on the Schuylkill River and founded the city of Germantown. There he guided the new settlers with a wisdom and a founding spirit which deserved his inclusion among the great names inscribed on Penn State's buildings.

He had given up his great status and position in Germany to come to the frontier of civilization to participate in the growth of a new people. His spirit in poetry infected the spanking new Commonwealth:

> *Men must go for, what 'ere the weather*
> *And now we must go forth together,*
> *Jacob! Up the morn is fine!*
> *Be not then so sad and moping,*
> *Dawns the freedom you are hoping,*
> *Comes another brighter mood,*
> *What God wills is luck and good!*

Neither Pastorius nor his plucky and optimistic spirit are as well known today as they once were. But they are not completely lost, either.

Thomas V. Pastorius, the ninth generation direct descendant of Francis Daniel Pastorius, and a Penn State graduate (master of business administration, 1971), is once again, in the family tradition, opening up new worlds in Pennsylvania. Young Tom Pastorius has just founded the new "Pennsylvania Brewing Company" to help restore the old feeling and the old Pennsylvania pride.

On June 23, 303 years after his famous ancestor arrived on these shores, he introduced "Pennsylvania Pilsner" to the palates of Pennsylvanians. "Pennsylvania Pilsner tastes like beer used to taste in Pennsylvania," he says.

Tom Pastorius stopped in my office last week for a tasting of his new beer. Space doesn't permit me to tell you more about Tom and his Pennsylvania Pilsner in this column. But I promise to bring the story of Pennsylvania spirit up to date in my next column with a report on how well Tom Pastorius' beer is made, and even more, how much it is enjoyed.

Ein Prosit der Gemutlichkeit!

New Lager with Old-Time European Taste is Brewed in Pennsylvania

August 24, 1986

Pennsylvania has joined the microbrewery revolution. It now has its own specialty brewed beer and joins the nationwide trend toward crafted super-premium beers with the old-time taste, body, and flavor most enjoyed by Europeans.

Pennsylvania Pilsner is a new lager brewed by authentic German brewing methods. It was introduced to Philadelphia beer drinkers on June 23, 1986, and this month is being introduced to beer lovers in Central Pennsylvania.

The beer is being introduced by the new Pennsylvania Brewing Company founded by Thomas V. Pastorius, the ninth-generation direct descendant of the first German settler in Pennsylvania, Francis D. Pastorius. The elder Pastorius was the founder of Germantown near Philadelphia and a personal friend of William Penn who welcomed him to Pennsylvania upon his arrival in 1683. As I recounted in my previous column, F.D. Pastorius is one of the great men of history whose names are inscribed in stone on the facade of Sparks Building on the Penn State campus.

Young Tom Pastorius, who received his masters of business administration from Penn State in 1971, lived for 12 years in Germany. He first served there in the Army as a First

Lieutenant. Later, he founded his own information consulting firm.

Tom Pastorius visited State College a few weeks ago to talk to people about his new brew. It seems he was led to go into the brewing business because of his love of the German-style beers which he could not find back in America. During his 12 years in Germany he said he fell in love with German beers and made a personal quest of trying to taste as many of the beers of Germany's more than 1,300 breweries as he could.

Viewing the development of microbreweries, he felt the time might be ripe to re-introduce real German-style beer to America. So he selected the beer he liked best in Germany. It was the beer of a small brewery in the Odenwald near Heidelberg.

Heidelberg, as some may recall, is the site of a famous University and the scene for the popular musical, "The Student Prince," in which one hears some of the greatest drinking songs of all times. Heidelberg, on the Neckar River, is a storybook land of famous characters and famous taverns, such as "Zum Schwarze Ritter," which I visited a few years ago. One can still feel there, in the entire atmosphere of the place, the tradition of riotous good fellowship and laughter which generation of disciplined German University students bequeathed to the world when they put their books aside and went out to "let go" and have fun.

Tom Pastorius brought back samples of the beer he had found and delivered them for testing to the Siebel Institute, which is the center of brewing studies in the United States. There the beer was subjected to every conceivable analysis in order to be able to duplicate its rich body and deep tastes.

Pastorius then enlisted the aid of Dr. Joseph Owades, the most famous brewer in the United States. Dr. Owades is the brewer who developed the first light beer in the U.S., and has since been the man chosen to develop America's most popular new beers. These include Samuel Adams Boston Lager for Bostonians, New Amsterdam Amber Lager for New Yorkers, Olde Heurich which was just introduced this spring in Washington, D.C. and the new Colony XIII for Savannah, Georgia.

Pennsylvania Pilsner follows the strict Reinheitsgebot of German Purity Law of 1516. That means that it is a "pure" beer. It contains only two-row barley malt, Tettrang and Hallertau hops, water, and a special yeast to ferment the beer.

The beer is presently being brewed by the Pittsburgh Brewing Company under special contract, and under the supervision of Dr. Owades. Eventually, however, Pastorius intends to build his own microbrewery to produce his favorite beer.

Besides the fidelity to the German brewing style, one of the main features of Pennsylvania Pilsner is its freshness. Beer is made from grain, just like bread. Imported beers are usually several weeks — sometimes several months — old by the time they reach the American consumer. Without the addition of chemicals or additives, their flavor changes. Thus few imported beers taste the same as the same pure, fresh beer tastes in its homeland.

Pennsylvania Pilsner is pure beer. It contains no rice, no corn, no chemicals, and no additives. It is delivered fresh within a matter of days after it is bottled.

Tom Pastorius says, "We believe that this beer will appeal especially to those connoisseurs who know and appreciate the beers and who have been seeking a comparable beer locally. Now there's no need to go to Europe to taste this German beer. It's here."

How well is it liked? The day after my last column on the great history of the Pastorius family, John Dombroski of State College gave me a call: "Where can I get some of that Pennsylvania Pilsner?" he asked.

He explained that he had been in Philadelphia in July and had been among the first to try Pennsylvania Pilsner in one of the famous old Taverns there.

"That beer is great," he said. "My son has been asking me for months what I wanted for my birthday. Now I know — I've asked him to bring up a case of Pennsylvania Pilsner from Philadelphia."

I've called around to check the Centre County beer distributors. Nittany Beverage in State College tells me they plan to have it in stock within a week or so direct from the brewery in Pittsburgh.

If you want to try the taste of a fresh and truly German Pilsner, it's on its way.

Ein Prosit der Gemutlichkeit!

A Legend in a Bottle

September 7, 1986

In Anno Domini 1854 — just a year before the founding of Penn State — a man by the name of John McSorely founded one of the most venerable and sacred institutions of the city of New York. It was a saloon — the most famous, most frequently written about and painted and honored saloon in the country. McSorely's Old Ale House is a monument to ale, male companionship and character.

McSorely's Original Cream Ale is now available in bottles in Centre County through Sam Nastase Beer Distributors in Bellefonte. So I thought I might share with you the story of this characterful saloon and the men who inspired it and served its ale for just a little longer than Penn State has been around.

John McSorely was an Irish immigrant who came to America to build a pub just like the one he had frequented in Ireland. Old John hated change, and the ocean voyage to the New World was apparently as much change as he was going to put up with in his lifetime.

John McSorely would undoubtedly be considered strange by today's standards. He didn't give two hoots about pleasantries. John was a man of a different age, when character was much more important than interpersonal relations.

And John viewed time very differently too. It was not something to be passed through as comfortably as possible until one passed away. On the contrary, for Old John time was a challenge. He was determined to defeat it by creating something that would last long after he had gone.

John did it by just being himself: ornery, surly, singular. No one ever told him about modern day niceness, and if they ever had he certainly wouldn't have listened. "Old John was quirky ... subject to unaccountable fits of surliness," wrote Joseph Mitchell in a famous essay on McSorely's written for the "New Yorker" magazine in 1940.

John was a man of principle. His motto was, "Good ale, raw onions and no ladies." He was true to them all. No women were permitted in McSorely's. Old John believed it was "impossible for men to drink with tranquility in the presence of women."

Obviously women were much more powerful in those days than they are today. Nowadays a young man is not supposed to notice or care whether the person he's working with is a man or a woman; women are supposed to be interchangeable with men. No doubt if Old John were still around he'd simply shake his head and say, "No wonder the country's confused."

There had always been a back room at McSorely's. But Old John had nailed a sign outside which read "Notice. No Back Room in Here for Ladies." Things were clearer then.

Each day Old John had set out the same free lunch for his customers: soda crackers, raw onions and cheese. The cheese sometimes looked like the same cheese he had put out on opening day in 1854. But it was there every day, along with thick, fresh onions. Old John loved onions: "the stronger the better," he used to say.

And the ale. For a while Old John made it himself. But then he went to the old Fidelio Brewery down the street to have them brew it according to his recipe. As breweries closed over the years, the recipe moved from one brewery to another. But Old John believed in ale. He'd serve no hard liquor at his saloon. "The man never lived who needed a stronger drink than a mug of stock ale," he used to say.

Old John loved memorabilia. He covered his walls with things to which he took a liking. For years he saved wishbones of Thanksgiving and Christmas turkeys and strung them on a string between the gas lamps and the bar. In 1902 he hung a heavy oaken frame containing portraits of Lincoln, Garfield and McKinley and attached a brass plate at the bottom which read, "THEY ASSASSINATED THESE GOOD MEN THE SKULKING DOGS." He hung the front pages of old newspapers, photos of friends, engravings of famous events, banquet menus, autographs, starfish shells, theater programs, political posters and even worn-down shoes from brewery horses.

Around 1890, Old John's son Bill McSorely took over the day-to-day running of the bar. It was said of Bill that "He inherited every bit of his father's surliness and not much of his affability." Bill was so solemn that before he was 30 customers were calling him "Old Bill."

According to Joe Mitchell, "Bill worshipped his father, but no one was aware of the profundity of the worship until Old John died." After the funeral, Bill did not leave his apartment for a week. Then he went to the saloon and painstakingly nailed and screwed every one of his father's pictures and souvenirs to the wall. From that day on Bill's sole concern was to keep McSorely's exactly as it had been in his father's time.

Such was the power of this love that whenever something had to be changed or repaired, it appeared to pain him physically.

When he had to have the sagging floor fixed, he sat with his head in his hands and would not eat for several days.

Under Bill's care, from 1890 till 1936, the only changes he allowed were a switch from pewter mugs to earthenware, and the installation of a coin box telephone, which he refused to answer when it rang.

Bill was difficult as ever a man could be. He hated banks, cash registers, bookkeeping and salesmen. "If the saloon became too crowded," wrote Mitchell, "he would close up early, saying, 'I'm getting too much confounded trade in here.'" Perhaps he was the archetypal New Yorker.

"Bill was tyrannical," Mitchell wrote. "Reading a newspaper, he would completely disregard a line of customers waiting to be served. If a man became impatient and demanded a drink, Bill would look up angrily and shout obscene remarks at him in a high, nasal voice. Such treatment did not annoy customers, but made them snicker; they thought he was funny. In fact, despite Bill's bad disposition, many customers were fond of him. They had known him since they were young men together and had grown accustomed to his quirks. They even took a wry sort of pride in him, and when they said he was the gloomiest, or the stingiest man in the Western Hemisphere, there was boastfulness in their voice. The more eccentric he became, the more they respected him."

So, under Bill's stewardship, McSorely's plodded through the first third of the 20th century, growing in honor and in fame as a saloon owned by a man and not a management team.

Ein Prosit der Gemutlichkeit!

Memories Abound:
Many Drawn to Famous N.Y. Saloon

September 21, 1986

There are some people who believe that nothing is sacred. There are others who believe that only visitors from the next world — such as gods, saints, Buddhas, and angels — leave sacred places where they come to earth.

But for most men, sacredness is much more mysterious, much more indefinable. Somehow, from out of nowhere, and with sometimes no particular reason, a particular place or thing rises above the ordinary and attracts the reverence of men.

The Constitution of the United States is one such thing. Most European countries — such as France, Germany, and Italy — and most Latin American countries have had dozens of constitutions without their citizens ever dreaming that any of them were sacred or permanent. The American Constitution, we all know, is different. It is sacred. The Vietnam Memorial in Washington is another example. It calls forth a reverence which few other memorials in our capitol command.

Locally, Mount Nittany attracts similar feelings of respect for what outsiders see as nothing but an ordinary Pennsylvania hillock.

Thus, there is an instinct in men which mysteriously recognizes the sacred as something special, toward which one automatically behaves differently, as though called upon by a mysterious voice from within. It is as though every man possesses a third eye which can see a difference in something even though our two sensible eyes see it as only ordinary.

There is such a sacred place in New York known as McSorely's Saloon.

Last Saturday I visited McSorely's again. I had just written my earlier column on McSorely's a week before. At the same time I had written a second column to bring the story of McSorely's up to date. That second column was to have appeared this week. But the feeling that writing them evoked in me called for me to make another pilgrimage to McSorely's. And being there again led me to write this column and to record the experience while it was still fresh. So I'm offering this column now, and I'm saving the "McSorely's Up-to-Date" column for next time.

It was around 1 p.m. Saturday when I entered the place. I ordered an ale and sat down at one of the battered wood tables. The man at the next table was in a postman's uniform. I asked him if he came here often. "I remember when my grandfather first brought me in here 48 years ago," he replied.

It turns out that he was a retired policeman from the 62nd precinct who now had a part-time job at the post office nearby. His visit to McSorely's was the high point each day.

At the table on the other side of me were three younger college men. I overheard two of them explaining to a third in an indefinably respectful tone of voice the meaning of the sign above the bar which reads, "Be Good Or Be Gone."

They told the story of how they had been ordered to leave McSorely's once for acting up. They didn't resent the authority of the place: this was an unusual place where authority was respected. It was as though they were boasting of being disciplined by someone who meant something. It was a story they would probably tell their children someday with the same pride.

Two young men in their thirties standing across from me at the bar had the old torn Levis and calloused hands of construction workers. I overheard one telling the story to the other of how at one time women were not allowed to enter McSorely's. If a woman ventured into the place, the lights would go off and the men would stomp their feet and pound the tables with their mugs. Most women quickly got the point and left. If they didn't, they were escorted out.

Of course, all that changed with the rise of feminism. In 1970 the National Organization for Women went to court to force McSorely's to admit women. The court bowed to the winds of change blowing that day and issued the requested order. Today women can enter McSorely's and John McSorely's famous tradition of "Good ale, raw onions, and no ladies" is only two-thirds followed under threat of force.

I went up for another beer at the bar and asked the bartender if this chair above the bar was, according to legend, the one Abe Lincoln had sat in when he used to come to McSorely's to drink ale, eat 3-inch thick steaks, and pray with Old John at his Sunday evening Bible meetings. He replied with an unfathomable smile, "Only half the things they say are lies are true."

I told him that I write a column on beer for an obscure (to New Yorkers) newspaper in Central Pennsylvania and he asked me if I had read the book called "McSorely's Wonderful Saloon."

Yes, I replied, and told him I was borrowing from it heavily for my history of the place and hoped Joe Mitchell, the author, wouldn't mind. "Nah," he said, "Joe would love it." He told me Joe had just been in the week before and was writing another book on McSorely's to bring his 1940 piece up to date. "Joe's glad when anybody shares his love for this place with others."

I went back to my table and the postman was gone. He was replaced by two young couples. The women were talking about how inexpensive a ham sandwich was in this place for only $2. One woman held the jar of mustard under her boyfriend's nose and told him to smell the hot spicy odor.

Later, as we headed toward the door a newspaper clipping on the wall caught my eye. It was a picture of the 100th anniversary party for McSorely's in 1954. The caption explained that it was a picture of the bartender bringing a mug of beer outside to the owner, Dorothy O'Connor Kirwan, who inherited McSorely's from the third owner, Daniel O'Connor, in 1939.

Mrs. Kirwan, even though she was owner of the place, respected the tradition and would not set foot inside it. My wife read the same clipping over my shoulder and whispered, "Sic transit gloria mundi" which means, for those who didn't attend old-fashioned Catholic grade schools, "Thus passes the glory of the world."

Next week I promise we'll cover the rest of the history of McSorely's and bring it up to date.

Ein Prosit der Gemutlichkeit!

McSorley's Character

October 5, 1986

Old John McSorely died in 1910 at the age of 87. But he had already established the fame of McSorely's Old Ale House as a place of character. And he had passed the tradition on to his son, Bill, whose character was irascible enough to inspire artists for four decades.

Character — that's what the tradition of McSorely's was. Let's face it, most of the smiling people you meet in businesses and restaurants today are fakes. They are smiling at you because they want your money.

McSorely's was different. It was wonderful to go to a place where the owner was not trying to please you in order to get your money; in fact, he wasn't trying to please you at all. The only reason to go to McSorely's was because you wanted to be there. And you knew that the other people you met there were only there because they wanted to be there, too. It felt good to be with people who couldn't be used, and who weren't trying to use you.

At McSorely's you had to be tough just to get served a draught of beer. If Bill was reading the newspaper, you waited. If it was time to feed the cats, you waited till all 18 of them got fed. You weren't sure about your evening plans, because there was no set closing time; Bill just closed the saloon whenever he got tired. And if too many customers came in at once, he'd close the whole place, explaining fitfully, "I'm getting too much confounded trade in here."

It was because of this absolutely independent, unconditioned character that McSorely's became one of the most artistically celebrated saloons in American history. In 1882 McSorely's had acquired some fame by becoming the scene of one of Harrigan and Hart's comedies, called "McSorely's Inflation." Harrigan and Hart were considered the Gilbert and Sullivan of the U.S.A. back then.

But the real artistic fame of McSorely's began just shortly before The Great War. About 1911 several American painters, such as John Sloan, George Luks, Glenn Colemen, and Stuart Davis, began drinking together at McSorely's. John Sloan was inspired to do five paintings of famous scenes from McSorely's between 1912 and 1930. Sloan's paintings are often included in collections of American masterpieces. Today they are all owned by the Detroit Institute of the Arts.

Louis Bouche did another famous painting of McSorely's which is owned by the University of Nebraska. Reginald Marsh had done many sketches of McSorely's. "There is no doubt," wrote Joseph Mitchell in the Atlantic Monthly in 1940, "that McSorely's has been painted more often than any other saloon in the country."

What was the special character of McSorely's? This is how Joe Mitchell described it 46 years ago:

"To a steady McSorely customer, most other New York saloons seem feminine and fit only for college boys and women; the atmosphere in them is so tense and disquieting that he has to drink himself into a coma in order to stand it. In McSorely's the customers are self-sufficient; they never try to impress each other. Also they are not competitive. In other saloons if a man tells a story, good or bad, the man next to him laughs perfunctorily and immediately tries to tell a better one."

"It is possible to relax at McSorely's. For one thing it is dark and gloomy, and repose comes easy in a gloomy place. Also there is a thick, musty smell that acts as a calm to jerky nerves; it is a rich compound of smells of pine sawdust, tap drippings, pipe tobacco, coal smoke and onions. A Bellevue intern once said that for many mental disturbances the smell in McSorely's is more beneficial than psychoanalysis."

The special character of McSorely's Saloon was particularly noticeable during Prohibition. When Prohibition came in 1920, it closed all the taverns and saloons and breweries across the country. But not McSorely's. Character is character. Joe Mitchell described it like this:

"When Prohibition came, Bill simply disregarded it. He ran wide open. He did not have a peephole door, nor did he pay protection, but McSorely's was never raided." McSorely's was protected by a mystique of sacredness — and by most of the politicians, statesmen, and policemen of New York City.

Barney Kelly, a retired brewer from the Bronx, would come down three times a week during Prohibition to brew the ale in McSorely's basement. Everyone could smell it for a block, but no one ever complained. Barney's brew was described as "raw and extraordinarily emphatic," by Joe Mitchell. One's mouth waters at the thought of it.

Today the ale sold at McSorely's is brewed by Christian Schmidt's in Philadelphia. Some time ago I visited the Schmidt's brewery and had a tour of the ale house.

Schmidt's has two entirely separate breweries — one for lagers and one for ales. Because ales and lagers are made with different yeasts, they cannot be produced in the same building, and must be separated or the yeasts might contaminate each other. To my knowledge, Schmidt's has the only commercial brewery on the east coast capable of making a real ale for McSorely's.

McSorely's Cream Ale is a darker, heavier brew than your usual American beer. It has a heavier malt aroma, and a well balanced body; plenty of hops and an excellent finish. It goes very well with food.

McSorely's also serves a dark beer. This is really Schmidt's Prior Double Dark. This beer is a modern rendition of the famous dark lager beers of Munich. It has a special old-time flavor and body which is entirely appropriate to the character of McSorely's and the ghost of the old Irish, German, and Ukrainian workmen who immortalized it.

McSorely's Old Ale House is presently owned by Matthew "Matty" Maher. He is as determined as his loyal customers to keep the spirit of McSorely's alive.

You can get in touch with the all-but-lost spirit of American independence by pouring a bottle of McSorely's Cream Ale into a pewter mug, letting it warm up on an old wood stove, sitting back and closing your eyes to dream of the days when men were men and they built nations and slew dragons and faced evil empires without flinching.

You can find McSorely's Cream Ale at Sam Nastese Beer Distributor's in Bellefonte, on tap at "Taps" on Sowers Street in State College, and in bottles at many restaurants and six-pack shops.

Ein Prosit der Gemutlichkeit!

A Layman's Introduction to Brewing from Milling to Bottling

October 19, 1986

I ran into a friend the other day and the conversation went something like this:

"I've been reading your column, Ben, about all these different beers, and I sure have been enjoying tasting," he says.

"That's great, "I reply. "Let's have a beer on that."

"But one thing I'd like to know," he says, ignoring my invitation, "is how the stuff is made."

"Barley, water, yeast, and hops," rolls off my tongue like a formula.

"I know," says my friend, "and there is lagering, aging, fermenting, and brewing. I've heard all the terms. But what I need is someone to explain how it all comes together. Do you lager first and then brew it or vice versa? What goes into the brew kettle and what comes out? When do you add the hops?"

"A most reasonable question," says I to my friend. Herewith is your very own short course on brewing, "on tap," as it were:

First, it must be understood that beer is a unique food product. It is biologically and chemically more complex than any other food product. There are more than 1,000 identified biological compounds in beer. But, paradoxically, beer starts out even more simple than wine.

Both beer and wine are made by a process involving yeast fermentation. With wine, the liquid which is to be acted upon comes in little purple or green packages called grapes. When the grapes are crushed, one gets the juice which is to be fermented. But with beer the liquid which is to be fermented must be made from scratch.

Malting. The basic raw material from which beer is made is barley. Barley is a cereal grain like, say, wheat or corn, except for one very unique characteristic: it is the only cereal grain that retains its husk.

For this reason, it is "the soul of beer. "

When Barley is harvested for beer, it is prepared for the brewing process by being "malted." The barley corns are moistened first with warm water and allowed to begin germination. They are then dried. The temperature at which the drying takes place determines the character, color, and flavor of the malt. The basic types of malt resulting from different temperatures of drying are crystal malt, caramel malt, and black malt. Malting is done by specialized companies which sell their malted barley to brewers.

At the brewery, the brewer decides what kind of beer he wants to brew and orders a combination of malts he needs in order to obtain the desired taste, weight, and color.

Milling. The malt is first prepared for brewing by being milled at the brewery. The milling crushes the husk of the malted barley so that it can be acted upon by hot water to begin its biological and chemical transformation.

Mashing. After being milled, the crushed malt is fed into the mash tun. There it is covered with hot water whose temperature is increased through stages to accomplish different chemical and biological reactions at each stage. The choice of temperatures of the hot water at each stage and the length of time at each temperature will determine many of the characteristics of the beer.

The liquid resulting from the milled barley and the hot water is drained from the mash tun into a lauter tun which filters out the husks and other solids. This is why the husks are so important — without them all one might get would be a gooey glue as you would if you mixed water and milled flour. The results of water and barley, however, after the husks are strained out, is a clear, sweet amber liquid called the "wort." It is this wort which is the liquid base of beer.

Brewing. The next step in the process is the actual brewing. The wort is piped to the brew kettle where two things happen. First the wort is heated up to boiling and second, the hops are added. Brewing produces flavor and color compounds in the wort, and at the same time brewing extracts the bitter and aromatic oils of hops. These hop oils will then provide aroma and bitterness to the beer.

Fermentation. After brewing the liquid is strained to remove the spent hops and it is cooled as it goes into the fermentation tanks. At the proper temperature the yeast is added. The yeast acts throughout the wort and ferments the sugars into alcohol and carbon dioxide. The yeast also imparts a very distinct flavor and character to the beer. The numbers of kinds of yeast are almost infinite. The yeast culture used by a brewery may be unique to that brewery and the one, true unreproducible secret of its brewing process.

As the fermentation proceeds, the yeast will gradually settle out of the wort, either by rising to the top (ales) or settling to the bottom (lagers). The yeast is then skimmed off and the now fermented wort, changed by the action of the yeast into a living substance, goes into the aging tanks.

Aging. In the aging tanks, the beer clarifies and mellows. For an ale, this might involve resting in a "ruh" tank for two through seven days. For a lager, it usually means storing or "lagering" the beer for at least 14 days and as long as 90 days.

Finishing. During aging there are a variety of processes which can be followed by the brewer to finish the beer. One is called secondary fermentation, which places the beer in the aging tanks before fermentation is completed. This results in a second and longer fermentation in the aging tanks. Another method is to add young fermenting beer to aged beer in the aging tanks. This second process is called "kraeusening." It allows the beer to mellow more effectively and also adds natural carbonation. Iron City Golden Lager is an example of a beer which uses this finishing process to produce a smoother, richer lager beer.

After aging, the beer is ready to be filtered, pasteurized, and bottled.

The process can sound simple, but it releases, as I said before, more than 1,000 biological and chemical compounds, each acting and reacting on all of the others. To keep that many actors in harmony is the challenge of the brewer.

Ein Prosit der Gemutlichkeit!

Autumn a Season of Beers

November 2, 1986

It is already November. The harvests are all in by now. The chill is back in the air for good. There's not a green leaf left on the trees. Last Sunday evening time itself changed to steal the sunshine from our evenings.

In Europe, where a lot of us have our roots, this season of the year was mysteriously important. Being farther north then we, our ancestors in Europe experienced the change of seasons in and even more extreme form. Since they are farther north, their summer days are much longer while their days in winter are so short as to breed the darkest fears that light and warmth might never ever come back.

We just celebrated Halloween which is the ancient Celtic prayer for the dying sun. In this time of the year when the nights are growing much longer, it seems to the Celts that the Kingdom of Darkness was encompassing the earth. It was the season when the dead were in the ascendant, when what was imagined became real, and ghosts and goblins arose from their graves and walked the earth. On ancient craggy mountaintops huge bonfires were lighted as signals of Thanksgiving to a dying warrior sun for the blaze of summer glory that his conquest of the night had won just one more time.

Autumn was also, at another level, a time of celebration. It was when the warriors came home. Lords in castle halls and poor knights and archers in country taverns assembled to toast the summer's exploits and keep together through the lengthening nights. It was the season when sports replaced real battles and the rampart guard could be relaxed.

It was, in a word, the season of beer.

And there is much reason to recall the ancient ways of our ancestors in these days. For these ancient ways, which follow seasons and cycles of their own, seem to be coming back.

One sure sign of the times is the growing availability of the ancient types of beer at the pubs and taverns. It was not long ago that most bars and taverns carried nothing but summer beers all year long. These were the light, refreshing local style pilseners, such as Yuengling, Rolling Rock, Stoney's, Schmidt's, Straub's and Iron City; a few out-of-staters like Genny, Bud, Miller, Pabst and Strohs; and a few imported light lagers such as Heineken, Molson, Moosehead and Beck's. All were of the same generic type and style.

But, as Bob Dylan said when I was a much younger man, "The times they are a-changing."

One of the exciting signs of the times is what has become the annual appearance of Oktoberfest beers from Germany. These have become seasonably available here from about the last week in September until the end of November. They appear each fall without fanfare or heralding. One only knows of them by the autumn sounding date on one's calendar, a certain itching in the mouth that can only be assuaged by a deeper, darker, maltier, stronger lager from Munchen, and the appearance of ubiquitous little standup cards on one's tavern table. Any one of these can tell you it's Oktoberfest time.

What is an Oktoberfest beer? Well, before the advent of refrigeration, it wasn't generally possible to make good lager beer in the summer. Lager beers have to be fermented at cold temperatures, normally about 35° Fahrenheit, and then aged for several weeks or months. In the summer, temperatures rose too high for this kind of fermentation.

So when the warm summer weather approached each spring the brewers of Munich thought ahead of the fall and brewed a special beer which would be fermented at cold spring temperatures, but which would age and last through the warmer summer in order to be ready for the famous Munich Oktoberfest which begins annually on the second to the last weekend in September.

Those special Oktoberfest beers were usually brewed in March, and thus are sometimes called "Marzen "beers. They are brewed with extra hops and a higher alcohol content in order to preserve the beer through the warm summer days. Oktoberfest beer is darker than our normal beers today, but is probably lighter than what it was back in the early 19th century when the Oktoberfest began.

Oktoberfest beers, with their extra bite and slightly higher alcohol, were the perfect beers for celebrating. They made warriors and hunters glad to be home. The hops encouraged a fine and glorious appetite. The slightly higher alcohol content induced good health and a greater openness to friends and good fellowship. And the deeper taste made them feel that there were things worth living for even when the glorious battles of summer were over.

Three Oktoberfest beers are being imported into Centre County. Hickey's is carrying Wurzburger Oktoberfest by the case. Or you can try a bottle of it with friends at the Tavern, the Rathskeller, Cafe 210 and Zeno's in State College, or Duffy's in Boalsburg. It's also available at many six pack shops.

Pletcher's in Bellefonte is carrying one of Munchen's most famous Oktoberfest beers — the superb Spaten Oktoberfest. Passing through an autumn without Spaten Oktoberfest is like an autumn without football. Life just wouldn't be the same. You can try it by the bottle amidst the students at the Phyrst or the Brewery or get a case direct from Pletcher's Distributors.

As of last Monday, Nittany Beverage had only four cases left of the Oktoberfest of the other famous Munchen brewery: Hofbrau Oktoberfest. These will probably be gone by the time you read this, though. If you didn't get any this year, don't miss the Spaten or Wurzburger, but remember to try all three next autumn. You, too, may find yourself lighting bonfires to the dying sun.

The good feelings of the autumn Oktoberfest is the reason for the famous Oktoberfest toast which says all that there is to say about characterful beer. The Muncheners sway back and forth with locked arms singing and shouting, "Ein Prosit, Ein Prosit, Ein Prosit der Gemütlichkeit!" over foaming steins of beer. Every soldier who has ever experienced the miracle of true camaraderie in battle knows the meaning of that: "A toast of good fellowship, good feelings, great taste, and true friends!"

As the days grow shorter and the sun almost seems to disappear from the sky, Oktoberfest beer reminds us of how important our friends are. Think of bonfires on the hilltops.

Ein Prosit der Gemütlichkeit!

Founding Fathers Quaffed Their Beers

November 16, 1986

In only 11 days it will be Thanksgiving. It may be well, then, to bring to mind some of the things for which our Pilgrim ancestors were thankful.

The Puritans who came over on the Mayflower were beer drinkers. In fact, in the 17th century everybody who intended to stay healthy drank beer. In those days the wells were generally contaminated and drinking water was much more dangerous than driving under the influence. The Pilgrims were deeply concerned that the "drinking of water would infect their bodies with sore sickness and disease." Thus it is recorded that they would not even consider embarking on their journey to the New World until they were assured that they would not have to drink water on the way.

Having received an assurance that the beer would be plentiful, our Pilgrim fathers, mothers, and children set off on the Mayflower to find a new colony at the mouth of the Hudson River in New York. But they never made it. As luck and poor planning would have it, they ran out of beer as they were sailing south along the Massachusetts coast. The diary of the voyage records, "We could not now take time for further search or consideration, our victuals being much spent, especially on beer." So they landed at Plymouth Rock.

It was a tragic time. The Pilgrims were "hasted ashore and made to drink water." They were filled with dark foreboding at the prospect, but fortunately the water in the area proved to be clear and pure and they did not suffer the "sore sickness and grievous diseases" which they had feared. Sometime later Governor Bradford writes that while the water "is as good as any in the world, still it was not so wholesome as the good beer and wine in London."

If beer was not available at that first Pilgrim Thanksgiving dinner, we know that it was sadly missed. Stanley Baron records that, "the Pilgrims were willing to put up with drinking water, as they put up with many other hardships, but they would have preferred beer, and indeed had beer as soon as it was possible." When John Winthrop arrived as the new governor of the Massachusetts Bay Colony, he came ashore with "42 Tonnes of Beere" (about 10,000 gallons).

Now that was truly something to be thankful about. Upon Winthrop's arrival, it is recorded, everyone celebrated and "they supped with a good venison pasty and good beer."

In 1663, a brew kettle was sent from England and the following year the governor decreed that the price of beer could not exceed one penny per quart, so as to assure wholesome beer to all the inhabitants. In 1665, Richard Mather, the Puritan minister and father of Cotton, happily noted that there was no shortage in the colony "of good and wholesome beere and bread."

What might there be for us to be thankful for on the upcoming Thanksgiving Day in the 365th year since that first day of Thanksgiving in the Plymouth Colony?

The first thing we might be grateful for is that we don't have to drink water. There is beer in store and even wine enough to make our Puritan forefathers feel that they did right well in helping found this "land of the Pilgrim's pride."

The second thing for which we might be thankful is the vast increase in the types and styles of beer available on tap in Centre County.

Good beer on tap is always the true beer lovers' first choice. Beer on draft means that the beer is generally (1) fresher and (2) not heat pasteurized. And that spells better body, better balance, and better taste.

The number of beers on tap has increased in Centre County dramatically. Several pubs and taverns, sensing a new appreciation for the ancient brew, have added new taps to bring the freshest and most varied assortment of beers to their customers. The largest number of beers available on tap is at the All-American Rathskeller, which has 20 different taps for beer. Next comes the Brewery with 11, Taps with 10, Gingerbread Man with eight, Post House and Zeno's with seven, and Cafe 210, Brickhouse Tavern, Lion's Den, and Phyrst, each with six.

But along with an increase in the total number of beers on tap, there is also a wonderful increase in the number of types and styles available on tap. For years all one could get on tap was a choice of a few American mass production pilseners. But now there is a growing trend toward specialty beers and imported lagers, ales, and stouts.

The new availability of the ancient styles of beer appears to be primarily concentrated among the students and the young people of the county. They, like young people everywhere, are returning to the ways of their ancestors and honoring the ancient traditions of our civilization.

One of the most promising signs is the appearance of the famed English pale ale. These pale ales are considered to be responsible for England's finest hours. Millions of Englishmen believe that they have spent their finest hours imbibing them.

Today they are available for future leaders of the Empire on tap at Cafe 210 and Brickhouse Tavern (Bass Ale); Zeno's (Watney's Red Barrel); and the All-American Rathskeller (both Bass and Watney's).

Guinness Stout, treasured as a priceless black pearl in the treasurehouse of fine beers, is newly available on tap at the Rathskeller and Brickhouse Tavern.

McSorely's Cream Ale, the pride and joy of Old John McSorely and made in huge wood vats at the Christian Schmidt Brewery in Philadelphia, is available on tap at Taps on Sowers St., State College, the Brewery, and the Rathskeller.

One of the finest styles of Old Europe is the dark Bohemian lager which is available on tap as Prior Double Dark at the Deli, Hi-Way Pizza, and the Posthouse.

Another famous specialty is Yuengling's Half & Half. This is a mixture of Yuengling Premium and Yuengling Porter. The English call for a quart of this combination by asking for a "Narfen narf." A half a quart is a "Narfen narfen narf." Both the Brewery and the Phyrst carry Narfen narf.

Of course, there are the Canadian lagers (e.g., Molson, Moosehead, Labatts), the European supers (e.g., Heineken, Kronenbourg, Dinkel-Acker, and Harp); the American super premiums (e.g., Michelob) and the standard American pilseners (e.g., Bud, Stroh's, Genny, Miller, Pabst, Rolling Rock, etc.) on tap at pubs and taverns too numerous to mention.

There are 11 days until Thanksgiving, and a cornucopia of things to be thankful for. Be humble. Think of how you can enjoy a draft of one of the things our Pilgrim fathers and mothers would have really appreciated. If you enjoy it just as much as they did, then you can be sure that the spirit of the Pilgrims is still alive.

Ein Prosit der Gemutlichkeit!

Beer Mixed Drinks Are Straightforward

December 3, 1986

One of the basic qualities of the American character is its love of straightforwardness. We like to look a man straight in the eye. We like to talk a straight answer and a straight deal. We like our steaks without fancy sauces and our contracts without small print. We are also accustomed to drinking our beer straight and unmixed.

But for every rule there is an exception, and the great diversity in human nature insures variety in every aspect of life. So, just about the time that you begin to appreciate the value of a purely brewed beer, made straight according to Reinheitsgebot, someone beside you at the tavern orders a mixed drink made with beer.

Beer mixed drinks were once quite popular in America and England. In fact, when the opportunity of making them was available to our Colonial forefathers, beer mixed drinks may have been more the rule than the exception. And today, in many parts of the world, beer mixed drinks are still very popular.

One of the most popular drinks of the Colonial period in America was "mulled ale." Mulled ale was ale warmed in the fireplace or on the Ben Franklin. But in addition to being warmed, it was also interestingly spiced. Here is a recipe for spiced mulled ale taken from the book "Drinking with

Dickens," by Sir Cedric Dickens, the great-grandson of Charles Dickens.

Take a pewter mug of strong ale. Add to it a teaspoon of sugar, a pinch of ground cloves, a pinch of nutmeg and pinch of ginger. Place the mug into the fire or on the stove until the mixture is hot, but not boiling. Remove from the heat, add a jigger of rum or brandy and stir. It's guaranteed to warm most people's spirits.

This recipe calls for "strong ale." That doesn't mean strong in alcohol content, but strong in taste.

An English pale ale, such as Bass Ale or Watney's, would be acceptable. So, too, would be Amber Liberty Ale or McSorely's. If you visit a large city, you might look for some Double Dragon Ale or Hercules Ale from Wales for this recipe.

Our Colonial ancestors also had a large number of other beer mixed drinks with fascinating names. A "Calibogus" was ale with a jigger of rum mixed in. A "Whistle-Belly-Vengeance" was a pint of ale with molasses and crust of brown bread ("rye and Injun") crumbled over the top. A "Marrathan" was ale with rum and sugar added, and a "Tiff" was ale with rum, sugar, and buttered toast steeped in it.

Probably the most popular Colonial party drink was a "Flip." This is one you might make for your friends over the holidays.

Start with two quarts of ale (perhaps McSorely's or Bass) and eight ounces of gin. Beat four eggs together with four ounces of sifted sugar. Add the beaten egg mixture to the beer and gin little by little, stirring all the while. Then pour the whole mixture from one pitcher back and forth to another pitcher a few times to create a blooming froth. This should be served in tall glasses with freshly grated nutmeg sprinkled on top.

A "Rumfustian" was another popular Colonial drink, but one which would take stout hearts to drink today. It consisted of a quart of ale, a bottle of wine or sherry and the yolks of a dozen eggs. Grated orange peel, freshly grated nutmeg and assorted spices, such as ground cloves and ginger, were added.

If our Colonial ancestors were able to drink a mixed drink like this one, it's a wonder they were able to stand up, take on and beat the British Empire in our American Revolution. But those Colonials were tough.

One of the standard tricks with both the Flip and the Rumfustian was to warm them up with a "loggerhead." A loggerhead was a small iron poker which was kept near the fireplace in Colonial homes. It was used to heat and stir drinks. The tip of the loggerhead would be placed in the fire and heated to red hot and then placed in one's mug of tea or soup or beer.

With a Flip or Rumfustian, the loggerhead would not only warm the drink but would also fry some of the egg mixture in these drinks. Frederic Bellingham described the result in the "Falstaff Complete Beer Book," this way: "There is a moiling and a broiling, while beer egg and all acquire a slightly burnt, bitter taste that only adds zest to the drink for the man who knows what he likes."

There are also many modern beer mixed drinks. Perhaps the most well known is a "Black Velvet." This is made with Guinness Stout and champagne mixed in equal portions.

A popular drink in modern England is a "Lager 'n' Lime," made with a good lager beer and a tablespoon or two of Rose's

Lime Juice. I would suggest trying this with Saranac 1888 Lager beer.

Out in Colorado and Wyoming, I have had occasion to try a popular mixed drink that appears to be available in many western taverns. Out west, it's called "Red Beer" and it's made with Coors beer and tomato juice in equal proportions. I find this particular combination to be strange to my taste buds, but the cowboys seem to like it a lot. (A Western "Red Beer" is called a "Tom Boy" by Easterners in the Mr. Boston's Guide to Mixed Drinks.)

A modern day "Shandygaff" is a pilsener beer with ginger ale mixed in equal parts.

Mr. Boston's Guide also lists a drink called a "Beer Buster" made with a jigger of vodka in a glass of ice cold pilsener, with two dashes of Tabasco sauce.

Of course, the steel towns of western Pennsylvania have contributed the "Boilermaker" to mixed drink history. This consists of a shot of bourbon or blanded whiskey with a beer chaser — usually Iron City Premium. A "Depth Charge" is a beer with a jigger of bourbon dropped into it, glass and all. Neither of these should be tried by anyone without a designated driver in the group.

So there you have it — straight talk on beer mixed drinks. They are well worth trying, but just remember that no mixed drinks should be mixed with driving.

Ein Prosit der Gemutlichkeit!

This Season Brews Fond Memories

December 17, 1986

It is only a week till Christmas eve. When I was a boy the Christmas season did not begin on the day after Thanksgiving. From the last Sunday in November until Christmas Eve it was a time of fasting and preparation. No eating between meals, no snacks, no movies, no parties and meat only once a day.

My mother baked for weeks on end, but we put all the cookies and cakes away in storage until the 12 days of Christmas. The Christmas tree was bought in advance but carefully stored on the back porch until Christmas Eve.

Christmas Eve was my favorite time. That was when we brought in the Christmas tree and decorated it. That was the official beginning of the Christmas season.

On Christmas Eve we always had the same traditional meal. My father set the Christmas table with straw placed under the table cloth and also a pile of straw on the top of the table cloth, in the center of the table, where we placed a special Christ child in the manager.

At dinner, holy bread, that had been previously obtained from the pastor, was broken and passed around. Then we ate mushroom soup, followed by poppy seed crusts soaked in milk and fish. Back then Christmas Eve was still one of the strictest of fast days.

For dessert we had our first taste of the weeks of Christmas baking, the wonderful poppy seed and walnut cakes and crescents.

After the dinner we opened our presents. Santa Claus, it was explained, always came early to the people of Slovak descent. But mostly we got the presents out of the way so that we could concentrate on the importance of Christmas day — the birth of the Savior.

In central Europe, Christmas Eve is the night all barn animals receive a voice and can talk. This was because the animals in the barn where Christ was born were the first to greet him and keep him warm with their breath. Thus every Christmas Eve one can go to the barn and hear the cows and sheep and chickens and pigs tell the story of the night that God became a creature of the earth like all of us. To this day I never think of Christmas Eve without thinking of cows and sheep and pigs talking about the night the Savior was born.

After the presents were opened, we cleaned up the Christmas wrappings, washed the dishes and prepared for midnight mass. Since I was a choir boy, we always arrived at church by 11 so I could get my cassock and surplice on for the Christmas caroling which began at 11:30 in the church chancel.

After midnight mass came the first party. We always went to Uncle Gus's for drinks and joviality. He wasn't really my uncle; he was a girlfriend's father. But he was as humorous and personal as any relative ever was. One Christmas Eve he offered me a thousand dollars to elope with his daughter. Gus didn't like his daughter's fiancé. But her fiancé was standing there when he made the offer. I thought it prudent to decline.

Christmas Day and the days after it were filled with one holiday dinner after another, first with one set of relatives and then with another. Neighbors were expected to stop in at all times and at various times we all bundled up to stop in at their homes.

At every home the men toasted Christmas with a shot of Old Granddad and glass of beer. The women drank pink ladies and we kids drank enough sodas to significantly decrease our Crest scores.

It was a wonderful time that lasted until the feast of the Epiphany on January 6. All of our Christmas trees stayed up until then and partying and visiting continued until then. Then, as abruptly as Christmas began, it ended.

Christmas was a very special time. It was a special 12 days when friends knew that they were always welcome and every one was expected to arrive for a jovial visit.

Today the Christmas season is different. There is greater wealth, but less magic. The Christmas carols begin and end almost before the old Christmas season used to begin. On Christmas day the television programming is designed to downplay any specialness to the day. People don't visit as freely either. Perhaps they are afraid that they'll drop in on a party to which they weren't sent an invitation three weeks earlier.

But there is a new conspiracy brewing to remember and relive the ancient spirit of the Christmas season. It is a small but open conspiracy to introduce a taste of Christmas past. It is the introduction each year of special Christmas ales and beers.

The most famous Christmas ale of the country is the special Christmas ale of the Anchor Brewing Co. Each year Fritz Maytag and the brewers at Anchor create a new Christmas ale to reawaken the ancient feeling. Each year it is acclaimed as a new feat of the old magic.

The Sierra Nevada Brewing Co. of Chico, California, makes a special Christmas ale which it calls Celebration Ale. I recently purchased some in Washington, D.C. I happened to enjoy it with an American diplomat just back from the arms reduction negotiations in Vienna who claimed the ale was one reason that we should never give in to the Russians. It was dark amber in color and had a fruity bouquet and deep taste, sufficient to warm even the spirits of our State Department.

The Boulder Brewing Co. of Boulder, Colo., makes an annual Christmas stout of superb quality. It is deeper and darker but milder than Guinness. I had some last year and it is a taste I can attest that one will long and fondly remember.

The Hibernia Brewing Co. of Eau Claire, Wis., is making a special winter brau of superlative quality. If anyone is traveling out that way, it's a must.

F.X. Matt of Utica, N.Y., always offers what it calls "Season's Best." It is a lager with 100 percent barley malt and a good dose of caramelized barley to give it deep amber color and special seasonal taste.

Hudepohl of Cincinnati, Ohio, always makes a special Christmas beer in a very limited edition to celebrate the holiday. I have never tasted this one despite its apparent proximity to us. But I hope that some will someday make its way to our valley.

The imports which I know of so far are only the traditional Noche Buena from Mexico and the Aass Jule Ol from Norway. Both of these are deep, dark and delicious.

These Christmas ales and holiday brews are but one small symbol that the spirit of Christmases past is not wholly lost. If you can find some Christmas ales and beers, save them for a quiet time in front of your fireplace. Pour them slowly; close your eyes, and think of the times when you were young and the spirit of Christmas was, too.

Ein Prosit der Gemutlichkeit!

Thomas Hardy Ale Arrives in America

January 7, 1987

While glancing through the December issue of All About Beer magazine a small article caught my eye. It was in the "What's Brewing" section of the magazine where announcements of new products and beer happenings are printed. The article announced "Thomas Hardy Ale arrives." It reports that Phoenix Imports Ltd., of Baltimore, Md., had just been appointed sole importers for Thomas Hardy Ale in America.

I have never drunk Thomas Hardy Ale, so I can't speak of it from experience. But the fame and legends about this beer long preceded its arrival to those shores. So I share with you the stories I have heard while we wait for a bottle of the nectar to find its way to our valley.

The story of Thomas Hardy Ale begins with one Thomas Hardy who was a late 19th early 20th century English novelist.

Hardy had a wonderful imagination for plot and circumstance. But he relied on this description of real places and things as the backdrops for his novels. His novels are generally set in his home district, Dorset. Scholars have had no difficulty in identifying the local towns and walks he wrote about even though they all have different names in his novels. The Thomas Hardy Society of England sponsors special events and lectures each June 3, the date of Hardy's birth, and also given tours to those party of Dorset featured in Hardy's novels.

But Hardy not only described local places in his novels, he also described local things. In one of his novels, "The Trumpet Major," appears the following description of a glass of beer he called "Casterbridge strong beer:"

"This renowned drink — almost as much of a thing of the past as Falstaff's favorite beverage — was not only well calculated to win the hearts of soldiers blown dry and dusty by residence in tents on a hill-top, but of any wayfarer whatever in the land. It was of the most beautiful color that the eye of an artist in beer could desire; full in body, yet brisk as a volcano; piquant yet without twang, luminous as an autumn sunset; free from steakiness of taste; but, finally, rather heady.

"The masses worshipped it," Hardy wrote, "the major gentry loved it more than wine, and by the most illustrious country families it was not despised. Anybody brought up for being drunk and disorderly in the streets of its natal borough had only to prove that he was a stranger to the place and its liquor to be honourably dismissed by the magistrates."

Hardy's description tantalized the tastes of beer lovers and Hardy scholars. Had Hardy imagined this "volcanic, piquant, luminous" beer, or, like so many other things and places in his novels, was he describing a real beer?

Research uncovered Thomas Hardy's affection for the beers of the Eldridge Pope Brewery of Dorchester. Dorchester, of course, was called "Casterbridge" in Hardy's novels. The Eldridge Pope Brewery was founded in 1874 and Hardy was a very good friend of Alfred Pope, one of the

279

brothers who founded the brewery. Hardy is known to have written a fable for the entertainment of his friends' family, and also wrote the introduction for the Pope family history.

Scholars pondered these facts and, so one of the stories goes, went to the Eldridge Pope Brewery in the 1980's to request that they try to recreate the famous beer described in "The Trumpet Major."

Another story is that in the 1980s one of the Pope family brewers stumbled upon 2,000 antique Victorian beer bottles and thought that it really might be a lot of fun to brew up a special beer to fill them. At the time there was a special Thomas Hardy Festival planned to commemorate the 40th anniversary of Hardy's death. So the thought was to brew a special old-fashioned ale to distribute in the Victorian bottles at the festival.

Whether it was at the request of academic scholars or whether it was simply because the brewery found 2,000 old bottles to fill, is unknown. What is known is that Ray Bottling, the brewmaster, went back to old recipes in the company files and brewed up a new beer designed to match the description in the book: strong, rare, special.

The result was called Thomas Hardy Ale. It is strong beyond doubt, with an alcohol content of 10.5 percent by weight (12.58 percent by volume). It is made of whole hop cones and a special strain of top fermenting yeast. After the ale is fermented, it is transferred to a vat to be matured for six months. It is then bottled with its natural yeast and continues to age in the bottle. The bottles are numbered in series and dates. Each carries a special notice on the back of the bottle. This one is from a 1979 bottle label:

"This bottle will improve if kept at 55 degrees Fahrenheit and will last at least 25 years. If bottle is disturbed before drinking, stand for 48 hours to allow sediment to settle and pour carefully. Do not open before 1989.

With its long aging time, Thomas Hardy's could not be made in great quantities, nor often. It was for years, therefore, a rare and scarce brew. It is not recommended that one drink it until it is at least three years old in the bottle and 10 years is the preferred earliest date to drink it. It will continue to age and improve in the bottle for decades. Thomas Hardy Ale comes in the famous 6.34 ounce size called a "nip," which is the usual size of bottle for an English barley wine.

Thus Thomas Hardy Ale has been called the "Dom Perignon" of beers. It is said that its taste is rare, scarce and unbelievably complex. One beer writer says that its taste is "as subtle and complex as Hardy's prose." It is one of the few ales to receive five stars in Michael Jackson's "Pocket Guide to Beer."

In 1963, the Duke of Kent came to the brewery to add Kentish hops to the brewing of Thomas Hardy's, as well as to inaugurate an expansion of the capacity of the brewery. The brew which marked the Duke's presence was specially marked with the word "Royal" on the label. There was only one brewing so to be marked and it is highly valued by collectors. But the event which it marked, i.e., the expansion of the brewery, appears to have made it possible for us in America to have a chance to taste this famous beer.

Let the word go forth from glen to glen that there shall be praise, joy and accolades for whomever first finds Thomas Hardy Ale and returns to our beloved Valley with a bottle of his precious nectar.

Ein Prosit der Gemutlichkeit!

Magazines, Newsletters
Give You Latest Beer Info

January 21, 1987

The other day a friend asked how one can learn about beer. "Do you read books?" he asked. There are some excellent magazines and newspapers on the subject of beer. And there are also some new books on beer which beer lovers might want to know about. This week I'll tell you about the magazines.

America's best magazine for the beer consumer is the one called "All About Beer." This magazine is now in its seventh year and carries articles in every issue on just about every facet of beer enjoyment. The magazine comes in a multicolored format and is published six times a year. A one year subscription costs $13. Write to Beer, P.O. Box 15690, Santa Ana, Calif., 92705-0690.

For the breweriana buff, one of the best magazines is the "American Breweriana Journal," the official publication of the American Breweriana Association. The ABA is a non-profit and tax exempt education corporation organized to advance the public knowledge of brewing and breweriana; to serve collectors of breweriana and brewery historians and dedicated to the preservation of the memories and artifacts of America's historic breweries.

The "ABA Journal" carries outstanding articles on brewery history, and information on collecting everything from labels and coasters to mirrors and tavern chairs. It is published six times a year. A one year subscription is $12. Write to the American Breweriana Association, P.O. Box 6082, Colorado Springs, CO 80934.

If you want to get into homebrewing, the outstanding journal in the field is "Zymurgy." This magazine is the official journal of the American Homebrewers Association. It is written for the homebrewer, and has carried articles by Cliff Newman of Port Matilda, the present of Happy Valley Homebrewers Club, as well as an expert in homebrewing.

"Zymurgy" is published five times a year and an annual subscription of $13. Write to Zumurgy, Box 287, Boulder, CO 80307-0287.

If you are interested in keeping up with the national microbrewery and brewpub revolutions, there are two magazines you can try.

The first is "The New Brewer." This is the bi-monthly journal of the Institute of Fermentation and Brewing Studies. "The New Brewer" is aimed at the professional trying to open up his or her own microbrewery operation; in this sense it is really intended as a trade journal. But it does have excellent information and profits. An annual subscription (six issues) is $18. Write to The New Brewer, Box 287, Boulder, CO 80306-0287.

If your interest is more as a consumer, the magazine you might want to subscribe to is "The Amateur Brewer." This magazine was started by Fred Eckhardt, who is the grandfather and St. Nicholas of American beer. About a year ago, Fred sold the magazine to Bill Owens who pioneered the brewpub craze in California. The magazine is trying to keep readers current with the best news in the microbrewery field. An annual subscription (four issues) is $13.50. Write to Amateur Brewer, Box 713, Hayward, CA 94543.

One of the more fun publications in the field is the work of Bunny and Mike Bosak of Ocean hills, Calif. Bunny and Mike have created "Beer Drinkers International." Their newsletters are gems of the beer movement. The newsletter comes on 8 ½ inch by 13-inch legal size yellow sheets of paper stapled together in a corner. The dot-matrix computer type was often hard to read, but they have a new PC and it's legible. They publish the best poetry, best recipes and best personal stories, with the best sense of humor in the business. They even list me as an associate editor and republish some of my columns. An annual subscription for 12 monthly issues is $12.97. Write to Beer Drinker's International. P.O. Box 6402, Ocean Hills, Calif, 92056.

But keeping up with American brewing is not sufficient for the true beer lover. Around the world are other nations where the same love of this noble brew spurs literary efforts.

The most revered of all other publications is the newspaper of the Campaign for real Ale of London, England. "What's Brewing" is the monthly newsletter of CAMRA which reports everything there is to know about the breweries and pubs of England. An annual subscription runs about $20, depending on the strength of the English pound. For information write to CAMRA, 34 Alma Road, St. Albans, Hertfordshire, AL1, 3BW, England.

The Campaign for Real Ale has also spread to Canada. The Canadian version of "What's Brewing" describes itself as "Canada's Only Magazine for Beer Lover's and Home Brewers." It covers all the fronts, from Canada's strange pub laws to brewery history and home-brewing. Membership in CAMRA

Canada costs $18.75 and entitles one to receive "What's Brewing" quarterly. Write to CAMRA Canada, P.O. Box 2036, Sta. D., Ottawa, Ontario KIP 5W3, Canada.

If you are interested in beer from Australia, you can join the Australian Beer Society and receive the monthly magazine called "Beer Matters. Dues plus out-of-country postage are about $23 (Australian). This is a journal with articles on Australian brewing, and also a lot more than you might expect on European brewing stories. Write to the Australian Beer Society, Box 123, P.O., Coolangatta, Queenland 4225, Australia.

There, if it tickles your interest, are the names of some of the major magazines and journals on brewing and beer enjoyment. If you've wanted to get deeper into the subject of beer, this is your chance to follow the foam with the magazine of choice.

Ein Prosit der Gemutlichkeit!

Slide Rule Provides Ratings on Brews

February 4, 1987

Did you know that there are almost 800 beers available in the United States today? To the average beer drinker, and even the beer lover, it presents a bewildering choice.

As beer has become more popular, the number of selections in restaurants and taverns and pubs has grown. Many places now carry 20 or 40 choices where before they offered only five or six.

One problem is immediately faced by the brave and intrepid beer explorer: How can I find my way through the thicket to try the best beers available?

This problem occurred to a number of people up in East Norwich, N.Y. In response they developed a guide called the "BeeRRateR" which provides ratings on just about all the beers which are available in the United States.

The "BeeRRateR" is a handy "Slide Guide," and with it in hand one can begin one's own survey of beer by borrowing the expertise of about 20 New York tasters. When I heard about the BeeRRateR, I wrote to the people who put it together. Here is their story as told to me by Terry Toth of BeeRRateR Inc.

The idea got started among a few friends. Each of them traveled a lot on business. One of them began bringing back unusual local beers from around the country and sharing them with his friends. Soon the others began to do the same. They began tasting and comparing them informally and one of them got the brilliant idea to rate them just like wines. One member belonged to a wine society and he designed a rating sheet like wine tasters use.

Soon the group got very systematic and began keeping track of all the beers they had tasted. They began looking for new beers everywhere they traveled. So far their travel has been extensive, for they have tasted about 800 brands of beer.

The nucleus of the group was originally five individuals. But the idea spread and soon others, including co-workers as well as beer lovers who heard of the tasting, joined the group. They formed a panel of about 20 tasters from all types of occupations, both sexes and various age groups. The idea was to get a real "mix" of people so that the ratings could apply to the "typical" beer drinker. They each tried all 800 of the beers and rated and scored them and compiled the results.

From all this research, the group developed a "slide guide" which one uses by inserting rating cards. So far the group has developed 27 cards each with approximately 40 beers listed. Each card has a different category of beers.

To read each card, one slides it through the guide until the beer one wishes to check out appears in a window opening. Beside the name one can see the panel's rating as to five characteristics: appearance, aroma, flavor, aftertaste and overall impression. Each characteristic is rated on a scale of 1 to 10. There is also a final BeeRRateR rating which weighs the ratings to give a final "overall impression" of each beer.

Each rating card also has another attraction. It is a special "value rating," which relates the quality of each beer to its price. In this category, the BeeRRateR shows, for example, that a relatively inexpensive beer with a 7.9 rating, which might sell for 40 cents a can in a six-pack, might be a better value than an import which sells for $1.65 and rates an 8.4. There are many people whose pocketbooks will appreciate this feature.

How is the BeeRRateR as a guide to beers? Since taste is very personal, it is merely someone else's taste. But the developers of the BeeRRateR have made an honest effort to taste all the beers and compare them systematically, something which most people simply do not have the time or funds to do. It seems that a bunch of professionals, much like those one might find in a college town, have had an idea about how to help others acquaint themselves with the field of beer, and have prepared a handy guide of their experience.

The BeeRRateR slide guide can be ordered from BeeRRateR Inc., P.O. Box 206, East Norwich, NY 11732. The initial card to come with each Slide Guide is the "Favorite 40" card listing the most popular beers in America. Additional cards can be ordered in 13 different categories. These include such categories as: Beers of the United Kingdom, Germany's Big Brews, Lusty Lagers, Dark Brews, etc., at a cost of from 60 to 80 cents for each card, depending on how many are ordered. The cost of ordering the Slide Guide with initial card is $5.95 plus 50 cents postage. To order the additional 26 cards costs an additional $12.95, which adds up to a pretty hefty total of $19.40 to get the whole kit. My advice is: It isn't worth it without all the cards.

The BeeRRateR Slide Guide is a handy guide to comparing beers and learning to spot the best buys. Is it worth the price? All About Beer Magazine says, "If you like to try a lot of different brews but don't want to spend money on any beer that might not be worth even 40 cents a can, yes, it is."

For the individual who travels and wants to find the best brews wherever he goes, the BeeRRateR can be a real help. It easily fits in one's pocket and can provide a fun guide to the best in beer.

Ein Prosit der Gemutlichkeit!

New Brews Might Be Worth a Taste

February 18, 1987

When this column first began two and a half years ago, there were only about 50 brewing companies in this country. Such has been the revolutions in America's tastes that in the short span of two and a half years, the number of brewing companies has increased to well over 100.

I have tasted many of these, either on travels across America or through local availability. But the speed of growth has been such that new ones spring up faster than I can get around to taste their beers and old brewers are continuing to bring out new beers and new styles of beer.

So this column is dedicated to letting you know of the existence of a few beers I have only heard about. We will leave it to intrepid Centre County explorers to search them down and let us know what they think.

Dock Street Amber. One new beer which I am looking forward to trying is Dock Street Amber Beer from Philadelphia. This beer was introduced last Sept. 15 in Philadelphia. It is being brewed by former chef, Jeffrey Ware, and is said to be modeled after the original style of ales that once made Philadelphia the brewing capital of the American colonies.

The name "Dock Street" is taken from an original brewhouse tavern which welcomed immigrants and sailors to

Penn's colony 300 years ago. Dock Street Amber Beer won third place in the voting for the best 10 beers at the Great American Beer Festival last October.

M.W. Brenner Amber Light. Last spring a new beer was introduced in New York by the Monarch Brewing Company of Brooklyn. The beer is called M.W. Brenner Amber Light. The company decided to name its beer after a mythical brewmaster, but someone suggested that they did not need to invent one since there was a real, live legendary brewmaster to name it after.

Mort Brenner is a consultant to more than 100 breweries around the world, and is also the brewmaster for Dock Street Amber. He's flattered, of course, to have a beer named after himself. So far, only reports in the "New York Times" confirm its existence. We're still trying to find a real bottle of it.

Acme Beer. A year ago I visited San Francisco for a seminar on brewing and heard about a new brewery in Santa Rosa, California, called Xcelsior. An old college friend of mine, Gordon Griffin, knew the brewers, and arranged for me to have lunch with them. The owners, John Senkevich and Peter Eierman, have great senses of humor, and we exchanged jokes, stories and puns for two hours. Then they took me on a tour of the then only half-finished brewery. The reports are that the beer was finally introduced last fall under the name "Acme," which was a famous beer brand in Northern California just prior to World War II.

The brewery is located just off the fashionable "Railroad Square" in Santa Rosa. A report by a beer tasting expert in the "San Francisco Chronicle" said, "I found this beer to be one of the finest I've ever tasted, domestic or imported." If this beer is only half as delightfully sociable as its brewers, it should be a real joy to taste.

Vienna All Malt Lager. Out in Eau Claire, Wis., one of America's famed small brewing centers, there's a new beer called Vienna All Malt Lager. It is deliberately designed to be a recreation of the 1880's style Viennese beer by brewmaster Gary Bauer. It placed 8th in the top 10 at the Great American Beer Festival last fall, and I suspect it will be one of the special tastes in beer with which every beer lover will want to be familiar.

Twentieth Century Ale. The only commercial brewer on the East Coast with facilities to make a real ale is the Christian Schmidt brewery in Philadelphia. There are reports that they have produced an "absolutely incredible" ale under the label of "Twentieth Century Ale." The label comes out under the name of the Adam Scheidt Brewing Company, which originally produced famed Prior Double Dark. Schmidt's of Philadelphia purchased the company in 1954 and promised never to tamper with the recipes. It's a limited edition and we hope a few will be sent to the Centre County market.

Catamount. Another set of beers I would like to try are Catamount Gold and Catamount Amber, the new beers from White River Junction, Vt. The word "catamount" is another world for mountain lion which might have some interest locally.

The beers made their debut last August. We're hoping Terry Dalton, former CDT political reporter, who is now teaching up that way, will give us a report.

These are just a few of the new American beers we've heard about. If you hear of others, drop me a line.

Ein Prosit der Gemutlichkeit!

Writer Pleasantly Surprised with New Beer

March 4, 1987

In my last column, I wrote about a few beers that I had heard of but not had the opportunity to taste.

One was Catamount Beer from White River Junction, Vt. I didn't have much hope of tasting this one, since I did not have any trip north planned for the next year.

Imagine my surprise, then, to come back to my office on the following Monday to find a six-pack of Catamount waiting for me.

It seems that "intrepid Centre County Explorer" Fred Houlihan had been to Burlington, Vt., to visit his daughter, a student at the University of Vermont.

Fred tells me that he had gone out to dinner at a nice restaurant, and when he asked to order a beer, the waiter suggested a new one that had just been introduced the week before. Fred tried the brew and liked it.

In fact, he liked it so much he went out and bought a couple of six packs. He decided that he'd bring a few back to share with his friends.

The nice thing about it, besides getting the beer to taste, was that Fred and I have probably never met. Fred has simply found something that he liked, and immediately thought of sharing it with others who might also enjoy it. He figured I might enjoy it and share it with you.

I called Fred to thank him for the sampler and it turns out that Fred graduated from Penn State the same year I did. Fred was a frat man from the old days, and a true lover of beer. Of course, almost all frat men back in the old days were beer lovers.

Fred was a brother in Alpha Tau Omega, and I was a Teke. Maybe we did meet, because I remember some great parties at his fraternity during my college days.

Since Fred enjoyed the beer so much, I thought I would find out more about it.

Catamount started brewing about two weeks ago. The brewery is the project of Allen Davis and Steve Mason, who have been working to put together a brewery for about four years.

Steve dreamed of making beer and went to England to apprentice at an English brewery to learn how it makes good ale.

Catamount makes two ales. The first is called Catamount Gold. It is a light-bodied ale that tastes very much like a full-bodied pilsener such as Pilsner Urquell.

The second Catamount brew is Catamount Amber, a heavier, copper-colored brew.

I can report that both are excellent. They are delightful additions to the tastes in beers available from American breweries.

The Catamount Brewery is the first microbrewery of ale on the East Coast, and probably only the second or third brewery east of the Mississippi capable of brewing ales.

The Schmidt's Brewery has a separate brewery for ales in Philadelphia, and the Newman Brewery in Albany brews ales. But as far as I know, those are the only ones.

Interestingly for Penn Staters, the mascot of the University of Vermont is a mountain lion. The word "Catamount" is a local word in Vermont for a mountain lion. The beer is named after the mascot of the University.

I have received some material on the backgrounds of the men who started the Catamount Brewery, and hope to tell you more about it soon. It has been featured in Time magazine. A national public radio segment about the brewery is planned for airing on "All Things Considered" in the next few weeks. So I hope to have a lot more to tell you about Catamount Beer in the future.

Ein Prosit der Gemutlichkeit!

Iron City Beer a Part of Growing up in Western Pennsylvania

March 18, 1987

When I was growing up in Johnstown, more years ago then I care to remember, television was just making its debut.

Back in 1948, when we got our first TV, there was only one hour of programming a night, and even the test patterns were only on for an hour before that.

Such was the attraction of that electronic box that I can still recall staring at the test patterns for the hour before the programs came on.

But the fact was that before television became the central point of American social life, there really was a social life. I remember the picnics that brought families together at Ideal Park and Stackhouse Park through the summer, and the ethnic day celebration all year long. Then there were the funerals which lasted two days and the weddings which took a whole weekend of celebrating.

In those days we had to entertain each other. People told stories to while away an evening. And to tell stories well, something was needed to wet the tongue and mouth.

It was beer. And the label I remember most was Iron City.

When I grew up Johnstown was a steel town. From where I lived every evening we looked east toward the valley where the steel mills stretched for 12 miles and checked the sky to get our financial report for the day.

If the sky were red, times were good. It means that the mills were working the giant open hearths that cast their red flames out bright enough to light up the entire sky above the valley.

All of my father's brothers worked in the steel mills. One was a foreman and the others held a variety of jobs in the mills, in offices and in the various divisions. Steel was central to our lives.

And when the family got together, there was Iron City. It was as much a part of social life as a chardush, a polka or a massurka.

Iron City beer was part of what it meant to grow up. It was part of story telling and the sharing of experience. The old men with the calloused hands and the quiet ways sat and drank Iron City while telling of the strike of 1921 or the organizing battles of the 1930s.

Back in those days, according to the legends, Pinkertons patrolled the roads, and one needed more papers to travel a few miles out of town than it takes to visit behind the Iron Curtain today.

The earliest beer in the area of Pittsburgh is recorded to have been brewed in 1758, just after the French and Indians were defeated and the colonials captured Fort Duquesne and changed its name to Fort Pitt.

In 1861, just on the eve of the American Civil War, Edward Frauenheim founded the Iron City Brewery.

The Iron City Brewery was one of the first to produce the new lager type of beers — the pilseners — which were so popular in Europe. This kind of beer could only be made in America after the invention of the "Yankee Clipper" ship. Until then, the yeasts necessary to make lager beer could not survive the long ocean voyage. But the Yankee Clippers cut the voyage time so much that the yeasts could finally make it.

A consortium of Pittsburgh Brewers in the 1850s had gotten together to bring some of the yeast over on a clipper ship so they could make some of this lighter beer for the thirsty millworkers of Pittsburgh.

Iron City Beer has prospered for 126 years as one of America's foremost regional brewers. Today, in addition to the famous Iron City beer, it also brews IC Golden Lager, one of the finest super premiums available. It is also the contract brewer of four of the beers voted into the top 10 at the Great American beer Festival. These are Pennsylvania Pilsener, Samuel Adams, XIII Colony and Olde Heurich.

Iron City is now bringing out a "sampler" of these four beers: a case with a six-pack of each, which is available at local distributors.

Of course, there will always be Iron City, and for men who make steel there's always time to "pump an Iron."

Ein Prosit der Gemutlichkeit!

Did Beer Make the Beginnings of Civilization?

April 1, 1987

Scientists have pondered the question: What was it that caused fierce prehistoric hunting tribes to ever settle down?

"The question has long tantalized anthropologists and archaeologists," according to a recent article featured on the front page of last week's The New York times' science section, "Because once that answer is clear, they will know what sparked the long transformation of humans from wandering hunters to literate city dwellers."

Some anthropologists have speculated that population pressure may have been the cause of civilization, while others have suggested ecological or environmental causes.

But the real cause, according to The Times' article, may now be known: It was, of course, beer.

According to The Times' article, "Does Civilization Owe a Debt to Beer?," it was the need to settle down and cultivate grain for beer that transformed fighting savages into peaceful, industrious, studious, literate men.

Who says the media report only bad news?

The article is an account of the recent scholarly studies of Professor Solomon H. Katz, an anthropologist at University of Pennsylvania. Professor Katz's findings were published in the latest issue of Expedition, the journal of the Museum of Archeology and Anthropology in Philadelphia.

The event which caused the transformation of fierce hunters into peaceful, literate city dwellers, according to Professor Katz, "was the accidental discovery by prehistoric humans that wild wheat and barley soaked in water to make gruel, if left out in the open air, did not spoil. Instead, natural yeast in the air converted it to a dark bubbling brew that made whoever drank it feel good."

"On top of that, the brew made people robust." The article goes on to report that, at the time, beer "was second only to animal protein as a nutritional source."

"My argument," Katz reportedly explained in an interview with The Times reporter, "is that the initial discovery of a stable way to produce beer provided an enormous motivation for men to settle down and form more peaceful societies."

The report of Katz's findings were so interesting that I decided to check them with other scholars in the field.

Dr. Fredrick Matson, a Penn state archeologist, confirmed that beer may be man's earliest beverage. But, he said, "While no one single factor caused men to become civilized, the idea that beer is one of the bases of civilization has been around for a long time."

But, Matson said, early man did have a lot of grain. Beer was a way of preserving and getting a nutritious beverage.

Early man had one beer, and the idea might have occurred to him that sitting down and having a second one would be a good idea," said Matson.

Matson also pointed out that beer was covered in the earliest legal code known to man. The Code of Hammurabi had a provision which, roughly translated, said "Thou shalt not talk politics over beer." The penalty in the code was death for concocting political conspiracies while drinking beer.

Presumably, according to Matson, conspiracies discussed without beer were less important. I also decided to check out the story with my old fraternity brother, Dean Michael Steffy of the anthropology department of Queens College in New York. It was he who originally sent me the article from The Times.

When I asked him what he thought of the Katz findings, Steffy replied "While I'm not sure the evidence proves that beer alone caused the transition of hunting and gathering tribes into complex civilization, it was perhaps the basis of more friendly civilization. After all, beer does promote conversation and sociability."

Steffy also pointed out that in most Neolithic societies there was a large cult for sacrificing and eating cattle. He suggested this might have been the genesis of the first "Steak & Brew."

Getting back to The New York times article, Katz also presented some conclusions which may be of local and topical interest.

"Almost invariably," Katz has written, "individuals and societies appear to invest enormous amounts of effort and even risk" in the pursuit of beer.

"In many cultures the use of alcohol has been made so central to social ... practices that any disruption of its supply would be seen as a serious problem."

Perhaps Katz should be consulted by the State College Police Department. Who knows? If Katz is right, cutting off the beer supply to college fraternities and apartments may reverse the course of civilization, causing students to revert to the stage of prehistoric hunters and gatherers..."

Ein Prosit der Gemutlichkeit!

Catamount Brewery:
Young Men's Dream Realized

April 15, 1987

Alan Davis is 43 years old. He was raised in Boston and has a master's degree in history from Boston University.

A few years ago, he emigrated to Vermont to teach school. He is also a bluegrass musician and so became the coordinator of the Vermont Council on the arts' artist-in-residence program.

Stephan Mason is 31 years old. He was raised in a Detroit suburb, went to Bowdoin College for a while but graduated with a degree in social sciences from the University of Michigan.

He emigrated to Vermont to attend Norwich University for a master's degree in physical education and to become a physical education instructor in Vermont.

A few years ago, these two gentlemen met in a bar in Montpelier, Vt., to enjoy the reality of a good beer and to share the fantasy of making a really fine, fresh beer for New England. Both Mason and Davis dreamed of building a brewery. That night they decided together to make their dream come true. That night saw the birth of the Catamount Brewery.

That was more than three years ago. The biggest job in bringing a brewery to birth was convincing investors. But the hardheaded Yankees of Massachusetts and Vermont gradually came to see what the investors of the West Coast had seen much earlier: People want deeper tasting beer. So gradually the three-quarters of a million dollars that Mason and Davis needed was raised.

In the meantime, as Davis assembled both the investors and the brewery equipment, Mason went to England to apprentice at the Swannell Brewery to learn how to make English Ale.

On February 17, 1987, the ales were introduced. These were the beers that Fred Houlihan of State College encountered on his trip to visit his daughter at the University of Vermont. He brought back a couple of six-packs to share with friends here in Nittany Valley.

The Catamount Brewery makes two distinctive ales, Catamount Gold and Catamount Amber. The only other real ales produced on the whole East Coast are McSorley's Cream Ale made by the Schmidt brewery in Philadelphia, and the ales served at the Manhattan Brewery in New York. All of the other "ales" east of the Mississippi are really lagers made a little darker.

Catamount Gold is an ale with body. It looks like Harp Lager in color but the robust flavor of this beer in our mouth is the first thing you'll notice. You won't mistake it for a Miller or a Stroh's.

Catamount Amber is what the English call a "pale ale." It has the warm copper color of Bass ale, but, perhaps because of its freshness, it has a special feel and body you won't forget. Stephen Morris describes the color as, "aged wood, worn and finished like an antique, with a patina that suggests timeless history.

"The taste is full and round," he says, "slightly sweeter than the Gold, with a balance of complex flavors and carbonations that suggests that all is in harmony with the brewing gods."

I enjoyed Catamount as much as Steve Morris had. So I put through a call to the brewery. Phil Gentile, marketing director, spoke with me. Gentile had once been the owner of a restaurant in Montpelier but had gotten bitten by the enthusiasm of Davis and Mason, sold his restaurant and entered the brewery business.

We aren't getting rich," says Gentile, "but it's just a beautiful thing to do. People are knocking on our door with a smile to say, "Please let me try your beer." It gives you a purpose in itself."

The great thing about Catamount beer, Gentile says is that "people have discovered that they can sit down with a beer and not drink a whole six-pack. Palates have discovered that there is a whole lot of taste in beer. It awakens their senses."

Catamount ales are ales to savor. Gentile says, "You pour a Catamount, go out and chop wood, come back and finish your glass. It's still good. It keeps its character. You can't "do that with a regular American beer."

Catamount beer is only distributed in Vermont, New Hampshire, Massachusetts and northern New York. It isn't pasteurized, which is one reason it has so much flavor. But that means its shelf life is short.

This summer, when you travel north, the New Englanders you meet with have a little bit more pride. They now have a beer they can call their own.

En Prosit der Gemutlichkeit!

Students Decry Happy Valley's Loss of 'Natty Bo'

April 29, 1987

There are a few things in this world which still capture the loyalties of a man so much as his dog and his beer.

I don't have any new dog stories to tell, but the other day I received a letter from some truly loyal beer drinkers.

The letter tells a tragic story: The disappearance from the shelves of local distributors of a once famed beer.

Since loyalty is such a rare and precious quality in this crass and commercialized age, I cannot help but share with you the letter in which this virtue was so eloquently expressed.

The letter is from a student, J.D. Savage, a junior in geography at Penn State, and his friends from West College Avenue. J.D. hails from Rockville, Md., but he has been here in Happy Valley for the past three years happily enjoying his favorite hometown brew until it was recently discontinued.

"Dear Mr. Novak," J.D. wrote me, "We were extremely disappointed the other day when we made our pilgrimage to the beer Mecca of Nittany Beverage and discovered that our supply of the nectar and ambrosia of the gods was no longer carried by that once fine institution.

"I am, of course, talking about that fine elixir called National Bohemian Beer."

"As college students, my friends and I could easily appreciate the economics of Natty Bo. We could buy a case of 16-ounce returnable for under $7. In fact, our coin of realm became the case of Natty Bo. For example, I offer these two snatches of conversation:

"'Hey Jack,' hollered Peter, "try some of this wine. It costs $56 a bottle.'

"'Fifty-six dollars a bottle!" Jack cried in amazement. 'You could buy eight cases of Natty Bo for that!'

"And then there was this classic:

"'Bill, what would you do if you won a million dollars in the lottery?'

"'Why, I'd buy 140,000 cases of Natty Bo,' replied Bill before you could blink.

"National Bohemian," the letter continued, "represented tastes that were a cut above the beers of many so-called beer lovers. Sometimes one of these beer lovers would try to mooch a beer from our refrigerator. When they discovered our Natty Bo in the 'fridge, they would often mumble something about Moosehead and not being thirsty anyway.

"Occasionally an adventurous guest would down a bottle and would immediately either become a believer or would feel a sudden need to floss his teeth. I can think of few indicators which provided as much insight into a man's soul as a bottle of National Bohemian.

"National Bohemian represented the character of Baltimore, the 11th largest city in these United States of America, home of the Orioles and the Colts," Mr. Savage continued on tear-stained paper.

"Natty Bo was the liquid pulse of that hardworking, blue-collar town. Brewed from Sparkling Chesapeake Bay waters, National Bohemian was every bit a match for Iron City."

I called J.D. Sunday night to talk to him about his feeling for his friendly beer from "The Land of Pleasant Living."

He was crying in his beer at the time, and through the tears asked "Why would State College choose I.C. over Natty Bo?"

"National Bohemian's parent beer, National Brewing Company is sometimes called the "Pride of Baltimore," J.D. had written. What other city, I wondered, bottled its pride to provide so much to so many for so little?

"It ails me (pun fully intended)," J.D. had said, "to think that State College has become a 'national' disaster area."

Not since they tried to change the Coke formula have so many noble sentiments been penned about the loss of a beloved beverage.

A few days after receiving J.D.'s letter, I visited Beer World in Harrisburg located at 520 S. 29th St. Beer World is a Dauphin County distributor famous for having a large selection of domestic beers at discount prices.

There I picked up a case of National Bohemian for $4.99. I took a six-pack over to J.D. who was truly grateful.

The National Brewing Company was founded in Baltimore in 1885. It was bought out by Carling in 1975, but continued to brew Baltimore's finest.

How do others rate National Bo?

Michael Jackson, in his "World Guide to Beer," quoted this description of it from a national magazine: "clean and

307

pleasant, but no innocuous ... generally placed high on taste tests ... by discriminating judges ... against still opposition."

National Premium did even better. "For some time we were convinced that this beer was the best in America."

Who would have thought that a local, unsung beer from Baltimore would stir such feelings? But there you have it.

This Friday is J.D.'s birthday. He plans to be enjoying it with a beer in his hand. But this year, for the first time since he came to Penn State, it would be with a National Bohemian in his hand.

I learned the phrase for this in high school Latin class: "Sic transit Gloria mundi," the Romans used to say. It means, "Thus passes the glory of the world."

Ein Prosit der Gemutlichkeit!

Light, Dark Beer:
The Possibilities Are Endless

May 13, 1987

In my last column I printed a letter from several distraught Penn State students from the Baltimore area.

They had eloquently described their sadness upon discovering that their local distributor no longer carried National Bohemian Beer, which is the local brew of every local son of Lord Baltimore.

But no sooner had my column appeared than Pat Daugherty of the Tavern Restaurant called to tell me that there was cause for "joy in Mudville."

In appears that the W.R. Hickey Beer Distributor on Benner Pike has picked up the account for "Natty Bo," and Bill assures me that there are sufficient quantities in stock to satisfy all the local Orioles fans.

I have also received another letter that has brought back a flood of old memories.

It is from one of the greatest mentors of my youth, Professor John A. Mourant of Corl Street.

Professor Mourant is one of those men whom if you had once encountered while a student, you would never forget. Professor Mourant was the "Mr. Chips" of Penn State, the great archetype of the English professor of philosophy. In a word, he embodied the classical idea of what a professor was meant to be.

About a quarter of a century ago I studied medieval philosophy under Dr. Mourant. We read Thomas Aquinas, Augustine of Hippo and Anselm of Bec. Professor Mourant made these men come alive through their writings until one almost felt as though one were sitting on a stone bench at Cluny listening to a saintly abbot as a beam of sunlight shone through a stained glass window onto the palm of your hand.

To this day, I secretly smile when I hear people speak derogatorily of "medieval" ideas, or make fun of something by calling it "medieval." These people never studied under Dr. Mourant who somehow had the power to make it all dazzlingly alive and new again.

With Dr. Mourant, Augustine and Aquinas came across in conversation as though they had just talked to him yesterday. He made it possible to look at the world with new eyes, and to understand it in ways one never would have thought possible.

Dr. Mourant's laughing eyes and smile, and his eternal sense of humor, made everything he thought take on an air of invincible civility. In Professor Mourant's classes, Western Civilization was not only taught but incarnated.

I was, therefore, delighted to hear from my old mentor again. It brought back warm memories.

But Dr. Mourant writes me this time, not of philosophy, but of beer.

It is appropriate that a medieval philosopher would inquire into the term "light." Professor Mourant asks that I address "what the brewers like to designate as 'light beer.'" The professor wants to know, "Do they mean light in color, light in calories, light in body, et cetera?"

"They have converted me to a dark beer," he writes, "but," he notes, "I can't help but wonder if they will soon bring out a 'light dark beer'!"

It all depends on the meaning of light.

Dr. Mourant's concern for the irony of a "light dark beer" is fully justified. Although I have not yet heard of the brewers bringing out a light dark beer, it is certainly, upon philosophical and biological reflection, capable of being conceived. That is philosophic talk for yes, it is possible.

The reality is that the term light, when used with beer, just as with other things, has more than one meaning. One meaning refers to color, another to weight or body and the third, the major concept of "light," really refers to the work of a new enzyme.

Originally, the term "light," when used to refer to a beer meant its color. When the Prazdroj, Brewery of Pilsen, Czechoslovakia, first brought out its famous Pilsener Urquell in 1842, its light color was its most well known characteristic.

Beer drinkers switched from ceramic mugs to crystal clear glasses to show off the light, "pale" color of his famous beer. Indeed, the pilsener shaped glass was specially designed for this brew because it was said that there was a golden flame of light that one could see in each glass of beer if held up to the light of the sun in a certain way.

Just as light is distinguished from dark when speaking of color, the word "light" is also used to distinguish from "heavy" when speaking of weight. In this sense, one is speaking of the amount of malt in the beer.

A heavy beer is a beer made with more malt that produces more "body"; less body makes a light beer, such as Corona or Coors or Rolling Rock.

But today's "light" beers really refer to a third concept. In this third meaning, the term "light" is used in reference to the amount of calories in your beer.

Fewer calories depend upon "better living through chemistry."

Let me explain this. Beer contains a lot of particles of starch. These starch particles exist as complex compounds with many branches. In 1967, an enzyme became commercially available that had the ability to break these branches.

The "light" enzyme is called amyloglucosidase. It allows the brewer to start with about one-third less barley and grain malt. The enzyme actually causes less malt to make more alcohol and carbon dioxide. Thus with one-third less malt, the brewer is able to produce a beer with the same amount of alcohol and carbonation as a normal beer, but with far less starch. That means fewer calories.

There is also another way to produce a light beer. This method is to produce a regular beer and then simply add water. One of the light beers that the weekend is supposedly made for is made this way.

It is, therefore, possible to conceive of a "light dark beer." It could be a beer made with richly roasted malt, but with the light beer enzyme to break the starch chains.

Or it could be a regular dark beer made in concentrated form with water added. Fortunately, a light dark beer has not yet been marketed.

Every advance of science and technology, no matter how great the benefits, seems to also entail an assault upon the simple understanding of our language and our words. The possibility of light dark beer leaves much for us to ponder over, with a dark, heavy beer, of course.

But at least I can still be confident in knowing, thanks to Professor Mourant, that no matter what science invents next, St. Thomas, St. Anselm and St. Augustine will never been considered "light" thinkers.

Ein Prosit der Gemutlichkeit!

Worldwide There Are 25 Distinctive Beer Styles

May 27, 1987

Have you ever wondered how many distinctive styles of beer there are?

The people at the American Homebrewers Association have an annual competition among homebrewers to decide the best brews made in America. They have studied the world and have identified 25 categories of beer which are internationally recognized. I thought you might like to know all the categories and different styles.

Ales

Ales are historically made with top-fermenting yeast and brewed at warmer temperatures. They generally have a more pronounced palate. There are 14 distinct styles of ales:

Altbier — The name means "old beer" and refers to the ancient ales originating in the Cologne (Kolsch) and Dusseldorf areas of Germany.

Barley Wine — An extra-strong ale as potent as wine with 6 to 13 percent alcohol content by volume.

Brown Ale — A sweet, brown ale originating in Southern England.

Cream Ale — Any American style of mild, pale, light bodied ale, often made by blending an ale and a lager.

Fruit Ale — Any ale made by adding fruit as an adjunct.

Flanders Brown Ales — A Belgian style distinguished by the fruity, spicy flavors obtained through the unique yeast strains of the country.

Herb Ale — Any ale using herbs or spices rather than hops.

Pale Ale — England's most famous style which is copper-colored and "pale" only by comparison with porters, stouts and brown ales. This style also includes India Pale Ale, brewed to withstand ocean voyages to India in the 19th century, and Bitter, the national drink of Britain.

Porter — A dark English medium-bodied ale made with black malt rather than roasted barley as in stout.

Saison — A Belgium summer seasonal beer.

Scotch Ale — A strong, usually dark, malty brew originating in Scotland.

Stout — A dark heavy ale made with roasted barley. It includes Dry Stout (such as Guinness); Sweet Stout which is very lactic and is sometimes called Milk Stout; and Imperial Stout which is an extremely rich black ale once specially brewed for the Czar of Russia.

Trappist Ale — Five Trappist monasteries in Belgium and one in the Netherlands have developed this distinct strong style of bottle-conditioned ales which continue to ferment after bottling.

Wheat Beers — These beers are made by adding wheat as an adjunct to the barley. The result is a lighter, maltier, sharper and more refreshing summer drink.

It includes four subcategories: Berliner Weisse, a sharp, sour beer called by Napoleon the "Champagne du Nord"; Weizen, which is a southern German style with a spicy palate; Dunkel which is a dark, malty wheat beer sometimes referred to as Weizenbock; and Lambic which is only fermented with airborne yeasts found in the air of Belgium.

Lambic includes Faro, which is sweet; Gueuze, made by adding gueuze; Framboise, made with raspberries; and Kriek, made with cherries.

Lagers

Lagers are made with bottom fermenting yeasts, at much colder temperatures than ales. They are usually lighter and smoother than ales due to aging. There are 11 distinct styles of lagers:

Bock — A strong, dark, malty, seasonal brew originating in Germany and normally served in the spring of each year. It includes Helles, such as Maibock; Doppel which is double strong; and Eisbock which is made by freezing the beer and removing some of the water which freezes first.

Continental Dark — A German dark lager with less sweetness and more hops and carbonation than brown ales.

Export — Originating in Dortmond, this is a strong, light colored, medium bodied lager.

Fruit Beer — Any lager using fruit as an adjunct.

Herb Beer — Any lager using herbs or spices other than hops as an adjunct.

Munich — This is the famous beer style of Munich: a malt accented, dark brown lager.

Pilsener — The original beer of Pilsen, Czechoslovakia an the most copied beer in the world. It is light in color and body, delicately hopped, clean, dry and refreshing. It includes the American Style Pilseners which are lighter in body an flavor and more carbonated than the original. It also includes the diet light beers, which are ever weaker; and the continental copies of the original which are lighter than Pilsner Urquell, but more flavorful than the American Pilseners.

Porter — A black, heavy brew with complex taste, originally brewed with an ale yeast, but now often made with lager yeasts.

Rauch Beer — A "smoked beer" made by roasting the malts in a smoke-house to impart a smoky flavor to the beer.

Steam Beer — An amber lager brewed at warmer ale temperatures creating an ale character to the taste. The only original American style of beer.

Vienna Style — This brew is copper-colored with a rich toasted malt aroma, smooth flavor, and clean bitterness. It includes the seasonal Marzen and Oktoberfest styles of beer.

The American Homebrewers Association will be the host of the Ninth Annual Homebrewers Competition in Boulder, Colorado, in early June. The above are the categories for judging each beer.

It's a good guide to the beers of the world, and a good guide for all beer lovers to become familiar with the taste of each special style, most of which are available in Centre County.

Ein Prosit der Gemutlichkeit!

About the Author

Ben Novak, born in Johnstown, Pennsylvania on February 15, 1943, graduated from the Pennsylvania State University in 1965. As a student he served as president of the Undergraduate Student Government in his senior year and as a brother at Tau Kappa Epsilon.

In 1968 he graduated from Georgetown University Law School. From 1968 to 1970 he served as a Captain in the U.S. Army, Infantry, including a year in Viet Nam where he won the Bronze Star.

In 1968 Novak was admitted to the Bar of Pennsylvania. He practiced law in Pennsylvania for more than 30 years, with his own firm in State College and Bellefonte.

While living in Centre County for more than three decades, Novak was widely involved in the community. He was, at various times: founder of the Mount Nittany Conservancy; president of Lion's Paw Alumni Association; a Ph.D recipient in philosophy, history, and political science from Penn State; and an adjunct professor and assistant dean of students at Penn State. From 1988 to 2000 Novak served on Penn State's Board of Trustees.

In 2000 he retired, moving to Bratislava in Slovakia, his family's ancestral home. In 2008 he returned to the United States to advise students at Penn State, and has earnestly sought a renewal in University life according to the vision of Evan Pugh and the Founders of Penn State for many years.

www.bennovak.net

About the Publisher

The Nittany Valley Society fosters a spirit of community across time for Penn Staters, Central Pennsylvanians, and friends through a knowledge of our past, an appreciation for our present, and an affection for our spirit as a living treasury for our future. This finds expression through virtue, vigor, and soulfulness apparent in acts of honor, the cultivation of customs, and the Old State spirit.

The Nittany Valley Society is a non-profit, 501(c)(3) corporation in State College, Pennsylvania that serves as a cultural conservancy for the Nittany Valley, helping people to discover its many treasures and better share the story of this special place.

www.nittanyvalley.org